All About Adolescence

All About Adolescence provides a comprehensive and current introduction to all key aspects of adolescent development. Building on the success of *The Nature of Adolescence*, this book addresses the unprecedented changes affecting young people's lives, including the social media explosion, artificial intelligence (AI) emergence, pandemic impacts and growing climate emergency awareness. It covers critical contemporary topics including advances in neuroscience and brain development research, evolving discourses around racial and gender identity, mental health and well-being concerns and the lasting effects of Covid-19 on adolescent development.

What sets this book apart is the authentic voice of young people themselves. Interviews with individuals aged 14–18 from diverse backgrounds are woven throughout all 11 chapters, providing vivid, real-world insights into what it means to be an adolescent in today's world. The book emphasizes a positive perspective on adolescence while developing the innovative STAGE theoretical framework, examining how young people actively construct their own developmental pathways through this crucial life transition. From brain development and identity formation to peer relationships and resilience strategies, each chapter combines cutting-edge research with genuine adolescent perspectives.

This authoritative text is essential for anyone studying human development at undergraduate and postgraduate levels, as well as professionals including teachers, social workers, health workers, counsellors and youth workers seeking to understand and support young people navigating this complex and formative period.

John Coleman trained as a clinical psychologist and was formerly a senior research fellow at the University of Oxford. He is the founder of a research centre studying adolescents and their families, and during his career he has also run a special school for troubled teenagers and worked as a policy advisor for the government. He was awarded an OBE for services to young people in the Queen's Birthday Honours in 2001.

"Coleman grounds scientific findings in real-world experience. This is an essential text for anyone wanting to understand and support today's adolescents."

Professor Sarah-Jayne Blakemore, *FRS. Professor of Psychology and Neuroscience, University of Cambridge, UK*

"John Coleman has written a uniquely informative, balanced and readable text. This book will be welcomed by students, researchers, practitioners, parents, and all who have an interest in this important phase of life."

Professor Ingrid Lunt, *Professor of Education, University of Oxford, UK*

"Drawing on decades as a pioneering voice in adolescent development, Coleman once again brings the needs, challenges, and perspectives of young people to the forefront. An essential book for all who work with young people in the health field."

Professor Dougal Hargreaves, *Professor of Paediatrics and Child Health, Imperial College, London, UK*

"A terrifically insightful book. Too often adolescence is misunderstood and misrepresented – like adolescents themselves. This book, rich with theory and research yet highly accessible, is a superb counter to this. An outstanding book for anyone working with young people."

Dez Holmes, *MBE. Chief Executive of Research in Practice, UK*

"From one of the giants of the field, John Coleman's *All About Adolescence* is an outstanding contribution to a better understanding of this important phase in human development."

Professor Patrick Alexander, *Professor of Education, Oxford Brookes University, UK*

"This important book is a must read for anyone working with adolescents – or living with them."

Professor Lord Layard, *Co-Director of the Community Well-Being Programme at the London School of Economics, UK*

"This authoritative text is an invaluable resource for anyone seeking to understand adolescent development, and to identify effective ways of supporting young people as they navigate this complex and formative period."

Professor Amanda Holt, *Professor of Criminology, University of Roehampton, UK*

All About Adolescence

Understanding Development in Today's World

John Coleman

Routledge
Taylor & Francis Group
LONDON AND NEW YORK

Designed cover image: Getty Images @Jose Calsina

First published 2026
by Routledge
4 Park Square, Milton Park, Abingdon, Oxon OX14 4RN

and by Routledge
605 Third Avenue, New York, NY 10158

Routledge is an imprint of the Taylor & Francis Group, an informa business

British Library Cataloguing-in-Publication Data
A catalogue record for this book is available from the British Library

ISBN: 9781032640426 (hbk)
ISBN: 9781032624303 (pbk)
ISBN: 9781032640433 (ebk)

DOI: 10.4324/9781032640433

Typeset in Melior
by KnowledgeWorks Global Ltd.

Contents

Acknowledgements

The writing of this book would not have been possible without the help and support of many people. I should first acknowledge Fiona Factor for her amazing skill in finding and carrying out the interviews that contribute so brilliantly to this book. There is more about the interviews in a separate section. I want also to offer a huge thanks to Ann Hagell, who has been my colleague throughout. We planned this book together, and she has been a constant source of help and encouragement. I am hugely grateful to her. I would also like to acknowledge all the kind people, including Laura Coleman, Joanna Gilar, Alison Hadley, Debi Roker, Chris Warren-Adamson and Peter Wilson, who read various chapters and offered helpful comments on the text.

I want to recognize the support of the organizations I have worked for or been involved with during the years my ideas for this book have been evolving. These organizations include the Association for Young People's Health, the Department of Education at Oxford University, the Centre for Economic Affairs at the London School of Economics, Family Links (now the Centre for Emotional Health), Family Lives, Parental Minds and the Trust for the Study of Adolescence (later known as Youth in Focus). Throughout this whole process, my wife, Jenny Pearce, has read the chapters and offered wisdom, support and encouragement. She has continually suggested improvements as the book has progressed. She has been the steadying hand that has kept me going, and I owe her a great debt of gratitude.

Preface

The fourth edition of my book *The Nature of Adolescence* was published in 2011. Since that time, I have been encouraged to write more about adolescence, and this completely new book – *All About Adolescence* – is the result. The world has changed in so many ways since 2011, and a new book about adolescence written in 2025 has to cover many different topics and take a different view of the challenges inherent in this life stage. The most obvious changes in focus and in content will include new information about the brain, the role of the internet, including social media and artificial intelligence, the importance of the pandemic of 2020/2021, climate change, new discourses about gender and ethnic identity and a wider, more detailed approach to the mental health of young people.

Interview quotes

I feel like parents are now more aware of the things that could be dangerous. I feel like there is more control over being a teenager now than there might have been, in, say, the '80s. I feel like every generation perceives that they have it harder than the last person.

(Young woman, aged 15)

I think it is quite rewarding, because you are like the same thing, but different. You have all these responsibilities, but you have none at the same time. So, like, you get to enjoy life and experience it, but it's sort of contradictory. People expect so much of you, but then nothing at all from you!

(Young man, aged 16)

I think being an immigrant child, when you go through teenagerhood, you become stuck in the crossfire of where you belong.

(Young woman, aged 17)

I'm kind of, like, always stressed, and I'm always worried. But then I know it's just in my head, and I kind of go, the time will pass, you don't have to do amazing, just go through it. But yes, stress comes like a freaking brick to me.

(Young woman, aged 17)

It's hard, like, older generations, they're, like, pooping on our parade and stuff. And like a lot of them, so we're lazy, and we don't do this, and we don't do that. But I feel we're more hard working than they are. And also, for us, to be hard working, we've got our phones that distract us so easily.

(Young woman, aged 16)

The worst part of being a teenager ... it's probably going on your phone. You're being so obsessed with your phone, and like technology, that you kind of forget the social side. That's been tough. And, like, obviously, the hate on social media, that, like, really affects you.

(Young man, aged 15)

It's like there's a million and one different thoughts doing cartwheels and zigzagging across your mind. It feels excruciatingly difficult to find a clear space in your head to focus on one thing at a time. Sometimes it feels like you're being carried away by a rip current composed of all your worries and deadlines and thoughts.

(Young woman, aged 17)

Chapter 1

Introduction

Adolescence – how can we understand this stage of life? Is it one stage or many? Is it a troubled time, or a time when young people grow and flourish? Is it a time of dread for parents and carers, or a time of greater companionship and mutual support? How can we make sense of all these changes, if it is a time of maturation in body and mind? There is no one way to navigate the adolescent years, and an acknowledgement of individual differences is essential for an understanding of any one young person.

> I like being a teenager. I think it is quite fun. I like social media. I like dressing the way I do, and doing my make-up and hair, just the way I like it, not because I feel any sort of social pressure. It is very like 'freeing', and I do what I like.
>
> (Young woman, aged 16)

For my purposes, in this book, I consider adolescence as a stage in human development. By this, I mean that it is a time of constant change. It is a process as the individual moves from childhood to being an adult. This process takes time, and because it is a process, it means that nothing stays the same for very long. To help us understand this, I have proposed the STAGE framework. I will outline this towards the end of the chapter when I discuss theories and models of adolescence.

In recent years, there has been much debate about the possible frailty of young people. The phrase *the snowflake generation* is one that has received attention from commentators, implying that the resilience of previous generations appears to be lacking today. A book that has received considerable attention is titled *The Anxious Generation* (Haidt, 2024). This and other publications focus on an increased level of mental health problems among the young. Many argue that this rise may be associated with, or even caused by, the widespread use of social

DOI: 10.4324/9781032640433-1

media, as is argued in the best-selling publication "*Stolen focus*" by Johann Hari (2022). This is a theme I will explore in detail during the course of this book.

> The worst part of being a teenager ... it's probably going on your phone. You're being so obsessed with your phone, and like technology, that you kind of forget the social side. That's been tough. And, like, obviously, the hate on social media, that, like, really affects you.
>
> (Young man, aged 15)

In my own work over the last decade, I have been concentrating on the changes that take place in the adolescent brain (Coleman, 2021, 2024). It is a remarkable fact that until the early 2000s, it was believed that the brain stopped developing at the end of childhood. Until the advent of brain imaging or scanning, there was no way of learning what happens in the brain. This new knowledge has completely changed the way we understand this stage of development. I will explore our understanding of the adolescent brain in Chapter 2.

In the world of academic research, it is disappointing that so little attention is paid to this life stage. There is hardly any focus on this topic within universities, even in courses on developmental psychology. In the professional training of teachers, social workers, health workers and others, very little time is devoted to understanding teenagers. Yet this stage is one of the most important in the whole of the life course, since experiences during these years have long-term implications. Not only that, but it is also one of the most fascinating stages in human development, since so much happens during the years from 10 to 20. The transition from child to adult occurs across every domain, including the biological, cognitive and social domains.

It is especially important to understand this life stage now, since so much change is taking place in the world which has serious repercussions for young people. The spectre of global warming hangs over this generation and is undoubtedly having an impact on the mental health of young people. Emigration and the movement of people create new challenges that will continue to grow in the future.

The digital world is evolving so rapidly that it is hard to keep up, with the possibilities offered through artificial intelligence (AI) changing the face of education and personal relationships. In addition, we have experienced one of the most serious pandemics since the Spanish flu of the 1920s. It remains unclear what the long-term effects of Covid-19 will be on the generation that missed school in 2020 and 2021. I will return to this later in the book.

There are huge rewards to be gained by studying this life stage. Adolescence is both a challenge and a delight. It is a time when new skills develop, and when a more differentiated and complex social life becomes possible. It is a stage when family relationships are transformed. There is an opportunity for greater separation from parents, as well as for more closeness and equality. It is a stage when serious questions about values and attitudes come to the fore. The individual starts to grapple with some of the biggest questions about identity and the future. Adolescence is a delight because there is great pleasure to be gained for adults in the idealism and enthusiasm for life apparent in this stage of a young person's development. It is a challenge, however, because there are undoubtedly many difficulties and obstacles to be overcome if adults and teenagers are to get on well with each other.

> I think people think of a teenager as being moody, lazy, can't do anything, stays in the room all day. But really most teenagers aren't like that. From my perspective I am quite a bubbly person, sociable, sometimes lazy, but that is me. I think people put teenagers in a box, they put every teenager in that box, and that is ridiculous.
>
> (Young woman, aged 15)

What exactly is adolescence? For many people, this life stage is a puzzle. It is far from clear when the stage starts and when it ends. Where do the boundaries of adolescence lie? Even in the last decade, these questions have come to the fore, with children appearing to become mature earlier, and older teenagers remaining in the home and delaying work for longer. It has been argued that adolescence starts at puberty and ends at the age of 20. Is this too simplistic? For some purposes, the age of 13 is a good starting point. After all, this is when a child officially becomes a teenager. Clearly this may make sense in one way, but some aspects of adolescence are apparent, even at age 10 or 11.

An individual grows up in the context of social, political and economic circumstances. As I have indicated, we are living through times of great change, and these changes are bound to impact the lives of young people. So, how much has the experience of adolescence changed over the past 30 years? There are many different pressures and demands on young people and on their parents today, and it will be obvious that in many important respects, adolescence in the 2020s is different to what it was in the 1980s or 1990s.

> I don't really know if it is more difficult because I have no experience of being a teenager at any other point. But yes, I feel like parents are now

> more aware of the things that could be dangerous. I feel like there is more control over being a teenager now than there might have been, in, say, the '80s. I feel like every generation perceives that they have it harder than the last person.
>
> (Young woman, aged 15)

For many, this stage is perceived as a problematic one. The notion of "storm and stress" is still current among the general population. Notions about offensive behaviour, the use of drugs or youth violence are common. This image is one often highlighted in media representations of youth. Then there are the experiences of parents and carers of teenagers. In my work with groups of parents, I see, time and time again, the sense of dread at the approach of the teenage years. Families are convinced that this is going to be a difficult time. It is a fascinating question as to how this belief is engendered, and what can be done to reduce the possibility of family conflict.

There is a nice quote from the famous diary of Anne Frank which illustrates how young people experience parents at this stage:

> If I talk everyone thinks I am showing off, when I am silent, they think I am ridiculous: rude if I answer back, sly if I get a good idea, lazy if I'm tired, selfish if I eat a mouthful more than I should, stupid, cowardly, crafty etc., etc., etc.
>
> (Frank, 1993, page 57. (first published 1947))

One of the great conundrums of adolescence is whether adults see young people in an excessively negative light. It might be argued that the adult world exaggerates the more problematic features of this stage. Others take the view that negative perceptions of young people are directly caused by their own behaviour. This is one of the many questions that will be discussed in this book.

There are many academic questions which challenge anyone seeking to understand adolescence today. Does it make sense to talk of this as a single life stage? Perhaps it is more complex than that, since adolescence lasts more than 10 years. There has been some suggestion of a new stage, called "emerging adulthood". This would apply to those in the later teenage years and into early adulthood, as, for example, ages 18 to 25. Are there other stages, such as the "pre-teen" stage, that could be applied to those between 9 and 12? Many writers have attempted to divide this period of life into the three stages of "early", "middle" and "late" adolescence. Does this work? We will consider this further in a moment.

Then there is the question of how different theoretical perspectives can be combined. Is adolescence a biological phenomenon, or is it socially constructed? In this book an attempt will be made to incorporate both approaches. As I have noted, our knowledge of the brain has completely altered the way we understand human development during these years. However, we would be blind if we did not look too at the way society construes this stage of development. The context in which young people grow up and the influences that operate in the family and in the wider society evidently have a profound impact on how adolescents navigate this period of their lives. It is essential to incorporate both a biological and a social perspective.

There is a third perspective which is also of importance here. This is the perspective that sees young people as agents of their own development. To put it another way, adolescents may be constructing their own development. For too long, it has been assumed that young people grow up in a world constructed by adults. However, with an increasing focus on notions of agency and a realization that teenagers influence the way adults behave, there may well be an argument for saying that adolescents themselves play as big a part as any other factor in determining their own development.

Finally, there is the question of how research findings and academic theories can be brought together with the actual life experiences of young people and their families. How is it best to study this life stage? Should we rely only on longitudinal research that follows groups over long periods of time? What is the best method that helps us make sense of this hugely complex life stage? We will also need to consider how young people themselves describe their own life experiences. What do they feel about the notion of "storm and stress"? The voices of adolescents and their parents should never be too far away in any search for an understanding of this stage of life.

> I'd say it is very enjoyable, because you have one of the most freedoms you'll probably ever have in your life. You do have stresses, not just in education, some people worry about how popular they are, and that is an extra stress. You might worry, say, about sexual things, but I'd say it is also a great time. You have lots of friends, you have opportunities to go out and so on. You've not got to worry about bills and stuff like that, well hopefully you don't, so that is also a good thing.
>
> (Young man, aged 17)

Adolescent development takes place against a backdrop of changing social and political circumstances. The chapter will view this stage as a major transition, and will consider the elements of transition and their impact on young people. The chapter will conclude with an outline of four different theories, frameworks and models which will contribute to an understanding of adolescence.

The nature of transition

In much of the writing about adolescence, starting with G Stanley Hall's major work published at the beginning of the twentieth century, it has been customary to describe this stage as a transition (Hall, 1904). In many ways, this has seemed to be the best way to encapsulate the nature of the adolescent experience, as the individual moves from childhood to maturity. Yet, there are certainly complications inherent in this approach. It is unclear when this stage starts and when it ends. Furthermore, a stage that lasts 10 years or more cannot simply be seen as one transition. So how best to approach this?

Some writers have attempted to talk of sub-stages, such as early, middle and late adolescence. Here again definitions are slippery, and it is far from clear what the exact meanings of such sub-stages are. Steinberg (2023) suggests 10 to 13 as the early stage, 14 to 17 as the middle stage and 18 to 21 as the late stage. Readers can make up their own minds as to how useful this is. Each of these sub-stages might be considered to have different transitions involved. So, for example, the early sub-stage might involve transition from primary to secondary school. The late sub-stage might lead to transitions from school to college, or even from the family home to independent living.

There is, of course, an inherent problem when using chronological age to describe the different sub-stages, since there is such great variation between individuals in their developmental progress through the teenage years. This is apparent when we consider puberty, something that can occur as early as 9 or 10 or as late as 13 or 14. I will be discussing puberty in the next chapter. In my work with parents of young people, I often say: "*Inside every teenager is both a child and an adult*". This highlights the complexity of this stage of life. It is a theme I will return to later in the book.

> Like you can go through difficult patches a lot. I feel like, certain things happen. I mean one minute you can be happy and joyful and smiling. The next, something happens and then it's just like you've gone quiet. You're like proper keeping it to yourself, and you don't want anyone talking to you. Now I think I have become an anxious person, but it just sort of happened overnight. It just hit me. Like in Year 8 I was fine, I didn't really care about

anything, but now it's just, like so much anxiety about everything. It's quite hard to deal with.

(Young woman, aged 16)

Another way to think about transition is to divide it into three separate domains. Thus, writers have considered transitions to fall within biology, cognition and the social sphere. Evidently, the biological transition will involve the pubertal process as the individual experiences the physical changes of growth and bodily alteration, together with sexual maturation. The biological transition also involves the neurological changes occurring in the adolescent brain. These are a hugely important feature of our current understanding of adolescence, and Chapter 2 will be devoted to this subject.

Alterations in thinking and reasoning contribute to cognitive transitions. During this stage, the individual begins to develop the capacity for abstract thinking, and the ability to construct contrary-to-fact hypotheses. There will be much more about this in Chapter 4. Lastly, social transitions apply both to the changing nature of peer group relationships as well as to the legal restrictions that society applies to this age group. At what age is it allowable to drive a car, join the army or insist on a confidential medical consultation? This three-way division into the biological, social and cognitive areas is important and is certainly one way to conceptualize the various perspectives that may be applied to this age group. It is a division that we will be following throughout this book as we separate topics into different chapters.

I think it is quite rewarding, because you are like the same thing, but different. You have all these responsibilities, but you have none at the same time. So, like, you get to enjoy life and experience it, but it's sort of contradictory. People expect so much of you, but then nothing at all from you! So, it's sort of my family are quite laid back, so they will let me go and do things and experience life, but then they also expect me to do well in school, get good grades and so on. So, it's sort of you have no responsibilities, but you have so many at the same time.

(Young man, aged 17)

When considering transitions, we may want to consider both the entry into adolescence and the move to maturity at the end of this stage. It will be apparent to readers that both these moments in the life course have undergone substantial change in the recent past. There is a significant level of debate about the age of puberty, something I will be reviewing later. For the moment, it is sufficient to say that most commentators believe that some aspects of physical puberty are occurring earlier than in previous decades. However, there is also the question of what has become known as social puberty. This refers to the fact that children from the age of eight or nine onwards are displaying behaviours that were previously seen in older age groups. Examples include greater awareness of sexuality, interest in more adult types of leisure activity, engagement in social media and more evidence of confrontational and challenging relationships.

Turning now to the other end of the age spectrum, we know that leaving adolescence and entering the world of adulthood has become harder as a result of the major social changes of the last 20–30 years. It is interesting to note that writers in the 1990s, such as Jones (1995) and Coles (1996), noted three main status transitions:

- The school to work transition, when an individual leaves school and enters the labour market;
- The domestic transition, in which a young person attains independence from the family of origin;
- The housing transition, involving a permanent move away from the parental home.

It is striking to consider these transitions 30 years later and to note how much has changed. Few today move directly from school to work, with the great majority continuing in some form of training or college education. Also, of course, most have to accept temporary or low-paid jobs before they can expect any permanent employment. Similarly, the domestic and housing transitions are fraught with difficulty for most young adults, with many remaining in the family home or returning home after college education.

> For me it has been quite difficult, overwhelming, all the different things, it's like a transition into adulthood, but you don't really want to … …. Like obviously before people ask you, like, what do you want to do in the future, but now you've actually got to think about what you want to do in the future. I don't really know, and I feel like it's quite a lot of pressure. I don't really want these responsibilities, like having to make my own choices. Like when you're younger you just get told what to do, but now you have to pick for yourself. And that's quite … … it's hard.
>
> (Young man, aged 17)

In addition, of course, there are new transitions which early writers did not consider. These include the transition in the health field at age 18 from paediatric to adult care for those with long-term conditions. For those on welfare benefits in England and Wales, there is also the transition at age 16 from the Disability Living Allowance to the Personal Independence Payment. Such transitions make life especially difficult for the most vulnerable.

Today the concern of many commentators has to do with what is known as navigation through the alternative routes to independence. The effects of poverty and deprivation, or the challenges of having a disability or of being care experienced, are very much at the forefront of the discourse about the later stages of adolescence. There is also a much greater focus on transition for different groups of young people. Issues to do with gender and ethnicity are central here, and have attracted huge debate in recent times. I will be addressing these issues at various points in the book, especially in Chapters 5 and 6.

Many writers have argued that the prolonged transition and the difficulties of entering the labour market may lead to some groups being permanently marginalized. Those living in rural areas, with poor access to resources and services, have greater difficulty than those living in big cities. The impact of the period of austerity in the UK, as well as the ongoing consequences of the pandemic between years 2020 and 2022, continue to act as key factors in the determination of the outcomes for this generation of young people.

An alternative approach to transition is that described by Graber and Brooks-Gunn (1996). Although this paper was published three decades ago, it remains of importance today, and it has been elaborated by authors such as Steinberg (2016). These authors take the view that, while the notion of transition remains critical, we need another concept if we are to fully understand this stage of life. They argue that the additional concept is what they call "turning points". These moments might be a move from one school to another or major changes in family circumstances.

The key point here is to be able to identify circumstances in which turning points within transitions may be more problematic for particular individuals. Graber and Brooks-Gunn see these as being:

- When the turning points within transitions create additional stress, as for example, with delayed puberty;
- When cumulative or simultaneous events occur, so that the individual has too many things to deal with at one time;
- When mental health issues arise at the same time as the turning points are required to be negotiated;

- When there is a lack of "goodness of fit" between the context and behaviour during transition, as for example, a poor school environment for an academic young person.

Such ideas will be especially helpful when we come to consider theories of adolescence in the next section. Both the emphasis on the context of development, as well as the recognition of the timing of events, as key determinants of outcomes is especially important in this regard. Good examples of the relevance of turning points may be found in the literature on foster care (Shaw and Frost, 2013). These authors highlight the concept of turning points in considering how young people adjust when faced with the transition of leaving foster care.

There are many ways of looking at the concept of transition. There are, of course, other transitions in the life course, such as the menopause for women in middle age or retirement from employment in the later stages of life. However, there is little doubt that adolescence is one of the major transitions, and the move from child to adult over a number of years is never going to be all that easy. Transitions can be said to have a number of characteristics. These may include:

- An eager anticipation of the future;
- A sense of regret for the stage that has been left behind;
- A feeling of anxiety in relation to the future;
- A major psychological readjustment;
- A degree of ambiguity of status during the transition.

These characteristics may not apply to all transitions, but it will be clear they certainly apply to adolescence. Adulthood beckons, and with it, freedom and opportunity, which appear very attractive. Yet there is also sadness for what has gone before – the safety, support and love that the child receives from key adults may be lost in adolescence. Young people do worry about what is to come – more so perhaps than for previous generations.

When jobs, housing and the state of the planet are uncertain, it is hardly surprising that adolescents have anxieties about the future. As will be described in this book, a substantial readjustment is required during the course of the adolescent years. This is true in all spheres – with family, in the peer group and in the individual's sense of identity. A number of themes run through the adolescent period, including an intensified concern with status and the realignment of roles. Thus, it makes sense to consider adolescence as a major transition, while at the same time acknowledging that within this stage there are turning points which will have significance for later adaptation.

Theories, models and frameworks of adolescence

In the process of outlining the nature of adolescence, it will be essential to consider some of the major theories and models that have been proposed to explain this stage of life. We will now explore four different approaches:

- The "storm and stress" viewpoint;
- Developmental contextualism;
- The focal model;
- The STAGE framework.

Storm and stress

Looking first at "storm and stress", writers since the time of the Greeks have described adolescence as a problem period. It is often assumed that young people were only seen as troubled and troubling in the 1950s, when the word "teenager" came into fashion (Savage, 2007). Different styles of clothing, musicians such as Elvis Presley and Buddy Holly and films such as *Rebel Without a Cause* appeared to capture a new mood among the young and to mark the arrival of a generation that was "all shook up". Yet in 340 BCE, Aristotle wrote: "Young men have strong desires, and tend to satisfy them indiscriminately. Of the bodily desires, it is the sexual by which they are most easily swayed, and in which they show absence of self-control". He went on to write: "They are changeable and fickle in their desires, which are violent while they last". (*Rhetorica*. In *The Basic Works of Aristotle*. Quoted in Muuss, 1996).

In later centuries a similar view was common. Shakespeare wrote in a number of his plays about the problems of youth, and the poet John Keats, writing in 1815, said:

> The imagination of a boy is healthy, and the mature imagination of a man is healthy, but there is a space of life between, in which the soul is in ferment, the character undecided, the way of life uncertain, the ambition thick-sighted: thence proceeds mawkishness.

In modern times it was undoubtedly the publication of G. Stanley Hall's monumental work of adolescence that set the tone for much of what was written in subsequent decades (Hall, 1904). Hall's exhaustive two-volume study ushered in a new approach to the understanding of adolescence. He described it as a period of "storm and stress", a phrase he took from the Romantic writers of the nineteenth century such as Goethe and Schiller.

This was a literary movement which embraced idealism, passion and suffering. The movement also believed in revolution and the rejection of the old order. Hall argued that the adolescent passed through a turbulent, transitional stage, and that this was necessary for the "higher and more completely human traits" to be accepted.

Hall's view of adolescence was given added weight by the fact that well-known psychoanalytic writers, such as Sigmund and Anna Freud, took a similar view of this stage of life. The psychoanalytic view of adolescence took as its starting point the upsurge of instincts which was believed to occur as a result of puberty. This increase in instinctual life, it was suggested, upsets the psychic balance which has been achieved by the end of childhood and causes internal upheaval. This, in turn, leads to a greatly increased vulnerability of the personality (Freud, 1937).

As might be expected, later psychoanalytic writers, such as Erik Erikson (1968), have elaborated on these early theories. In so doing, they have also moved beyond the notion of "storm and stress" and have worked to explore the contribution of psychoanalysis to different aspects of adolescent development such as identity and family relationships. In addition, more recent writers, such as Frankel (1998) and Brady (2016), have continued to focus on the more troubling aspects of adolescence. There seems little doubt that such theorizing gives continuing impetus to the general view that there is somehow more upheaval in adolescence than in other stages of development.

In retrospect, and knowing what we now know about the changes in the brain in adolescence, the views of Freud and others about turmoil and upheaval make complete sense. As we will set out in Chapter 2, the technology of scanning has made it possible to describe the development of the brain during and after puberty. It is now possible to understand that what the psychoanalysts saw as being caused by an "upsurge of instincts" is much more likely to be caused by changes in the brain at this time of life.

During the 1960s and 1970s, a series of studies appeared challenging the "storm and stress" viewpoint. These studies reported that a majority of young people passed through the adolescent stage without serious emotional difficulties. Studies, such as those of Douvan and Adelson (1966), indicated that the majority of adolescents got on well with their parents and seemingly were able to cope adequately with the challenges of adolescence. Commentators such as Meeus (2019), who looked at evidence from many longitudinal studies, argued that the early theorists did not have access to empirical evidence from large populations. It was assumed that psychoanalysts were making judgements based on adolescents seen in their clinics, where it would be expected that those attending were likely to display higher levels of distress than normal populations.

There is no doubt that there is a minority of young people who do struggle during this stage. It is often argued that most psychiatric conditions appear first during adolescence, and, as we shall show later in the book, the incidence of mental health disorders has increased over the last decade in most Western countries. We are left with a number of contradictions when we consider the "storm and stress" viewpoint. We can be confident that this does not apply to all young people. However, there is a small group who experience problems during their adolescent years. This minority, and the difficulties associated with this group, loom large in the public mind. The notion of adolescence being a "problem" stage is hard to eradicate.

Developmental contextualism

The two theoretical approaches to be considered next highlight different viewpoints, one stressing the context of development, and the other considering how young people cope with the challenges of adolescence. The ideas outlined above relating to transitions and turning points are close to what has been called the life course perspective. This implies a belief that human development can only be understood by taking into account the historical time and place of the individual's life, as well as the actual timing of transitions and major life events (see Hendry, 2015).

The life course perspective is similar to, and associated with, what has become known as developmental contextualism. It is to this set of beliefs that we will now turn. The key figures in the history of this approach are Urie Bronfenbrenner, Paul Baltes and Richard Lerner, as set out by Hendry (2015) and Steinberg (2023). The main elements of developmental contextualism are as follows:

The context, or ecology, of human development is essential to its understanding. The intention here is to underline the importance of the environment in the widest sense, including not only the family, but also the geographical, historical, political and social context or setting in which the child or young person is situated. Glen Elder, who studied the Great Depression of the 1930s, put it like this: "The life course of individuals is embedded in and shaped by the historical times and places they experience over their life-time" (Elder, 1998, page 2).

Timing is critical. This principle implies that when events happen is as important as the events themselves. Elder phrases it as follows: "The developmental impact of a succession of life events or transitions is contingent on when they occur in a person's life" (Elder, 1998, page 3).

There is a continuity to human development. This principle is important in two respects. In the first place, it draws attention to similarities and differences between stages. In this sense, a consideration of the adolescent transition can be compared with other life transitions. The principle is significant also in that it points out the fact that the adolescent stage does not suddenly arrive out of the blue. It is a continuation of development during childhood. Too often writers treat adolescence as a stage unconnected to other life experiences. This principle highlights the interrelation between childhood and adolescence.

Individuals and their families reciprocally influence each other. This principle makes reference to the fact that neither a child nor an adult is an isolated entity. Each grows, develops and changes, and in so doing influences the other at all times. The young person's maturation produces changes in the family. At the same time, alterations in the behaviour of key adults have effects on the adolescent's development.

Individuals are agents of their own development. This is one of the key principles of developmental contextualism. Attention is drawn here to the part that all individuals play in shaping their own development. This is irrespective of age, so it is just as relevant to teenagers as it is to adults or to younger children. This principle has wide-ranging implications for social science and for our recognition of the nature of human growth and change. With respect to adolescence, it is only recently that commentators have come to see young people as "active agents" in shaping or determining the course of their development. The idea that young people both shape and navigate their own paths through the teenage years is influencing the research agenda and has links with the focal model, which we will consider in the next section.

> *When studying the interaction between person and context, attention should be paid to the concept of "goodness of fit".* The "goodness of fit" concept takes into account the relation between the individual and the environment in the widest sense. It considers to what extent the needs and goals of the individual are congruent with the context. Thus, whether a developmental outcome is adaptive or not does not just depend on the characteristics of the individual, or on the nature of the physical or social environment. Rather, the outcome depends on whether these two systems fit together.

There are numerous examples in the literature of research programmes that have used the framework of developmental contextualism. Some of these are summarized in Meeus (2019). Here he discusses longitudinal studies that have explored adolescence using the life span model. The work of Eccles and colleagues (Eccles and Roeser, 2003) on school transitions is a good example of the use of the notion of "goodness of fit". These authors show how the needs of the individual young person and the characteristics of the school environment either work together or lead to dysfunction. Another example is the work of Kerr et al. (2008), who draw on the concept of agency to show that monitoring and supervision by parents only has an effect if the adolescent is willing to cooperate.

Developmental contextualism draws together many strands of thought. As Bronfenbrenner (1979) acknowledged, his theoretical notions were themselves based on earlier studies by commentators and scientists such as Lewin and Vygotsky. Today it is no longer acceptable to consider only one side of the picture. The person and the context are inseparable. In addition, it is no longer possible to ignore the fact that the individual young person shapes her or his own world, an idea that fits with the focal model, which will be explored next.

The focal model

The focal model grew out of the results of a study of adolescent development (Coleman, 1974). In brief, large groups of boys and girls at the ages of 11, 13, 15 and 17 were given identical tests which elicited from them attitudes and opinions about a wide range of relationships. Material was included on self-image, being alone, heterosexual relationships, parental relationships, friendships and large group situations. The material was analyzed in terms of the positive and negative elements present in these relationship situations and in terms of the common themes expressed by the participants. Findings showed that attitudes to all relationships differed as a function of age. More importantly, the results also indicated that concerns about various issues reached a peak at different stages of the adolescent process.

It was this finding that led to the formulation of the focal model. The model suggests that at different ages particular sorts of relationship patterns come into focus, in the sense of being most prominent. However, no pattern is specific to one age only. The patterns overlap, and different issues come to the fore at different times. Simply because an issue is not the most prominent feature of a specific age, this does not mean it may not be critical for some individuals.

In many ways, this model is not dissimilar from any traditional stage theory. However, it carries with it a more flexible view of development. Thus, it differs from the traditional theories in three ways. Firstly, the resolution of one issue is not seen as a prerequisite for tackling the next. In fact, it is clearly envisaged that a minority will find themselves facing more than one issue at the same time. Secondly, the model does not assume the existence of fixed boundaries between stages. Issues are not specifically linked with a specific age or developmental stage. Finally, there is nothing immutable about the sequence involved.

As I have mentioned, empirical research shows us that the majority of young people appear to cope relatively well with adolescence. Only a minority struggle with this phase of development. So, how, it was asked, is it possible for young people to experience such a range of transitions, while at the same time managing without undue stress or difficulty (Coleman, 1978)?

One possible explanation for the successful adaptation of so many young people is provided by the focal model. The answer suggested by the model is that they cope by dealing with one issue at a time. They spread the process of adaptation over a span of years, dealing with one issue at a time. Different problems, different relationship issues come into focus and are tackled at different stages. The various stresses resulting from the need to adapt to new modes of behaviour are rarely concentrated at one time.

It follows from this that it is precisely among those who, for whatever reason, do have more than one issue to deal with at any one time that problems are most likely to occur. Thus, for example, when puberty and the growth spurt are delayed while at the same time difficulties in the peer group impinge on the young person, it thus becomes so much more difficult to manage well. Over time, there have been a number of studies which provide support for the notions implied by the focal model. Kloep (1999) showed that among Norwegian adolescents it was clear that they adapted by addressing one relationship issue at a time. Call and Mortimer (2001) showed that where adolescents have at least one source of support they are better able to deal with stresses in other arenas. They put forward the notion of "arenas of comfort", something that has been picked up by other authors commenting on coping in this age group (Frydenberg, 2019).

There is one other key aspect of the focal model that needs to be emphasized. This is the notion of agency, one already mentioned earlier. The focal model argues that the young person is an agent is her or his own development, managing the adolescent transition – where possible – by dealing with one issue at a time. While at first sight this idea may be difficult to grasp, a little thought will show that it is not so far-fetched. Consider for a moment the range of choices open to a young person. In any one day, an adolescent may choose to confront a parent at the breakfast table, to argue with a sibling or to stand up to a teacher. Every one of these situations offers the young person a choice. It is quite realistic to suggest that most young people pace themselves through this transition. Many will hold back on one issue while they are grappling with another. Most sense what they can and cannot cope with, and will be active agents in their own worlds.

It has to be recognized, however, that not all young people will have the same freedom to shape and manage their development. As has already been noted, when many events occur at one time, it will be more difficult for the individual to manage the transitional process. In addition, those who grow up in circumstances of deprivation, who face adversity due to illness or disability, or those who experience prejudice and discrimination will inevitably face constraints in terms of options and choices for their life course. Nonetheless, there is every reason to believe that, in the majority of cases, it can be said that the young person is constructing their own adolescence. Imagine a young person talking to a youth worker, or to a prison officer. Even in these situations, the individual will be making choices and deciding how to respond. They will be planning what to disclose and what to hold back, how to shape the interaction. It is in this sense that agency plays such a key role in human development.

> I can't really explain it .... I think, looking back at what was happening 20 years ago, teenagers' lives were totally different. There was nothing to judge against, like there were no people to look at and be like – I want to look like her, look like them. Now I feel you're getting people on the internet that are different, and I think it is quite good to look at and be like – would I like to be this, would I like to be that?
>
> (Young person, aged 17)

A number of commentators have given support to the notion of the adolescent as constructor of her or his own development. Within studies of gene-environment interaction there have been suggestions of what is known as "niche-picking". Here individuals are shown to select the environments that best suit their developmental needs. In studies of family relationships, researchers have looked at what is known as information management. This identifies the process whereby young people actively select which information to share with their parents, and which information to hold back (Keijsers and Laird, 2010; Marshall et al. 2005). When investigating problem behaviour, researchers have shown how the actions of young people both predicts and moderates the way parents respond (Reitz et al. 2006).

Many of the quotes used throughout this book Illustrate how adolescents actively work to shape their own developmental pathways. More will be said about this process throughout the book.

The STAGE framework

This framework is in a somewhat different category from the three previous approaches. It originated in my work with parents. It came about as a result of one parent asking me: "Do we really know what is good parenting for a teenager?" I considered this and came to the conclusion that I could summarize the key research findings about parenting into a short mnemonic. It was in this way that the STAGE framework came to be proposed (Coleman, 2019). Each of the letters in the word STAGE represents an essential element in effective parenting for young people.

I use the word *stage* since I want to emphasize that this is a stage of life, and thus it will involve constant change and development. Adolescents will not remain the same. If there are struggles and conflicts, it is important to remember that things will change as the young person matures. It is a process, although one that may not always be visible to adults who live with or work with young people on a daily basis. I will give greater detail about the framework in Chapter 8 when I discuss parenting and the family. For the moment, I can summarize it as follows:

S stands for *significance*. This refers to the significance of parents. While young people may want to push parents aside, all the research shows that parents are hugely significant in the lives of adolescents. Parents really do matter.

T stands for *two-way communication*. This underlines the fact that good communication involves both talking and listening. Parents often use one-way communication with young people. Yet, one-way communication does not encourage open talk between parents and teenagers.

A is for *authority*. The use of parental authority in the adolescent stage has to be different from the way authority was exercised during childhood years.

G represents the *generation gap*. This underlines the fact that parents and young people have had very different experiences in growing through these years. It is important that parents do not judge their young people by the experiences and standards that operated in their youth.

E stands for *emotion*. This refers to the emotions of both parents and young people. Emotion regulation can be hard for adolescents. Yet, parents too will experience difficult emotions in their relationships with their teenagers. It is essential for parents to learn to manage their emotions, so that two sets of difficult feelings do not become magnified and thereby get in the way of good relationships.

The STAGE framework has been used in many contexts since it was first proposed (Coleman, 2019). It has been used in telephone counselling, in one-to-one work with parents and in group settings. I have outlined examples of how the framework has been used in group work relating to the teenage brain (Coleman, 2024). The advantages of the STAGE framework are that it is simple to remember and that it is based on research findings relating to the parenting of adolescents (Roker and Coleman, 2007).

Conclusion

Adolescence is both a stage and a transition. It is important to recognize it as a stage in the life course, since there is significant change in all domains. Calling it a stage underlines the point that this is a process of development, as the young person moves from childhood to maturity. It is also a transition, possibly one of the major transitions in life. As with all transitions there is uncertainty as well as opportunity. One of the major alterations in our understanding of adolescence has been the availability of new knowledge concerning the changes taking place in the adolescent brain. I believe this knowledge offers an important opportunity to rethink adolescence and to open up new perspectives on this life stage. In this chapter, I have outlined theories and models which have been proposed to help explain adolescence. I have emphasized the point that young people are agents of their own development, navigating their way through the many decisions and turning points inherent in the passage to maturity. In the next chapter, I will provide a description of the human brain and outline how it alters during adolescence.

Chapter 2

The adolescent brain*

Introduction

As I pointed out in the previous chapter, our understanding of the teenage brain has altered the way we make sense of adolescence. Understanding the brain leads to a completely different picture of the teenage years. For centuries, adolescents have puzzled, confused and infuriated adults. Why is it that young people have to argue about everything that adults say? Why are they so confusing – happy one moment and cast into despair the next? How is that the normal chatty child has turned into a bad-tempered recluse?

The clue is in the brain. Once parents, carers, teachers and others learn what is happening in the teenage brain, they can see that the confusing behaviour makes sense. For the last few years, I have been running groups for parents in which I outline the main facts about brain development. The result? Parents talk about a *light-bulb moment.* They report a complete change of attitude to their son or daughter. "*Wow! I really didn't know all this*" said one parent to me. "*I will be so much more sympathetic now*". Another said: "*This will change the way I relate to my 15-year-old*". Lastly, this comment was especially powerful: "*If only we had understood this earlier so many problems might have been avoided*".

This knowledge really does have the potential to change family relationships. Of course, there are other factors at play. I will discuss these at various points during the book. One big factor is the social circumstances that affect all teenagers. At what point are they grown up? When can they make decisions for themselves? What rights do parents have over health and educational choices? These questions highlight the fact that the teenage years are a transition from child to

* I have not referenced the material in this chapter. It is a summary of the basic science which will be found in all good textbooks. I have given a list of these at the end of the chapter. The material can also be found in my books: "*The Teacher and the Teenage Brain*" (Routledge, 2021) and "*The Psychology of the Teenage Brain*" (Routledge 2024).

DOI: 10.4324/9781032640433-2

adult. And transitions can be uncomfortable. It will be much easier to deal with the questions thrown up by the process of transition if we take into account the impact of the changes in the brain.

Understanding the brain

The brain is a mystery. It is also a thing of wonder. The human brain is the most complex entity in nature. It is quite small – you can hold it in your hands. It is an organ, but it acts as a machine, a controller and a manifestation of human evolution, and it is the single most determining feature of each and every one of us.

It is a mystery because there is still so much we do not know about the brain. While neuroscience has made huge strides in the last 20 years, we are still at the very beginning of the search for a full understanding of the brain. Some writers call the brain "the inner cosmos". This is because it has a capacity that is so vast and because it is mostly as yet unexplored.

It is a thing of wonder, because the feats the brain performs are remarkable. Our brains manage our emotions, determine our actions, store our memories, create our dreams, help us deal with threats and keep us alive by regulating temperature, blood levels, energy and the sleep/wake cycle.

In this chapter, I will explain the basic processes that take place when we think, feel, relate and respond to our environment. Until quite recently, it was believed that the brain stopped developing at the end of childhood. We knew very little of what happens to the brain in adolescence. Since the advent of scanning, the picture has changed completely. We now know the brain undergoes major change during the teenage years. These changes have implications for the way adolescents behave and the way they deal with the challenges of this stage of life.

A short description of the human brain

The brain contains billions of cells. You will have heard people talk about "little grey cells". Your brain contains in the region of 80 billion "little grey cells". These cells are known as neurons. This is an unimaginable number! In fact, the joke is that the human brain cannot comprehend that number of neurons! This is a number that is greater than all the stars in the galaxy, nearly eight or nine times more than the entire global population.

All these billions of neurons are connected to other neurons in patterns and networks. We still know little about how these neurons combine together. It is hard to understand how the billions and billions of neurons can work together without getting into a tangle in the small space that is the human brain.

All our bodily systems are powered by the oxygen in our blood stream, and the brain is no exception. The brain also uses electrical and chemical processes to send messages along the pathways that connect the neurons together. These pathways are the nerve fibres that stretch across and around the brain. Each neuron has a number of nerve fibres reaching out to other neurons in the system. Messages or impulses are carried around the brain along these nerve fibres.

One remarkable feature of the brain is that there is a tiny gap in the nerve fibre or branch that reaches out from every neuron. This gap is called a *synapse*, and it means that the message or impulse has to jump over the gap to reach the next neuron. This is an important part of the picture, and I will say more about the synapse in a minute.

In order to understand the brain, we need to picture the different roles that various sites perform. The brain is immensely complex, so I will just concentrate on the most important sites. The first part to mention is known as the *prefrontal cortex*. This site is associated with thinking, reasoning and problem-solving. Some people like to call it the "command and control" centre. It is located at the front of the brain and can be considered the rational, sensible part of the brain which helps us think about the consequences of our actions.

The second site to mention is the *amygdala*. This is located deep in the middle of the brain, and is the part that processes and manages our emotions. The amygdala is that feature of the brain that determines our feelings, but it is also the site that is most affected by stress and difficult experiences. The third part of the brain to mention is the *hippocampus*. This is where memory is processed and stored for a short time until it is passed on to long-term memory (Figure 2.1).

The synapse

I have already mentioned the synapse. This tiny gap plays an important part in the story. Within this gap are what are known as neurotransmitters. They are essentially chemical messengers, as they help or hinder the sending of impulses along the nerve fibres. Another way to think about the synapse is to think of it as an on/off mechanism. The chemical messengers within the synapse are a bit like traffic lights, showing green to indicate go, or showing red to indicate stop.

Some people liken this system to an air traffic control setup. I prefer to think about it as a railway network. If a railway network had no signalling system, the trains would bump into each other, and the system would come to a standstill.

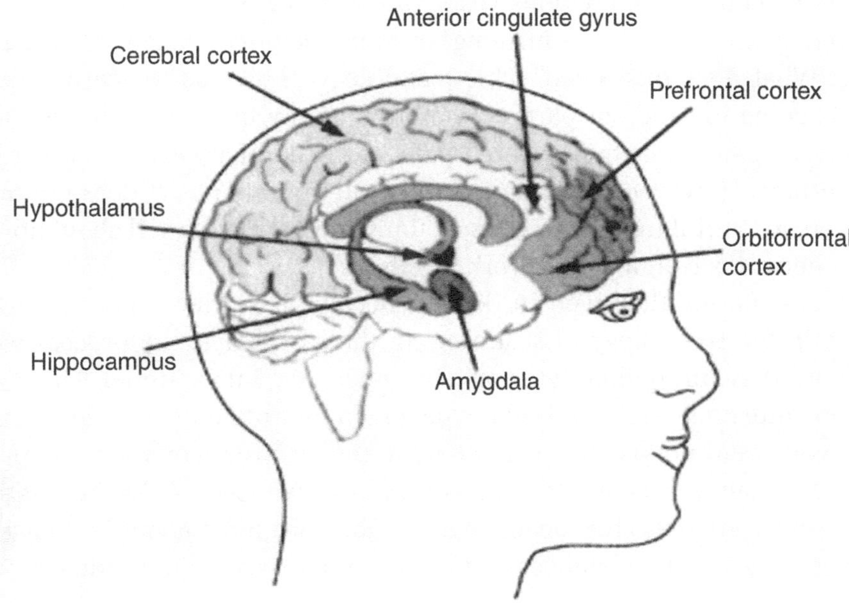

Figure 2.1 Illustration of the sites of the brain

Imagine the multitude of neurons and networks all sending trillions of messages all the time in your brain. Without some form of signalling, there would be chaos!

Take a moment to think about yourself while you are reading this. You are bombarded by an enormous number of stimuli. You could concentrate on the noises outside the room, the ache in one of your muscles, the memories you have about what happened at breakfast, the worries you have about the work you are meant to be doing and so on. It is easy for us to become overwhelmed with the sheer volume of possible stimuli. We would not be able to concentrate or pay attention if we did not have a system for blocking out the distractions.

This system is called inhibition, or the inhibitory process. This is especially important for young people in the classroom. The on/off mechanism is essential if they are to be able to concentrate. And yet, there are those who find this difficult. For them, the mechanism is not working as well as it should. I will return to this topic later in the book when I discuss neurodiversity.

Scanning

The last 20 years have seen a gigantic leap forward in our understanding of the human brain. This is because of the development of the technology of scanning. It is now possible to take pictures of the brain as it functions, without any distress or discomfort. In previous years, this would have been impossible. The technology is known as brain imaging, or to be technical, magnetic resonance imaging. What does this mean? This technology allows us to see how much oxygen is going to different parts of the brain at any one time. This is a huge advance, as it enables us to see which parts of the brain are active under different conditions. However, scanning can only tell us so much. It does not tell us what a person is thinking. There is also a limit to what we can tell about how the different networks combine and work together.

It is worth noting that even in the last decade or so there have been huge advances in the technology of scanning. In the early days, the process would have involved the individual lying on a bed and going into a tunnel. This would have been quite noisy and required the person to lie still for 30 to 40 minutes. As a result, you could not use the technology in the classroom or when the person was moving around. Recently the technology has advanced, so that mobile scanners are now available. This means that we can learn more about brain activity in a wider range of circumstances and with a wider range of individuals.

The changing teenage brain

The adolescent period can be a confusing and contradictory time of life. The young person is growing and changing. While still a child, the individual is also becoming an adult. This contradiction means that things are often topsy-turvy. The young person can be happy and sad, grown-up and needy all at the same time. Most importantly, in this context, the contradiction is reflected in the brain.

On the one hand, the brain is maturing, allowing the young person to develop new skills and capabilities. On the other hand, the brain is also undergoing a major re-organization, leading to times of confusion and uncertainty. I will deal with the positives first.

All parts of the brain will mature during the years from puberty onwards. This maturation leads to increased skills and capacities in all areas, whether these be physical abilities, sexual maturation or cognitive functions. One of the key areas here is the prefrontal cortex. It is this part of the brain which is most active during the learning process. Maturation here allows for better memory, improved vocabulary and the development of scientific reasoning. Better communication skills will also be developing. Adults sometimes find this hard to comprehend, but watching young people with their friends makes this plain to see.

In addition to the maturation of the brain, other things are happening too. During the period around puberty, there is an over-production of neurons and connections. At first sight, this may seem a strange thing to happen. In fact, this has happened earlier in childhood as well. What happens then is known as *pruning*. More neurons have been produced than can be accommodated, and as a result the brain allows the unwanted neurons and connections to die away. In the long run, this leads to a positive outcome. We sometimes say it leads to a "*meaner, leaner machine*"!

It is inevitable that this process leads to a significant re-structuring and re-organization of the brain. Scientists reckon that, on average, some parts of the brain lose 17% of the grey matter during the teenage years. Imagine what you would think if I were to tell you that you were going to lose so much of your brain in the next few years! It is a daunting thought. And it is no wonder that the process leads to times of confusion and uncertainty. As I have said, the outcome is positive. It allows the brain to function more efficiently. However, there is some cost in the process of actually getting there.

Hormones

One other fact should be considered here. This has to do with the role of hormones. This is a period when there is an upset in the hormone balance. Readers will know that the teenage years are sometimes described as a time of "raging hormones". We can see this in common behaviours such as mood swings and the flip-flop of emotions.

One of the things we have learnt as a result of research on the teenage brain is that there is a marked level of variation in the hormone balance in this age group. All of us have some daily variation in the balance of hormones in our brains. The variation for teenagers, however, is much greater than for other age groups. Thus, the level of any of the key hormones may be going up or down to a significant extent in any one 24-hour period. It is not surprising then that this affects behaviour and means that emotion regulation is that much harder for young people. There are dozens of hormones that circulate both in our bodies and in our brains. I will describe a few of the ones that are most important for teenage brain development.

The first hormone to mention is *cortisol*. This is one of the key stress hormones, along with adrenaline. Cortisol is released in the brain when we are anxious, stressed or vulnerable. On a short-term basis, cortisol can be useful. When we are under threat, this is the hormone that prepares our body to respond appropriately. This is the famous "fight or flight" response. However, too much cortisol has a detrimental effect and leads to poor functioning.

The next hormone to consider is *serotonin*. This is the hormone which is released when we are happy, relaxed or at ease. This is the hormone that helps keep our mood steady. Low levels of serotonin can be a factor in low mood or depression. Variation in serotonin levels may play a part in leaving young people at the mercy of feelings of sadness or misery. Teenagers may have extreme reactions to minor setbacks. Common difficulties may lead to the belief that "the end of the world has arrived". Such catastrophic reactions are related to levels of serotonin which affect the amygdala and other sites in the brain.

The third hormone to discuss here is *dopamine*. This is commonly known as the reward hormone. We have learnt that there is more dopamine in the teenage brain than in the adult brain. There are more dopamine receptors in the brain during these years, and this has a profound effect on behaviour. Readers may have heard people speaking of a "dopamine rush". Dopamine is a hormone that is especially active in the brain during the teenage years. This can lead to a sensitivity to rewards, as well as motivation to seek rewards.

Finally, I will mention *melatonin*. This is the hormone that makes us feel sleepy and signals that it is time to go to bed. As a result of research on the brain, we have learnt that melatonin is released later at night in young people than it is for adults. This means that it is harder for many teenagers to get to sleep, and this has implications for the amount of sleep that teenagers are getting on school nights. Sleep is extremely important for all of us, but it is particularly important for teenagers. I will deal with this in greater detail in Chapter 3.

Sites of the brain

In talking about the brain, I have mentioned the amygdala. This is the predominant site that processes and manages our emotions. However, the brain is extremely complex, and many sites play a part in determining our moods and emotions. The amygdala itself is part of a larger system known as the limbic system. It is also important to remember that the brain is in two halves – two hemispheres. Each of the sites exists in both hemispheres, so each site is mirrored on both sides of the brain.

This raises the question of how the two halves of the brain work together. The term *connectivity* refers to the processes that allow the two halves of the brain to be coordinated. The bridge in the middle of the brain that makes this connectivity possible is called the *corpus callosum*. One of the ways we measure maturity in the brain is by seeing how this bridge gradually becomes more sophisticated and elaborate as the young person grows older.

Another part of the brain that is important to mention here is that associated with reward processing. In years gone by, before scanning was available, scientists believed that there is a reward centre in the brain. This notion was based on research on animals. It was a great surprise when results from scanning confirmed this belief. It turns out that there is, indeed, a site in the human brain that processes rewards. This site, known as the *nucleus accumbens*, can be seen to become especially active and aroused when rewards are presented or even imagined.

In addition to connectivity across the two halves of the brain, there is also the question of how the sites are coordinated. So, for example, it is important to consider how the prefrontal cortex is networked with the sites processing emotions. This is pertinent, since the stronger the networks between these two areas of the brain, the more likely it is that the individual will be able to manage and control the hormones that activate emotional behaviour. It is probable that, during the teenage years, the networks that connect the prefrontal cortex and the amygdala will gradually strengthen. While these networks remain immature, the individual may struggle to control emotions. As the networks become more mature, this process becomes easier, and more adult behaviour becomes possible.

Risky behaviour

Questions to do with risk and risk-taking have a long history in the study of adolescence. From the time that the idea of "the teenager" came to public notice, from the 1940s onwards, risk-taking was considered to be a key element of teenage behaviour. This led to a big debate about whether this idea was unfair to young people. Many argued that not all teenagers take risks. And, furthermore, some risk-taking may be necessary in order to explore the world and experiment with what is safe and what is harmful.

This is where the study of the brain comes in. It is important to note that the brain matures from back to front. This means that the amygdala, part of the limbic system in the central area of the brain, may mature earlier than the prefrontal cortex. After the advent of scanning (say from the years 2000 to 2010), research was appearing that suggested this was the reason that young people are risk-takers. If the areas of the brain to do with thinking, reasoning and problem-solving are maturing more slowly than sites to do with emotion and sensation, that may explain why young people find it hard to consider whether their behaviour is safe or unsafe. In other words, here is the reason why young people take risks without fully considering the consequences of their actions.

In recent years scientists have become much more cautious about this explanation. As more studies have been published, it has become apparent that early conclusions were premature. Extensive studies have shown very large differences between individuals. While in some, the brain may mature from back to front, this is not the case for everyone. And then, in addition, it should be obvious that many factors affect risk-taking. The level of hormones in the brain has an impact. And, the brain and the environment interact, so that social factors will also influence risk-taking.

Earlier in this chapter I mentioned the hormone dopamine. This is the reward hormone, and there is more dopamine in the teenage brain than in the adult brain. For some young people, at some points in time, higher levels of dopamine may lead to a push for rewards and exciting experiences. This push may easily encourage risky behaviour.

We should also note the impact of social factors, such as the influence of other members of the family. Parents and older siblings may act as role models and thereby offer examples of certain types of risky behaviour. We also know that the peer group plays a part here too. I will discuss this in greater detail in Chapter 9. However, at this point it is important to note that studies clearly show higher levels of risk-taking when peers are present.

One interesting focus of recent research has been an attempt to distinguish between what are called "hot" and "cold" situations. This links with what I was saying about self-control and being able to hold back before taking action. What does this mean? The distinction refers to the amount of emotion present in the situation. So, for example, a "hot" situation may be one where the young person is at a party, surrounded by friends or one where the stakes are high in terms of relationships or attractive rewards. Brain imaging shows that areas of the brain, such as the amygdala, are more active in such situations. In these circumstances, it is harder to engage the prefrontal cortex and thus to avoid risky behaviour.

It may be useful to describe the adolescent as a "trainee adult". After all, there are many situations where individuals can be described as trainees. So, for example, in a work setting, individuals at the start of their placement are trainees. In such circumstances, they are not expected to get everything right the first time. We allow the trainee to make some mistakes, as this is part of the learning process. The same could be said for the teenager. Adults should be able to take this into account. So, when a young person appears to get something wrong, it is important to "cut them some slack". They won't get everything right first time. That is fine, as it is all part of the process of growing up and learning how to be an adult.

Reward processing

As noted previously, dopamine is known as the reward hormone, and there is more of this in the teenage brain than in the adult brain. It is for this reason that there has been a strong focus on the topic of rewards and reward-processing in recent research. Dopamine has two functions. On the one hand, it encourages behaviour that may lead to a reward or a sensation of pleasure. On the other, it also has a separate role, in that dopamine is released following a reward, causing a feeling of well-being and satisfaction.

Many studies, using both animal and human subjects, have shown a peak level of the release of dopamine during the adolescent period. This means that young people are more sensitive to the potential rewards that come from the use of social media, and from using drugs, going to parties or eating fast food and sugary snacks. This finding has big implications for understanding teenage behaviour. It also has relevance if we want to identify the things that are most likely to motivate young people, whether that is in the classroom or at home.

I will mention a couple of studies here that illustrate this point. The first makes use of "the wheel of fortune" game. Here participants spin the wheel, as in roulette, and the number the wheel lands on determines the level of reward. Both adults and young people take part while their brains are being scanned. The results indicate that teenagers show more activity than adults in the reward areas of the brain when they win.

Another similar study has the participants seeing three cues on a screen. Each cue is associated with a different level of reward. The goal is to identify the cue that gives the highest level of reward. The earnings associated with each cue are then shown on the screen. Participants can then get feedback on how much reward they will receive. The results demonstrate that areas in the brain associated with reward are activated to a greater degree in adolescents than in other age groups. Also of interest is the fact that these areas continue to show a higher level of activation for a longer period after reward in the teenage participants.

These findings have great significance. The knowledge we now have about the importance of rewards for young people should change the way adults engage with this generation. Why? Because we know that, in the relationships between adults and young people, there tends to be less focus on reward and more focus on nagging, complaints and general negative feedback. Once adults recognize how sensitive teenagers are to reward, a shift in behaviour becomes possible. This is relevant as much to the school setting as it is to the home.

Some may say, what rewards? Of course, rewards should be age-appropriate. What may be rewarding for a 12-year-old will not be suitable for a 16-year-old. Rewards associated with consumer behaviour, whether money, toys, gadgets or similar things, should be avoided. The most effective rewards are praise, recognition, support and the giving of appropriate responsibility. Adolescents need recognition and endorsement from adults, and these will prove more powerful than any other type of reward.

Drugs and alcohol

These topics link closely with notions of risk and reward. When I give webinars about the teenage brain, one of the most common questions has to do with the use of alcohol, cannabis or other drugs. Participants usually want to know whether the presence of particular hormones in the teenage brain explains why some teenagers are especially attracted to the use of substances. Naturally this leads on the question of what we can do about addiction or the over-use of drugs and alcohol.

In thinking about the effects of alcohol on the brain, the impact will, of course, depend on how much the individual is drinking. In addition, we know that, again, there are individual differences in alcohol tolerance. Alcohol affects three key areas of the brain – the frontal areas, the hippocampus and the cerebellum. The frontal areas have to do with thinking and reasoning, the hippocampus is where memories are processed, and the cerebellum is the area controlling physical movement.

Why is drinking appealing, especially to young people? The immediate effect is that alcohol impacts the hormones that affect anxiety and stress, so that drinking leads to disinhibition and a greater sense of ease in social situations. In addition, alcohol leads to the release of dopamine, inducing a sense of well-being. However, as with all addictive substances, as time goes on, more alcohol is needed to keep up the dopaminergic effect.

Cannabis is another substance that is commonly in use among this age group. It is now known that THC is the psychoactive agent that leads to the perception of relaxation, pleasure and even euphoria. Anxiety is usually decreased, but it can sometimes be increased, causing depression or low mood. The important thing to note is that the amount of THC varies greatly in different types of cannabis. There are many forms of cannabis now available, and the higher the amount of THC, the greater the psychoactive impact.

The worry about cannabis use is that, frequently, young people do not know the level of THC in the cannabis they are using. High levels of THC may lead people to experience lower inhibition, causing troubling behaviours such as aggression or even violence. It is also the case that frequent cannabis use may be a precursor to mental health problems. Using cannabis more than three times a week is undoubtedly a risk factor for psychotic illness.

A brief mention of other drugs is in order here, including ecstasy, heroin and cocaine. These substances have similar effects on the brain as cannabis and alcohol, but the impact is often greater and more intense. Such substances are, in addition, more likely to be addictive, since they have the effect of altering the reward structures in the brain to a greater degree than a substance such as cannabis. In addition, the effect on a variety of hormones is more powerful here. As an example, studies of the use of ecstasy show that this drug affects every area of the brain and has an especially powerful impact on levels of serotonin.

Stress

When there is a discussion of stress, the phrase "fight or flight" is often mentioned. In essence, the brain releases two main chemical messengers in response to the presence of a stressor. These chemicals prepare the body to respond in a way that will protect the individual from threat. In other words, these substances in the body enable the individual to respond to danger by raising the heart rate, increasing oxygen levels, redirecting blood to the muscles and so on.

These responses are part of our primitive history when we lived in times of ever-present danger. Today, threat is likely to be different, and the "fight or flight" response may not necessarily be appropriate. For teenagers, threat may come in many forms. These may include anxiety about tests and exams, conflict with parents, rejection within the peer group, not receiving many likes on social media and many other social circumstances.

We have learnt a considerable amount about how stress affects the teenage brain. In particular, we know that the brains of young people do not respond in the same way to stress as adult brains. Stress affects the amygdala and other areas of the brain that help process emotion. The teenage amygdala has less capacity to deal with fear and anger, thus leading to more extreme or inappropriate responses to these emotions. The emotions of worry, anxiety and stress are all associated with levels of cortisol in the brain. Research has shown that cortisol levels are somewhat higher in adolescence than in adulthood.

As mentioned in the section on risk, a different perspective on stress comes from studies of self-control. This evidence comes from examples of placing young people in situations where a good decision involves holding back until more information is available. Where teenagers are calm and relaxed, they show just as much self-control as adults. However, under conditions of stress or other strong emotions, the self-control of a teenager deteriorates. This can lead to poor decision-making. Thus, it is clear that young people can think about consequences in some situations, but not in all situations.

Blog "Why teach brain development to secondary school pupils?"

Our knowledge of the changes in the teenage brain is not exactly "new knowledge". It is 20 years now since reports of research on the teen brain starting appearing in the media. However, there is a long way to go before the field of education catches up with these exciting developments. There are many who argue that a collection of brain scans does not help us plan the curriculum or organize the school day.

This is to misunderstand the value of knowledge about the teenage brain. In talking to teachers, it becomes clear that, in the main, they see this knowledge as extremely helpful. They don't value it for lesson planning but as a vital tool for helping them to understand their students.

They want to understand why some are drowsy in the morning. They want to make sense of the emotional meltdowns and to know why young people develop at such different rates. Why do some mature early, while others lag behind? How can teachers help their students become more mindful of the consequences of their behaviour?

In addition to this, there is another important possibility which arises out of our knowledge of the teenage brain. This is the possibility that we can actually teach young people about their brains and about the changes that are taking place. Why is this important?

The fact is that most teenagers are puzzled about what is happening to them. They want to understand why they experience a rapidly shifting kaleidoscope of emotions. They want to know more about how memory works. They are keen to understand how best to revise and how to manage the stress that they all experience. While we concentrate on teaching them science or history, they would really like to understand themselves better.

Our understanding of the brain has made this possible in a way that was unimaginable 20 years ago. We now know that the teenage brain undergoes a major re-structuring and re-organization during these years. This knowledge provides us with an insight into teenage behaviour. Such an insight has value not only for adults – parents, teachers and others – but for young people themselves.

In my own experience delivering lessons on the brain to students, as outlined in my book *The Teacher and the Teenage Brain*, this knowledge is hugely reassuring to young people. Those in the first years of secondary school tell me they are grateful to learn about this, while those in the "A-level" years ask: *"Why didn't we have this earlier? It would have made so much difference!"*

In my view, this is a matter of a human right. Young people have the right to know what is happening in their brains. After all, we now take it for granted that we teach young people about puberty. In years gone by, it would have been assumed that this should happen in the family (if at all) but not as part of the school curriculum. Knowledge of the changing brain is the same. I predict that in 20–30 years it will be seen as extraordinary not to be including this topic in the curriculum.

In making this point, I should not under-estimate the challenges involved. We have a long way to go in designing lesson plans for different age groups. Some initiatives are under way (e.g., Brain Waves in Oxford), but this is an exception. There is also the question of who should teach this topic. Many teachers are cautious about taking this on, as it is seen as a "new" subject.

In spite of all this, I remain convinced that, in time, this will be seen as an accepted part of the curriculum. Before too long it will be recognized that this knowledge is helpful, not only for teachers, but also that it leads to improved learning among students. Most importantly, it helps young people understand themselves better, resulting in happier, healthier teenagers. Who can argue with that goal?

12.01.23

How does the brain mature?

I have talked about maturation, but what does this actually mean? There are a number of processes that contribute to this. In the first place, there is a change in myelin. This is a substance that surrounds or encases the nerve fibres. Myelin is extremely important because it protects the nerve fibres. It also ensures that they remain separate from each other. If you remember how many neurons there are, and thus how many nerve fibres, you can see that it is essential to have a means of preventing the billions of fibres from getting tangled up.

As for maturation, during the teenage years the myelin gets thicker. Clearly this is at an infinitesimal level, but nonetheless the myelin gets thicker. This enables impulses to travel a round the brain faster and more efficiently. This process takes some years, but it contributes significantly to a more mature and effective brain.

The second element that contributes to maturation involves the way the two halves of the brain operate together. As I have noted, the two hemispheres are connected by the corpus callosum. This becomes stronger and more elaborate during adolescence. Connectivity increases with age, allowing the individual to draw on greater capacities from each hemisphere and thus function more effectively and in a more mature manner. In essence the more connectivity there is, the better the person's thinking abilities. In order to understand intelligence, we need to look at connectivity. In earlier times, it was believed that the size of a person's brain was a clue to their intelligence. We now know that this belief is false. Intelligence is not related to size but to the degree of connectivity between the two halves of the brain.

There is considerable controversy about the roles that each hemisphere plays. Some have argued that it is possible to think of the left brain as the site of logical thinking and the right brain as the site of emotion and creativity. However, this is not a conclusion that is universally accepted, and there continues to be debate and discussion over the roles of the two hemispheres.

One last point about maturation. During the teenage years, maturation does not occur equally across different parts of the brain. In fact, in most individuals the brain matures from back to front. This is important because it means that the prefrontal cortex, the site of thinking and reasoning, is maturing at a slower rate than other sites in the brain. Of course, the prefrontal cortex is maturing, but it is just maturing more slowly than other parts of the brain.

The brain and the environment

What determines the way the brain develops? This is a perennial question. Is it down to the person's genes? Is the structure of the brain set from the very early years? How does the environment make a difference to the way the brain develops in the teenage years? Do early experiences have later consequences?

This is not an easy question to answer. The first important thing to note is that the brain and the environment interact. Each has an influence on the other. The environment affects brain development, but the capacity of the brain will influence the way the individual responds to circumstances. As one example of this, it is probable that enriching environments lead to healthier brain development. On the other hand, environments that are restricted in one way or another are likely to hinder brain development.

This was a question that scientists were asking in the 1960s, when I was at university. We were taught about studies that placed rats in two different environments. One was full of toys and stimulating experiences, while the other environment was bare and spartan. The results were clear. The rats brought up in the stimulating environment were quicker learners and performed better at solving puzzles and finding their way around mazes.

In recent times, the experiences of Romanian orphans have given us a real-life opportunity to study this question. Readers may remember that, during the Ceaucescu era in Romania, orphans were placed in extremely restricted environments, left in their cots with very little human contact. Many in the West offered to adopt these orphans, and this led to a number of natural experiments.

In the UK, the Institute of Psychiatry in London studied these orphans as they grew up, went to school and developed into teenagers. The results are fascinating. I will just mention two main findings. Firstly, the earlier the orphans were adopted, the easier it was to overcome the early deprivation. Those adopted before the age of one did better than those adopted between two and three years of age. This makes sense, as those adopted at a young age had a shorter experience of deprivation, and presumably there was less damage to the developing brain.

Those adopted later, however, also showed the capacity to recover. These adoptees were able to make good relationships with the adoptive parents and were able to perform adequately at school. In spite of this, there remained some challenges for those adopted after the age of one. Once they got to secondary school, they struggled with friendships and showed other signs of finding it hard to adapt to changing circumstances such as the move to a new school.

One other strand of work casts some light on this question. In recent years, a number of studies have looked at teenage brain development in those who had been the subject to adverse childhood experiences (ACEs). Such experiences usually include abuse, bereavement, rejection and other types of trauma. Results of these studies do show that, in some young people, early experiences lead to altered brain function. However, studies also show that the brain has the capacity to recover. Where the individual receives strong support and care, it would appear that earlier disadvantages can be overcome. There is a further discussion on trauma and its effects in Chapter 7, which is concerned with mental health.

From all this we can conclude that the environment really does make a difference. One key aspect of the environment for young people is, of course, the adults who surround them. This is an important message. Adults have a key role to play. All the research shows that the outcome for young people is very much affected by the support and encouragement that is available from the adult world. This applies whether the adult is a parent, carer, teacher or other practitioner. The brain and the environment interact, both influencing each other.

Conclusion

Understanding what happens in the brain leads to a significant change in the way we make sense of adolescence. In this chapter, I have covered the main changes that occur in the brain during the adolescent period. I have discussed scanning and outlined what it means to say the brain is maturing. I have outlined the relation between the brain and the environment and showed that each influences the other. One young man in the classroom said to me: "*So, my brain is changing. Nothing much I can do about it then*?" I was able to reassure him. The brain is not fixed. The environment makes a difference. There is a lot we can do to assist healthy brain development.

Chapter 3

Physical health and development

Introduction

As I have argued in the previous chapter, the adolescent period is one of enormous change in all areas. I have outlined what happens in the brain during these years and shown how significant neurological developments are for all aspects of adolescence. In this chapter I will start to look at health from a wider perspective. There was a time when adolescent health was a marginal focus for health professionals. This was partly because of the high priority attached to the early years. It was believed that if interventions in the health field were to be pursued, there was a greater gain to be achieved by focussing on the first few years of life. In addition, the general negative stereotype of adolescence played into this scenario.

> Even women's health is severely underfunded. Serious illness relating to our gynecology is often ignored, and even if the case is considered we are popped onto a list that will end up waiting decades to be seen and properly diagnosed. I abhor it when people, especially women, are indifferent to the side effects of menstruation. Every girl gets it, only they don't get it, do they? They don't recognize how excruciating period pains are.
>
> (Young woman, aged 18)

Health professionals have tended to view young people as difficult to communicate with, unresponsive when offered health advice, and more likely than other age groups to engage in health risk behaviours. Interestingly, this picture has been gradually changing. Since 2010, there appears to have been a much greater interest in the health of this age group. This trend has been supported by initiatives such as the first Lancet Commission on Adolescent Health and Wellbeing (Patton et al., 2016), as well as the publications resulting from the WHO Collaborative study of Health Behaviour in School-Aged Children (Hulbert et al., 2023).

DOI: 10.4324/9781032640433-3

It is probably the case that the appearance of the pandemic in 2020 has also had an impact on the interest in the health of young people. Much concern has been expressed over the apparent increase in mental ill-health as a result of Covid-19, and numerous studies have investigated this and other aspects of health appearing after 2020. I will explore this in further detail later in the chapter. It is also the case that many new organizations have been developed with a focus on young people's health. In the UK, a good example of this is the Association for Young People's Health (AYPH) based in London.

Mortality and morbidity

While there have been major improvements in the health of children and in those over 60 in the last few decades, it would appear that this trend has not been as marked for those in the adolescent years. This may partly be due to the belief of health professionals that this is an age when health is at its best, and therefore there is nothing to worry about. Why put effort into an age group who are, in the main, healthy? However, this belief is being challenged, and today there is a more widespread recognition of the long-term implications of poor health during adolescence. As far as mortality is concerned, huge strides have been made in lower-income countries with improvements in the care of communicable diseases and other threats to life. However, in the West there has been little reduction in levels of mortality, with road accidents and self-injury remaining the main causes of death for those in this age group.

> I'm a rare person, because I've got something called Ehlers Danlos. Basically, it can be stage one, stage two or stage three, and I have stage two, which isn't the most livable stage. Stage two is you're ok to live, but it can affect your life. I guess. Basically, it means I can't run very far, but I still have to exercise. It's a hard thing to explain because it's not really a normal thing.
>
> (Young man, aged 15)

> (Note: Ehlers Danlos is a condition that affects the joints and the skin. There is no known treatment, and only in rare cases is it life-threatening).

Turning to morbidity, there has been a marked decline among young people in traditional health-risk behaviours. Levels of smoking, alcohol and substance misuse appear to have significantly reduced (Kang et al., 2026). This is encouraging, although there is some concern that vaping is taking the place of cigarette smoking for many teenagers. There is also concern over increasing levels of mental ill-health in this age group, especially eating disorders, anxiety and depression. This is a topic to which I will return in greater detail in Chapter 7.

One topic that has received considerable attention is that of health inequalities. There are many different types of inequality. Where health is concerned, inequalities may relate to poverty, poor nutrition and inadequate housing. In addition, there is the question of access to health services and gateways to treatment programmes (Patton et al., 2016). In the UK, this has been highlighted by the squeeze on services and the greater difficulty experienced by young people in having the confidence and social skills to get through the barriers that exist where resources are severely stretched. The presence of inequalities is highly relevant when we consider the health of young people living in different communities and coming from diverse backgrounds. Finding improvements in the health of young people will be greatly challenged where significant inequalities exist (Kang et al., 2026).

Puberty

The word *puberty* derives from the Latin word *pubertas*, which originally meant age of manhood. Among the general public, this stage is generally assumed to start with the onset of menstruation in girls and the emergence of pubic hair in boys. However, these two observable changes are only a small part of the total picture, since puberty is in reality a complex process involving many bodily functions. It is common knowledge that puberty is associated with sexual maturation, but many other things are happening at the same time. The obvious things that everyone knows about are maturation of the reproductive system, the growth spurt and the development of secondary sexual characteristics such as breasts and body hair.

In addition to all this, there are changes in the functioning of the heart, and thus of the cardiovascular system, in the lungs which in turn affect the respiratory system, in the size and strength of many of the muscles in the body and so on. On top of these changes, there are, as I outlined in the previous chapter, major alterations in the brain during the years during and after puberty. Puberty should be seen as an event in the physical life of the body with wide-ranging implications.

> It definitely was not a good experience. When I was in primary school girls and boys changed together for PE, and a boy once made fun of my underarm hair. I was so young, and I felt deeply embarrassed. Maybe it was shame, maybe embarrassment. It hurt when my obvious physical changes around

> my body became visible to others, and girls who I thought were my friends commented on my chest. I remember when I had extremely bad abdominal pains in primary school during my period and I was the only one sobbing and crying in pain, and I was given a hot water bottle to hug.
>
> (Young woman, aged 17)

One of the essential facts about this aspect of human development is that there are wide differences in the age of commencement of puberty, and these differences are both between individuals and between communities. Thus, for example, puberty occurs later in lower-income countries across the globe, as has been documented by Eveleth and Tanner (1977) and by Parent et al. (2003). In addition, research has shown that, among African-American young women early indicators of puberty such as breast development occur at significantly earlier ages than they do in White Americans (Wu et al., 2002). The primary explanation for variation in the age of puberty is likely to be genetic. However, it is important to recognize that genetic factors are not the only ones to influence the start of puberty, as environmental factors play a role too. The explanations for the international differences previously mentioned are likely to be variations in nutrition and health care. Other factors such as body weight also play a part. Young women who are very thin are likely to have delayed puberty, while those who are overweight or obese may start puberty earlier than their peers (Brooks-Gunn and Warren, 1985).

> That generational shame that has been born and fed through many generations. It's really, really difficult growing up and going through puberty in a positive light because of my own experiences. I just hope, if I have a daughter, I'm able to end the generational trauma, and, you know, the shame that comes with, or the humiliation, that comes with it. Educating both male and female, especially like traditional parents, who've come from another country, having to accommodate to their kind of understanding, it's so important.
>
> (Young woman, aged 18)

The growth spurt

Turning now to the actual events of puberty, one of the many changes involved here is known as the growth spurt. This term is usually taken to refer to the accelerated rate of increase in height and weight that occurs during early adolescence. Typical curves for individual rates of growth are illustrated in Figure 3.1. As noted previously, it is good to bear in mind that there are large individual

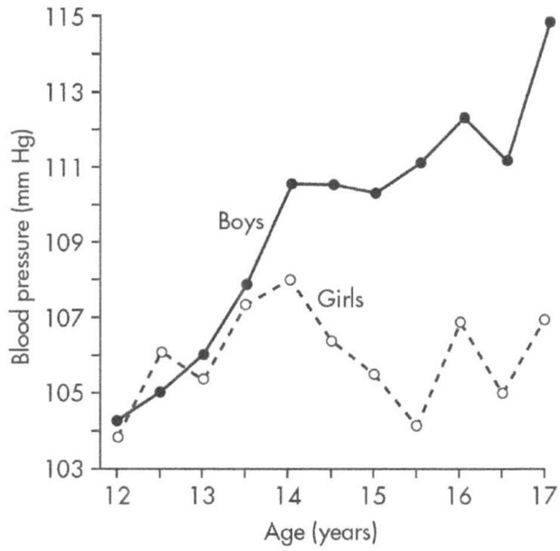

Figure 3.1 Differences in systolic blood pressure between boys and girls at puberty

Source: Montagna and Sadler (1974).

differences in the age of onset and in the duration of the growth spurt. Parents and young people themselves often fail to understand that a wide variation in timing is quite normal. This lack of information may cause a great deal of unnecessary anxiety.

> I went through puberty quite early, and I think that was quite isolating. There weren't any other girls, like any best friends, it was just me. There was nobody to relate to. It was just, yeah, quite hard. I am alright now though.
>
> (Young woman, aged 16)

In boys, the growth spurt may begin as early as 9 years of age or as late as 15, while in girls the same process can begin at 7 or 8, or not until 13 or 14 or even later. For the average boy, though, rapid growth is likely to begin at around 12 and to reach a peak somewhere in the 13th year. Comparable ages for girls are 10 for the onset of the growth spurt, and 11 for the peak age of increase in height and weight. Readers will note that girls, on average, are likely to commence puberty much earlier than boys. This fact has important implications for peer relationships at this age, a point to which I will return in Chapter 9.

> It's really difficult for some children who are, like, 13 or 14, because a lot of people start hitting puberty when they are in Year 7 or Year 8. Sometimes it's really early or really late, and I know it's really tricky for them. I know

a boy in my school who was really pooped by it, and he was telling me his hormones were, like, very tricky, and he used to break down in class because of it.

(Young man, aged 15)

As already mentioned, other phenomena apart from changes in height and weight are also associated with the growth spurt. Thus, the weight of the heart nearly doubles at this time, there is an accelerated growth of the lungs, and a decline in basal metabolism. Noticeable to young people themselves, especially to boys, is a marked increase in physical strength and endurance. Gender differences are also reflected in less obvious internal changes, as Bancroft and Reinisch (1990) point out. For example, changes such as the increase in the number of red blood cells, and in systolic blood pressure, are far greater in boys than in girls. The extent of such differences is likely to be evolutionary and is illustrated in Figure 3.1.

Sexual maturation

As readers will appreciate, it is sexual maturation which is usually understood to be the essential element of puberty. There are a range of bodily changes that accompany this stage of life. For boys, the first signs of puberty involve the growth of the testes and scrotum, together with the appearance of pubic hair. Approximately a year later, the growth spurt begins, and at this time there is also growth in the size of the penis. The appearance of other bodily hair, and especially facial hair, occurs quite late in the sequence, as does the deepening of the voice. Lastly the internal sexual organs, such as the prostate gland, develop about a year after the growth of the penis. This leads to the possibility of nocturnal emissions, or wet dreams.

For girls, there can be greater individual variation in the order in which the various changes take place. The following is therefore an approximation of what might occur for a typical girl. The first sign of puberty is usually early breast development, known as breast bud development. In about a third of girls, pubic hair may appear before any changes in the breasts are obvious. Breast development moves through a number of stages during puberty. James Tanner, the leader in identifying the key elements of puberty, showed that there are usually five stages of breast development, taking two or three years to complete (Tanner, 1962). In addition to this, there are internal changes taking place, including the growth of the uterus, the vagina and other reproductive organs. The growth spurt usually occurs during the early or middle stages of puberty, while menstruation itself happens towards the end of the sequence. This occurs only when a range of hormonal changes have taken place.

> The menstrual cycle, like you have to put on an appearance in front of friends. Like with me, when I am on my cycle, it's like, really painful, and I get to like, just have to put up with it. Like they don't really deem that you can go home, and you just have to sit there and engage in the lessons. And then the emotions, like everything is taken to heart, and then you laugh, you shout, and like, it's you are in front of people, even at home, and it's like you're not right!
>
> (Young woman, aged 15)

There has been much debate in the literature about how to measure puberty, and when puberty can be said to commence. While it is clearly easier to date puberty in girls from the onset of menstruation, this is too simplistic a measure, since so much else happens preceding the arrival of periods. However, there are no other obvious external markers. Carrying out a clinical examination of breast development or assessing dental age is expensive and time-consuming procedures. The situation with boys is even more difficult, as there is no externally obvious and agreed markers of pubertal status. Many different approaches have been used, as outlined in Coleman and Coleman (2002). In reality, there is no way of measuring pubertal status in a reliable fashion in boys without carrying out a clinical examination.

> I've grown really tall, and I didn't expect it. Little things you don't expect. Like the first time I had to shave, and I'd be, like, "Oh! Who do I ask?" Or whatever. And I'd feel awkward, but my Mum would say: "Don't worry about it. It doesn't matter". And she would buy me a razor. But it was still awkward.
>
> (Young man, aged 16)

The secular trend

One of the fascinating debates relating to puberty and sexual maturation involves what is known as the secular trend. This term has been used to describe any trend over time relating to the body, such as changes in height and weight. Over the past century, the physical growth of children and adolescents has accelerated, leading to faster and earlier maturation. This trend has been noticeable in the growth rates of two- to five-year-olds, but it also has many implications for

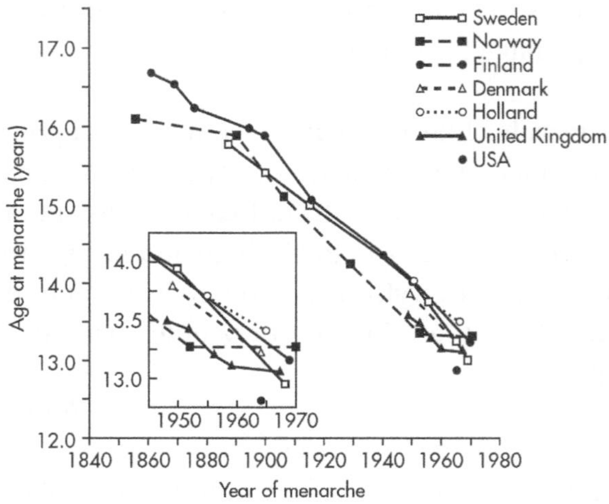

Figure 3.2 Secular trend in age at menarche, 1860–1970
Source: Tanner (1978).

adolescents. Full adult height is now achieved at an earlier age than was the case 50 years ago. Final adult stature and weight have increased, and many investigators are reporting that height and weight in adolescence are greater than they have been in earlier ages.

This trend is, of course, directly relevant to puberty. As can be seen in Figure 3.2, the age of puberty has gradually decreased over the years since records began in the middle of the nineteenth century. It is believed that at that time the average age of menarche was around 17 years of age, while today it is, on average, around 12 years and 6 months. A study of Danish adolescents (Brauner et al., 2020) found that five times more girls were seen as having "precocious puberty" in 2017 than had been the case 20 years earlier. Similar declines have been observed in many countries, such as China, where the average age of menarche was found to have dropped by nearly two years between 1991 and 2011 (Meng et al., 2017).

As might be expected, the secular trend is less well-documented in boys. As I have noted, there are fewer obvious markers for males than for females. One interesting exception to this is evidence concerning the age at which the voice breaks. Based on evidence from European children's choirs, it appears that the age of change in the voice for boys has dropped from about 18 in the mid-1700s to around 10 today (Mendle and Ferrero, 2012). Other studies have shown that the age of male puberty is continuing to decline, based on evidence from many Western countries (Herman-Giddens et al., 2012).

One other factor of interest is the possibility that the course of puberty may also be taking longer to complete. This means that children and young people are spending more time actually going through puberty (Mendle, 2014). There are, not surprisingly, many theories as to why the age of puberty is dropping. It is generally agreed that better nutrition and health care are the main drivers, but beyond that there may be other factors playing a part. Increased body weight is likely to be one key factor, as it is clear that the heavier you are, the earlier you will reach the onset of puberty. There are also some classic studies of ballet dancers, showing that when dieting and fasting take place to reduce weight, then puberty is delayed (Brooks-Gunn and Warren, 1985). Finally, on this subject, it is worthy of note that many commentators are highlighting the possible effects of chemicals in cosmetics, food and the environment as one possible reason for the secular trend in relation to puberty (Greenspan and Deardorff, 2014).

The psychological effects of puberty

The changes in the physical self inevitably have an effect on the way the young person thinks and feels. The body alters radically in shape and size, and it is not surprising that many young adolescents experience a period of clumsiness and self-consciousness as they attempt to adjust to these changes. The body also alters in function, as new and sometimes worrying experiences, such as the girl's first period, or the boy's first wet dream, have to be understood. Because these things are difficult to talk about, there is perhaps too little recognition of the anxieties that are common at this stage.

In their writing, Temple-Smith et al. (2016) have highlighted the remarkable degree of embarrassment, discomfort and concern about menstruation experienced by a wide range of young women, in spite of good health education in schools. A further consideration is the effect that puberty has on identity. As many writers have pointed out, the development of the individual's identity requires not only the notion of being separate and different from other people but also a sense of stability and self-consistency. To have a stable identity, one needs a firm knowledge of how one appears to the outside world, and a recognition that there is some continuity in how one looks to others.

In the next chapter, where I deal with the development of cognition, I will outline some facts about what is known as the social brain. As this develops, the individual experiences a stage known as "preoccupation with the self". This arises from an intense concern with how one appears to others. The maturing brain allows for the possibility of seeing the world through the eyes of others. This in turn leads the young person into a state where it feels as if the whole world is watching. The individual grows to feel as if there is an "imaginary audience", and as a result one's bodily appearance takes centre stage.

Much research on the psychological effects of puberty has concentrated on body image, and on the degree of satisfaction or dissatisfaction experienced by the young person at this stage. A book by Ricciardelli and Yager (2016) explores this in detail. In early adolescence, both boys and girls rely heavily on physical characteristics to describe themselves. As they progress through adolescence, they are able to make greater use of social and intellectual characteristics of personality to describe themselves. As a result, they begin to depend less on body image as a key element of their self-concept.

> Like people feel like people body shame them, so they walk around with really baggy clothes on, where they feel like they can't be themselves in public. Like for me, having to go out and buy baggier clothes, so everything is, like body shape, yeah, and like having bigger clothes, so because of how tight tops look on me.
>
> (Young woman, aged 16)

In terms of bodily dissatisfaction, girls experience this to a much greater degree than boys (Calzo et al. 2012). Boys are more likely to be dissatisfied with their height, while girls are more concerned with weight. This is closely linked to the question of dieting and anxiety over eating habits. As has been much discussed, the role of the media is also critical here. Whether it is through social media, films, television or the print media, a certain type of body image is portrayed as being of high value, and this in turn has a direct effect on the way young people, both boys and girls, feel and think about their bodies. Girls can see that female models, film stars and celebrities are, in general, portrayed as being slim and of low weight. The model for males has to do with muscle and fitness. While much focus has been on the way body image is illustrated in the media for females, the impact for males should not be forgotten.

> Like body shaming and stuff, it's a massive topic for girls, because a lot of girls I've seen they don't like the way they look, and it's not nice to hear. You're beautiful the way you are, don't change yourself. But also in a relationship, the boyfriend wants you to be someone you're not, then it's like you do it because you want to be with them. It's one of the main things I'm worried about in a relationship. But I know that I am strong enough and now old enough to make my own decisions. No one can control me.
>
> (Young woman, aged 15)

Early and late maturers

There has been a long-standing interest among social scientists in the effects of especially early or late development where puberty is concerned. This is sometimes referred to as "on-time" or "off-time", since one of the important implications of being early or late has to do with how the young person compares themselves with their peers. As I have noted, individuals mature at very different rates. One girl of 13 may be small, with no breast development, and look very much as she did during childhood. Another 13-year-old may look like a fully developed woman and appear to others as if she were 16 or 17. These differences have significant consequences for emotional and social development.

> I was about 9, and like everybody else was 12 or 13. So it was, like, three years and it was just me, and I was, like, just there, and nobody else like me. It would have been nice to have somebody else there. I felt so out of place for a while, like sticking out from everyone.
>
> (Young woman, aged 15)

By and large, studies have shown that, for boys, early maturation carries with it social advantages, while later development can be more of a problem (Temple-Smith et al., 2016). In essence, if boys are taller and stronger than their peers, they are usually better at sport and are therefore likely to be more popular. On the other hand, those who develop later than their peers are reported to struggle with schoolwork and to be more isolated within the peer group.

Not all studies show positive benefits for early maturing boys. In some cases, it would appear that being in this group may lead to lower levels of parental supervision and greater involvement in anti-social behaviour (Beltz et al., 2019).

For girls, the picture is different. Most studies show that early-developing girls have a disadvantage in that they are less popular with their female peers and are more likely to be popular with older boys. In addition, being popular with boys at an early age brings with it some obvious challenges. Concerns about body image could be more prevalent, and questions relating to dating may be difficult to navigate at an early age. Some studies also highlight higher levels of emotional distress in early maturing girls (Stumper et al., 2019). This evidence underlines the importance of good health education and awareness by parents and teachers of the psychological impact of early and late development.

One question of importance has to do with the relation between physical puberty and the changes in the brain, which are described in the previous chapter. Are the two developing at the same pace? How do these two critical features of maturity work together? There are some hints about this in Galvan (2017), but these are only some very preliminary ideas. Apart from her work, there is little else to draw on. This is something that will be a high priority in future research.

Covid-19

The pandemic of the years 2020 and 2021 was caused by the coronavirus, or Covid-19. An enormous effort has gone into attempting to understand the effects of this virus on the population in general. However, it is not surprising that the highest level of attention has been on children and young people. Even some years later, it is still the case that many impacts of the pandemic are still being explored. This is due to the fact that Covid-19 caused so many changes to people's lives that the impacts have been extremely wide-ranging. As far as young people are concerned, there was the fact that school was suspended. Not only was education itself disrupted, but all the social experiences associated with the school were also suspended.

> I mean, Covid was a real struggle for me. Because of my medical condition I wasn't allowed to leave the house until I actually had something to fight the infection. In the end I got it, but even so when I left the house, I would take gloves and face masks, face shields and hand sanitizer with me.
>
> (Young man, aged 15)

This in turn led to children and young people spending all day at home and thus significantly more time with parents and other family members. While this had a positive benefit for some, especially those with good housing and outdoor space, it was much harder for those living in poor housing where the whole family had to adjust to cramped conditions and greater stress on family relationships.

> I think Covid created a lot of health anxiety for me. It was just a constant worry. Being in public spaces with people, and going from not being in a room with more than five people to being in a supermarket with 50. It was quite intense.
>
> (Young woman, aged 17)

In the early days of the pandemic, there was much anxiety expressed about the impact of the expected loss of social life for adolescents. Commentators talked of "social deprivation" and speculated about how the loss of social life would lead to long-term deficits in social skills. In fact, adolescents kept in touch with their peers through the internet, and it has been difficult to establish whether there really was a phenomenon that could be described as "social deprivation". Nonetheless, some would argue that this is linked to the problems of school absence in the years following the pandemic. I will return to this later.

> It's been quite gradual, because, like, we missed so much, like we missed two years of our lives, and it was like Year 7 and Year 8. So, it was quite an impactful time in our lives that we missed. Because we were inside for so long, we missed loads of socialization, and like learning how to deal with these things.
>
> (Young woman, aged 15)

In terms of research, the primary focus has been on the increased levels of mental ill-health. While different studies point out a variety of implications on mental health, it is generally agreed that the most striking impact has been on eating disorders. In the UK, eating disorders increased significantly during this period, with the biggest rise being on girls and young women in the 13–16-year age range (Auger et al., 2023). It is hard to understand quite why this should be. Some say that this links to a sense of being out of control because of the pandemic. The experience of having no control over disease could possibly relate to a need to have more control over another aspect of life – e.g., nutrition.

Eating disorders were not the only aspect of mental health that appeared during Covid, as other symptoms such as anxiety and depression were also witnessed by many clinicians (Watson et al., 2023). There has also been a concern about the increase in health anxiety among young people. It is believed that this type of emotional disorder has been linked with experiences during the pandemic.

> Me personally, my puberty got all messed up, because when I was going through puberty, I am an eating disorder which messed up my hormones and kind of stunted it a bit. Then I ended up going on a progesterone pill to prevent it going any further. It paused my periods, and then my puberty never really kicked off, and sort of messed everything up.
>
> (Young woman, aged 16)

Overall, as might be expected, those living in more deprived regions suffered most during this period. It is also clear that of all populations of young people, those with disabilities and with special educational needs (SEND) were most affected. It was harder for parents to access services during this time, and there is no doubt that one of the long-term impacts of Covid has been on those families with SEND children and adolescents.

One of the concerns over the long-term impact of Covid-19 on young people has been the return to school. And this has proven to be the case. Absence from school is at a significantly higher level than was the case before Covid. This may involve difficulty in returning to the routines associated with attendance and the structure expected as part of the school day. For others, this might be caused by the return to the social situation and the difficulty in fitting back into the peer group. It is also the case that more parents have been working from home for a greater period of the week. For many young people (although not all), this makes home a more attractive place to be, with a more nurturing environment than would be found at school.

In summary, the pandemic has continued to have effects, and these are to be seen particularly in the lives of children and young people. I will return to the topic of Covid-19 and mental health in Chapter 7.

Sleep

Many readers will be aware that sleep is an important topic where adolescents are concerned. Young people struggle to get to sleep and are often drowsy in the morning when getting ready for school. Research has shown that the sleep patterns of teenagers differ from those of adults (Foster, 2022; Walker, 2018). This finding has been one of the most significant outcomes of last decade of research into the adolescent brain. We now know that the hormone melatonin (the hormone that makes us sleepy) is released later in the evening in young people and therefore plays a big part in affecting sleep patterns in this age group.

It is noteworthy that not all young people are affected by melatonin release. Studies show that approximately 25% of adolescents do not experience sleep difficulty, and some appear to go through this stage in their lives with no problem. It is also the case that there is wide variation in the timing of the change in sleep patterns. Some find this change happens shortly after the onset of puberty, while others do not experience this until later in adolescence.

I should note that melatonin is not the only factor that has an impact on the sleep patterns of young people. The powerful draw of social media and other opportunities provided by the internet are factors likely to interfere with a process of relaxation at bedtime. The element of light in the bedroom and that given out by smartphones and other devices also play a part in making the process of getting to sleep problematic.

We know that adolescents need more sleep than adults. However, because of the fact that many find it hard to get to sleep at night, and because of the fact that they have to get up for school in the morning, young people are getting less sleep than is helpful for them. Surveys differ, but it is clear that many adolescents are getting only six or seven hours of sleep, and some even less. Yet, if you put a young person in a sleep laboratory, they will normally sleep for nine or 10 hours.

I will consider the implications of this in a moment, but first let us consider why sleep is so important. Many people have the sense that sleep is a time of rest. However, research has shown that there are times at night when the brain is just as active as it is during the day. There are at least five phases of sleep, but here I will distinguish between the two most significant ones. One phase is known as deep sleep, when there are no rapid eye movements (NREM sleep). The second phase is REM sleep. During this phase, rapid eye movements take place, sleep is shallower, and it is likely during this phase that dreaming takes place.

There are three reasons why sleep is especially important for young people. Firstly, growth hormones are released during sleep, and since this is a period of rapid maturation, these hormones play a key role in adolescence. Secondly, sleep is a time of memory consolidation. During sleep, the information that has been built up during the day is sorted and stored in a different part of the brain at night. Lastly, a process takes place at night which that manages the waste products that accumulate around the neuron during the day. As the neuron fires, it produces waste, and this needs to be recycled and cleaned up. There are special cells, known as glial cells (sometimes known as helper cells) that deal with this waste.

It will be evident that, if students find it hard to get to sleep and have to get up early for school, they will be missing out on much-needed sleep. There has been a lot of concern in how this reduction in sleep affects young people. The terms "sleep deprivation" or "sleep deficit" have been used to describe this situation. These is clearly a very wide variation in the amount of sleep any one individual needs. However, most experts in the field agree that anything less than six or seven hours of sleep for a young person should be classified as "sleep deficit" (Coleman, 2024; Foster, 2022). Reports from teachers and parents seem to indicate that many adolescents are today sleeping for five or six hours at most. Evidence from numerous studies indicate clearly that too little sleep has a negative impact on both learning and emotion (Foster, 2022).

Because of the concern about sleep loss, many have looked at possible interventions (Sharman et al., 2020). Three approaches that have been explored. The first is starting school later in the morning. In the USA there has been significantly more pressure to act on this, and some states, such as California, have legislated for a start time no earlier than 8.30 a.m. In the UK, there has been little appetite for this approach, partly because the UK start times are later anyway, and partly because teachers and parents are unenthusiastic about changing their own routines. The third approach has been to introduce sleep lessons into the classroom. The evidence is not particularly encouraging here, although when parents as well as pupils take part in these lessons it is more likely that there will be some positive effect.

It will be apparent that this matter will be of concern to parents of young people. It is important to note that, in addition to the interventions just mentioned, there are approaches that can be taken in the family that may be of value. Of course, it is hard for families and teenagers to work together on this. However, if everyone in the family can be made aware of the importance of sleep for adolescents, some progress can be achieved, especially as it is the case that the melatonin effect can be overcome.

There are a number of things that can be done in the family which will contribute to better sleep for young people. These are:

- Turning off digital devices for a period before sleep;
- If possible, put smartphones outside the bedroom;
- Turning lights low;
- Using mood music or other activities to aid relaxation;
- Most important, getting into a good sleep routine.

One key factor here has to do with the behaviour of others in the family. If it is possible, it will help to introduce what may be called "a family digital strategy" (Hayman and Coleman, 2016). This involves getting together and sharing a set of rules or agreements about how everyone behaves in relation to the digital world. For example, it is not helpful if the young person is told to turn off all devices when parents or older siblings are online until at late at night. In general, there is still too little information available about sleep, especially sleep during adolescence. It is to be hoped that this situation will change with more books and media interest in this topic.

Long-term conditions

The numbers of young people with long-term conditions surviving into adulthood are increasing across the world. Chronic conditions include diabetes, epilepsy, cancer, juvenile rheumatoid arthritis and cerebral palsy. The trend of longer survival is related to early identification but also to better treatments. The group of conditions falling under the rubric of neuro-diversity should also be included here. Those diagnosed with autism and attention deficit hyperactive disorder (ADHD) suffer from long-term conditions, although treatment will be very different from the more evidently medical conditions. The implications for health care are considerable, since resources are needed to support those in these categories. It is also the case that there are significant challenges for families and for the young people themselves.

> I got my period at, like 12, and every time I got a period, I'd get a seizure, really heavy seizures. It is directly linked to the epilepsy, because my seizures started around 10, which is when my body started changing. It was a really difficult time. I just got so scared every single month, Yeah! Yeah! And then I was having seizures in between. We all noticed a pattern, and I started taking the Depo injection, which is a new seizure med. So, I stopped having periods, and I don't have seizures once a month now.
>
> (Young woman, aged 16)

Living with conditions like these means that there will be a need gradually for the young person to assume responsibility and control over the care and the management of their condition. This may mean compliance with any medication but will also involve paying attention to any limitations on lifestyle that occur as a result of the condition. A further aspect of living with a long-term condition involves the transition from pediatric to adult health care. This is often problematic, since the circumstances and support available in adult care will almost certainly be different from those available for younger age groups.

> I don't remember much of going through puberty myself, because I was in hospital most of the time. I had these other things to think about. Right about four years ago now I was diagnosed with leukemia, which is a blood cancer. I finished treatment for that about a year ago, and I'm in remission for the moment. It's fantastic. So, I mean with all the hospital stays, all the hospital visits, that basically took over my life.
>
> (Young person, aged 17)

In terms of specific conditions, a good source of information is the Association for Young People's Health (www.ayph.org.uk), as this organization produces annual data on the health of adolescents in the UK. Based on the information provided by their publication Youth Health Data, the peak age for type 1 diabetes is between 9 and 14 years of age. Type 2 diabetes, however, increases with age so that the peak comes much later in adolescence. Another condition of concern is asthma. While the overall rate of this condition has declined over the years, this is probably due to a reduction in rates of smoking among young people. However, with regard to international comparisons, it is unfortunate to have to record that the UK is the country in Europe with the highest rates of mortality due to asthma (Kang et al., 2026).

Many studies have identified the fact that long-term conditions such as asthma and diabetes are more prevalent in populations where living conditions are poor and where other indices of deprivation are more marked (Kang et al., 2026). For health improvements to be recorded, it is necessary not only to try to improve health services but to consider more widely the living circumstances of young people in countries such as the UK. I will move on to consider issues concerning health promotion and health literacy.

Health literacy and health promotion

Health literacy is a concept that has gained increasing salience in recent years. This is usually defined as the young person's personal skills that enable individuals to understand and manage health information and to apply this to decision-making and taking actions that will protect and improve health. One of the first to set out a scheme was Nutbeam (2000), who divided health literacy into three types. These were:

- Functional: Use written information and be able to use language to seek help and ask relevant questions.
- Critical: Understand what is credible health information, be able to assess evidence and health information websites and have the capacity to seek a second opinion.
- Interactive: Explain how to make an appointment, be able to ask for a repeat prescription and share ideas about health care with others.

Today we should include an element of digital literacy in this schema. To obtain health information through social media and AI is an everyday activity for adolescents, but of course they need to be able to assess the value and evidence base for any information obtained in this way (Yonker et al., 2015). Health literacy depends on awareness of the complexity of the appropriate health care system. It will vary depending on the health of the individual young person. Those with long-term or chronic conditions will evidently need a greater level of health literacy (Kang et al., 2026).

A number of research projects have explored the relation between health literacy and good or poor health. Most studies report a positive relation between health literacy and good health. One example may be found in the study by Fleary et al. (2018). They were able to show that health literacy (especially functional and media literacy) was related to higher health-promoting behaviours and improved information-seeking. Other studies have demonstrated similar results. Zhong et al. (2019) reported that young people with kidney disease or hypertension had better self-management skills and higher levels of communication with health care professionals if they had higher health literacy. From these research projects, it is clear that health literacy should be an essential element in any health education programme.

This is a good time to consider the role of education in health promotion. Much has been written about health-promoting schools (sometimes known as healthy schools). The World Health Organization has developed a framework for schools in this context (WHO, 2021). Gray et al. (2022) have written about how silos between health and education can be broken down by considering how schools can address the health needs of their pupils. Four key elements of the school environment will contribute to health promotion. These are:

- The built environment: safe spaces for play, clean water, safe and hygenic toilets and so on;
- Services provided: healthy nutrition, vaccination programmes, support for mental health;
- Curriculum: Appropriate health education, health topics across the curriculum;
- School leadership: Caring and nurturing environment, teacher well-being commitment from senior leaders.

It is clear that schools can play an important role in health promotion and in encouraging health literacy. However, schools cannot do all this alone. Other players, such as families, the wider community, and the health service itself must take this seriously. As more young people with chronic illness survive into adulthood, their ability to manage their conditions becomes even more important. In addition, there are many threats to health that impact all adolescents. I have mentioned health inequalities, but there is also the worry about poor nutrition, inadequate levels of daily exercise, and other challenges in the modern world. Health promotion will always be a hugely important role for adults who live and work with young people.

Conclusion

In this chapter, I have covered a wide range of topics relating to health and physical development. A central aspect of the physical change at the start of adolescence is puberty, and here I have considered the range of changes to the body, including the growth spurt and sexual maturation. The psychological impact of puberty is important, and various features of this have been outlined. Early and late developers face particular challenges, and it is helpful if teachers, parents, and other adults are aware of this. I have looked at the continuing impact of Covid on the lives of young people, and the chapter also reviews evidence on long-term conditions, sleep and health literacy.

Chapter 4

Thinking, reasoning and learning

Introduction

Following the outline of the adolescent brain in Chapter 2, it is now time to turn to a consideration of the ways in which thinking, reasoning and learning develop during this life stage. Before the advent of brain imaging, it was only possible to identify changes in thinking by observation of young people's behaviour. Developments in thinking were often considered to be a result of the school curriculum. It is now clear that changes in thinking are, to a large extent, due to the maturation of the brain.

The role of teaching, as well as observation of the behaviour of others, will also play a part in enabling the adolescent to develop new skills and become a more efficient learner. In this chapter, I will first consider some of the ways in which thinking changes during these years, so that the adolescent can contemplate possibilities, understand abstract concepts and explore contrary-to-fact propositions. I will then go on to consider theories relating to thinking, such as that of Piaget. The chapter will outline key ideas relating to learning and memory at this age, and will conclude by considering social cognition.

> I struggled with a lot of subjects at school, so when I get home, if I can't get the help, I sit there, even on my laptop, and I sit there and I have the AI generator on. It's like I'm asking them questions, but it's not me putting in my own words. It's me copying the words that they've put on something.
>
> (Young man, aged 15)

New ways of thinking

The ability to imagine possibilities becomes important as young people move into secondary education. It is often said that children think about what is real, while adolescents begin to think about what might be. One example of this is

DOI: 10.4324/9781032640433-4

thinking about how you might have been if you had grown up under different circumstances. "What would have happened if I had been born during a different historical period, or what might I be if I lived in a different family?" Of course, children can be imaginative and have a rich fantasy life. What happens in adolescence is that it becomes easier to move from one reality to another and to generate alternative possibilities in school subjects such as mathematics and science.

It is worth noting that the role of artificial intelligence (AI) may be playing a part here. As young people become more engaged with virtual reality in the games they play, and as learners increasingly turn to AI for assistance with a range of tasks in education, the notion of reality will be altering for this generation. This point was made regularly by our interviewees.

> Just like the internet and AI, like, gives you access to anything and everything, so it definitely helps with studying and stuff like that. If I don't have the knowledge I need, I can go and look it up, even, like on my iPad for example. I don't take notes in a book now, I take all my notes on my iPad, so it's all in one place, nice and simple, yeah!
>
> (Young man, aged 16)

Scientific reasoning involves the ability to generate possibilities systematically. "If it doesn't work like this, then let's try something different". The essence of the increasing ability to reason like this is the capability to construct "contrary to fact" propositions. Steinberg (2023) makes the point that this growing ability to think about possibilities contributes to the increasing amount of argument and debate in the family context. Young people begin to see things from so many different angles, and this allows them to challenge other people's views, especially the beliefs and values of their parents.

I can now turn to what is known as metacognition. Another way of describing this is to say that it is thinking about thinking. This involves the monitoring of one's own thinking (Devine and Lecce, 2021). Examples would include the checking of conclusions, and the ability to ask yourself – "how did I do that?"; "could I have done this differently?" In other words, the process of thinking becomes a subject of consideration, with the young person starting to consider the actual nature of thought. Thinking about thinking also leads to a greater degree of introspection and self-consciousness. This involves thinking more about one's emotions, wondering where they come from and how to manage them. This also leads to a greater concern with how others think about oneself. This is relevant to a consideration of egocentrism. It will also be a topic in Chapter 9, where there is an outline of what is known about the social brain.

> It's like there's a million and one different thoughts doing cartwheels and zigzagging across your mind. It feels excruciatingly difficult to find a clear space in your head to focus on one thing at a time. Sometimes it feels like you're being carried away by a rip current composed of all your worries and deadlines and thoughts. It's harder to find an anchor to secure you to the ground when the anchor slips from your grasp several times.
>
> (Young woman, aged 17)

Adolescent egocentrism

David Elkind (1967) first suggested that adolescence was a time of increased egocentrism. Anyone familiar with young people will recognize this, since for most there will be a time when there is an intense focus on oneself. Parents may describe this as the "me, me, me stage". This phenomenon is closely linked to the new ways of thinking we have been considering. A greater ability to look at alternatives leads naturally to a greater focus on what others are thinking, especially what others are thinking about oneself. There is no doubt that the awareness of a changing body that comes with puberty has some impact here. The impact of the physical developments and the sense of a changing body lead naturally to wanting to know what those changes look like to others.

Elkind proposed two aspects of adolescent egocentrism. In the first place, he suggested that there would be a period when the individual constructs an *imaginary audience*. In this sense, the young person will be imagining themselves on stage, with everyone looking at them. This notion is part of increased introspection, as I have noted. The idea of an imaginary audience is closely linked to the growing importance of friendship and the peer group. As young people become more attuned to the attitudes and values of the social group, their own identity becomes more salient to them. They need to know what others are thinking, so that they can fit in and avoid being isolated from important others. The concept of the imaginary audience is part of the cognitive apparatus that helps the young person adjust to their changing body and their altering identity.

The second aspect of egocentrism is what Elkind called the *personal fable*. He argued that the personal fable is part of an intensely individual view of life that develops at this time. This is the belief that one's own experiences are unique. This is a time when the young person has fantasies about achieving extraordinary things – becoming a great popstar or sportsperson. This enables the adolescent to combat a sense of unworthiness or low self-esteem. If one can believe that one's own life is special, then that provides a boost to the developing identity questions that come with increasing metacognition. It has to be to be said that there has been only limited research in support of these ideas. However, it is only necessary to be close to a young person as they move through puberty to know that these ideas are substantiated by lived experience.

The theoretical perspective of Jean Piaget

It was Jean Piaget who first pointed out that a qualitative change in the nature of cognitive ability, rather than any increase in cognitive skill, is to be expected at or around puberty. He and others (e.g., Inhelder and Piaget, 1958) argued that at this point in development, formal operational thought becomes possible. The crucial distinction he and his colleagues drew was between concrete and formal operations. During the stage of concrete operations (approximately between the ages of 7 and 11), the child's thought might be termed "relational". Gradually they begin to master notions of classes, relations and quantities. Conservation and seriation become possible, and the development of these skills enables the child to formulate hypotheses and explanations about concrete events.

These concrete operations are seen by the child simply as mental tools, the products of which are similar to those that can be sensed through vision, touch or hearing. In other words, the individual at this stage seems unable to differentiate between what is mentally constructed and what is perceptually given. When children formulate a hypothesis, it originates from the data, not from within the person. If new contradictory data are presented, they do not change the hypothesis, but rather alter the data or rationalize the situation in one way or another.

With the appearance of formal operations, a number of important capabilities become available to the young person. Perhaps the most important of these is the ability to construct "contrary to fact" propositions, something I have noted in the previous section. This change has been described as a shift in emphasis in adolescent thought from the "real" to the "possible". It enables the individual to think about mental constructs as objects which can be manipulated, and to come to terms with notions of probability and belief.

The fundamental difference in approach between the child and the adolescent was neatly demonstrated in what has become a classic study in the literature (Elkind, 1966). Two groups consisting of children aged 8 and 9, and adolescents aged 13 and 14, were presented with a concept formation task, involving a choice between two pictures. Pictures were presented in pairs, with each pair including both a wheeled object (e.g., a car) and a non-wheeled object (e.g., a spaceship). Choosing a wheeled object made a light go on, while choosing the non-wheeled object did not. The problem was to determine what made the light go on. Only half the younger group were able to arrive at the correct solution, and those who did succeed took almost all of the 72 allotted trials to do so. On the other hand, all the older group solved the problem, and most did so in fewer than 10 trials.

The tendency of adolescents to raise alternative hypotheses successively, to test each against the facts and to discard those that prove wrong was apparent in their spontaneous speech throughout the trials ("perhaps it is transportation, oh no, it must be something else, I'll try ...."). The younger group, however, appeared to become fixated on an initial idea that was strongly suggested by the data (e.g., tool or non-tool, vehicle or non-vehicle). They clung to this hypothesis even though they continued to fail on most trials.

Another, slightly different example of this situation is illustrated by what is known as the "dolls and sticks" problem. Nine-year-olds can arrange dolls or sticks according to size with no difficulty. Furthermore, they can match sticks to dolls according to height, no matter how the dolls or sticks are first presented. However, when the same problem is formulated in an abstract fashion, then this age group is unable to manage the task (Inhelder and Piaget, 1958). These researchers developed a range of ingenious problems for the investigation of various aspects of logical thinking at this age. The imaginative ways they found for the investigation of these phenomena remain a landmark in the literature on the developing mind.

Later writers (e.g. Murray, 1990) attempted to categorize the elements that make up formal operations. These are:

1. Duration. Operational thought will continue over time, so that the same result will be obtained no matter how much time has elapsed since the problem was first presented.

2. Resistance to counter-suggestion. Young people who are operational thinkers will not be influenced by persuasion or arguments which offer alternative explanations.

3. Specific transfer. The original problem-solving ability will remain unaffected, even when different materials or different situations are presented.

4. Non-specific transfer. Adolescents will show an understanding of the principles behind problem-solving, and will be able to apply learning obtained in one domain to any other domain.

5. Necessity. This notion refers to the idea of continuity in physical objects and materials. Thus, no matter in what form something is presented, of necessity it remains the same despite its appearance. Those who think in operational terms understand this principle.

Over the years, there have been many criticisms of Piagetian theory. In the first place, there have been arguments over what is known as domain specificity. It is suggested that what young people learn will be a function of what they are exposed to. Those who, for example, have more exposure to mathematics will do better in this domain than in others where they have had less exposure (Byrnes, 2003; Kuhn, 2009). Piaget's approach may be described as a domain-general theory. He believed that formal operational thought would be applied across domains, no matter how much previous exposure the individual had had. Most cognitive theorists now believe in domain specificity.

A second problem with Piaget's approach is that formal thought is more difficult to define than the earlier Piagetian stages. Not all young people are able to demonstrate formal thinking by middle adolescence. Indeed, some studies have shown that even some adults have not yet reached this stage of cognitive development (Keating, 2011). A third issue has to do with what Ward and Overton (1990) called the distinction between performance and competence. In essence, they argued that, even if young people were competent in logical thinking, they might not demonstrate that ability if they had no interest in the particular task. They demonstrated this neatly by showing that the relevance of the task makes a big difference to the degree of formal thought demonstrated by young people at different ages.

> I think people are a bit AI dependent. I don't like it. I have used it a few times. I can really see the use of it. It makes it so much easier to do things. I just think it is stripping people of being able to be creative. Like I hate generative AI, it's taking away from the art industry and stuff. Just copy and paste, I think that is cheating. I think if you are using it for ideas, and using it to help out, then that's fine, but if you are literally just copy and paste, I don't get it, why are you in school? Why are you pursuing an education?
>
> (Young person, aged 16)

Information processing

In many ways, the topic of information processing does overlap with the section on learning and memory. However, there are some differences in coverage. Here I will deal with attention, speed of processing and organization. Memory will be covered in the following section. When considering information processing, it will be obvious that this has been hugely influenced by the development of computing, and indeed now of artificial intelligence. In this respect, the focus here is on the way the individual codes information, retrieves information, compares different bits of information and makes decisions based on these comparisons.

During adolescence there is a clear improvement in the ability to pay attention. This applies both to selective attention and divided attention. With the former, the individual will need to focus on one thing at a time, while the latter involves being able to manage two or more tasks at the same time. Both of these aspects of attention are critical in the classroom situation. Unless the individual young person can manage these skills, concentration will be problematic, and thus learning will be affected. There are some interesting examples of strategies that are helpful in improving attentional skills, as for example using video games and other technologies that are familiar to young people (Coleman, 2021). Divided attention is linked to the process of inhibition, something I will discuss in the next section.

Another component of information processing has to do with speed. How quickly can information be processed, and how does this change during adolescence? Evidence shows that young people make a big shift in the speed of processing, with a gradual improvement apparent during the adolescent years. Kail and Ferrer (2007) showed that, regardless of the task, older adolescents do better than younger adolescents, and they in turn do better than children on this element of information processing.

A final element in this picture has to do with organization. Adolescents show a greater ability to plan the way they organize information and thus to use this information in the classroom. One example would be the use of mnemonics and other strategies which enhance the learning process. When faced with new material, we know that creating structure, writing notes and finding other ways to organize new content helps with the learning process. Children find this hard to do, while the skills involved in this process come gradually as young people move into adolescence. A good example of this is the development of metacognition. As I have noted, young people begin to be able to think about their own thinking, and that of course enables them to question themselves about strategies which will help their learning (Dehaene, 2020).

One interesting question has to do with whether these different aspects of information processing relate to each other. Do they improve at the same rate across the age range? Do they enhance each other? And do they work together, or are they separate capabilities? In an important study by Demetriou et al. (2002), young people between the ages of 8 and 14 were studied over a long period of time. The researchers were able to show that, although all aspects of information processing improved over time, the growth of each of the abilities was not affected by the state of the others at any one point in time. In other words, it appears that the growth of these skills may be affected by external agents such as the learning environment, rather than by some internal neurocognitive process. Demetriou et al. (2002) conclude that there is no single driver of cognitive change during this stage but a complex combination of factors that are both within the individual and within the environment.

> I've used AI sometimes to come up with, like you can write stuff from it. Where, I'm doing a PowerPoint for homework, or say I don't know how to explain something, I'll just type in the question, and it will give me, like a massive list. It's amazing. The teachers do spot it, but if you're doing a research task or anything, I don't think it really matters because we're only giving information. It's only drawing from Google or the internet, isn't it? It's just about what is real, it's out there.
>
> (Young woman, aged 17)

Learning and memory

The first question to consider is whether there is a difference between learning and memory. Most writers make little distinction between these two ideas. However, it seems important to explore this a bit further, as exemplified in Dehaene (2021). In the first instance, one could say that memory is a *capacity*, in other words a resource or a strength, something you can draw on. On the other hand, learning is a *process*. Learning is something that takes place in time, leading to a change in the brain. Furthermore, memory is essentially dependent on the capabilities of the brain. Learning, on the other hand, is influenced by a wider range of factors, such as family, the school environment and the teacher. Motivation and interest in the subject make a difference too.

One example might be that of learning a poem. It would be possible to say that you were memorizing it, or you were learning it. In this case, the two words are interchangeable. However, you would not say that someone was memorizing how to drive. You would say they were learning to drive. A trainee chef would not be memorizing how to cook. Such a person would be learning how to cook. Of course, they might be memorizing a recipe, which illustrates the point. In the case of activities that involve a range of skills, it is more usual to refer to the process as learning. When it is a case of rote learning, we are more likely to use the word *memory*. There is the conundrum. The words *learning* and *memory* have been here used in the same sentence! How can we tell them apart?

Does this matter? It is important for our purposes, since different areas of the brain are likely to be involved in the different processes. As an example, there is one type of memory that refers to our ability to recall facts and bring events and information into consciousness. This aspect of memory is most likely to be associated with the hippocampus and associated brain structures. Another type of memory refers to habits and routines linked to performance, such as riding a bicycle. Here we are carrying out an activity without much effort or thought. These types of memories are likely to located in areas such as the spinal cord and the cerebellum.

Where school learning is concerned, it is probable that the first type of memory is the one that is most engaged. This will help when I consider the sites in the brain that show change following various cognitive activities.

Executive function

Executive function is one of the key concepts used for understanding the increasing capacity of the brain during the teenage years. Executive function is the term used to describe certain processes that underlie learning. This is a field of study that has aroused great interest in the last decade or so (Thomas et al., 2020). This is because it can be shown that executive function is closely related to academic performance. There are good studies that indicate that the skills that combine to make up executive function can be used to predict performance on tests and exams in school. This evidence gives us a good pointer to the fact that it is not just good teaching that leads to success in the classroom. What is happening in the brain is making a vital contribution as well.

There are generally considered to be four elements that make up executive function (Peters, 2021). These are:

- Working memory;
- Inhibition;
- Resistance to interference;
- Flexibility.

I will now explore each of these aspects of executive function in more detail. It is only through an understanding of these four elements that we can fully understand the process of learning in the classroom (see Coleman, 2021, 2024).

Working memory

Working memory refers to our ability to hold a certain amount of information in our attention while we are processing it. This is a key skill and has been shown to increase gradually from infancy onwards. How much can anyone of us hold in our memory at any one time? A well-known psychologist once wrote a paper entitled "*The magic number seven, plus or minus two*" (Miller, 1956). This is a classic article in social science, and refers of course to the challenge – what exactly is working memory? What is the maximum number of bits of information that can be held in our active memory at one point in time?

This is significant for our understanding of learning in the teenage years. This is a capability that underpins intellectual activity. It is interesting to note that, until recently, this was a capacity that was believed to be fully developed by the end of childhood. Now we know that working memory, among other skills, continues to develop throughout adolescence. Working memory can be measured by varying the amount of time between the presentation of information and the demand to retrieve it. Another way of assessing working memory is to vary the amount of information rather than the timing. Readers will be familiar with the parlour game of placing a number of items on a tray, giving a certain time for those playing to memorize the objects and then asking how many can be recalled.

This can be replicated in the laboratory, where the number of objects to be memorized can be varied. In one task, there may be 10 objects. This number can then be increased gradually to test working memory at different ages. Studies show that working memory improves during childhood and up to the age of 15. The changes between ages 11 and 15 are more gradual than during childhood.

A different approach to this is to ask the participants to reorganize the material while they memorize it. For example, they may be presented with a string of letters – M, B, I, P, F, R, X, L. In order to memorize these letters, the subject needs to find a way of linking them together. This is a harder task. The individual has to do some work in order to carry out the memory task. This probably involves different parts of the brain. Here the difference between adults and young people is more marked. Research shows that this skill only develops gradually during the teenage years.

Working memory is an essential skill needed for many of the activities taking place in the classroom. A mathematics or science problem that requires the manipulation of figures or other types of information will be dependent on working memory. Designing schedules or planning activities during the school day, as well as subjects as varied music and language, all utilize working memory.

> Like, I used to be able to sit through a two-hour YouTube video, but now I can't. I think a lot of people in our group, they all have shorter attention spans. It's harder to concentrate for long periods of time and it's also like, distracting. I think social media is one of the reasons why people don't really knuckle down and focus, because I do it all the time where you are going "I have to study, but I'd much rather watch TikTok". So, I am just going to sit on TikTok for four hours. So, I had to download, like, app blockers, to stop me from going on it all the time.
>
> (Young woman, aged 18)

Inhibition

The skill implied here is the ability to stop oneself doing one thing while concentrating on another. In other words, being able to concentrate on a particular task while ignoring other things that might be distracting. This is an essential capacity for learning. In the brain the ability to activate inhibition depends on the receptors that I mentioned earlier. These are known as the "off" receptors. These are the ones that prevent or inhibit the passage of a message that travels along the nerve fibres.

There are a multitude of ways in which inhibition plays a part in learning. In fact, it would not be possible to pay attention in class without the ability to inhibit stimuli in the surrounding environment. Can you imagine to yourself all the things that might be going on in the classroom? You have to screen out the behaviour of other pupils, the things that are going on outside the window and in the corridor, and indeed your own bodily messages such as aches from muscles or feelings of hunger or thirst. In addition, inhibition is essential for learning since new learning often involves un-learning old material. Thirdly, we make assumptions about our environment depending on what is obvious around us. A good example is the belief that the world is round. It looks flat, but we have to inhibit that idea to learn that it is, in fact, round.

Inhibition is not just essential for learning. It plays a major part in the way our brain functions in almost every situation you can imagine. As was mentioned in Chapter 2, it is useful to consider the idea of a railway network. In such a network, you have to have a signalling system; otherwise, the trains would bump into each other and the network would come to a standstill. Other scientists like to talk about an air traffic control system, stopping planes from colliding in mid-air. The point is the same. In our brains there are literally millions of messages being transmitted every second. There has to be a system which allows these messages to be sorted into the ones that matter, and the ones that can be halted or put to one side. Inhibition is the process that makes all this possible.

While we know that the skill of inhibition increases with age, there are also individual differences between pupils of the same age. Thus, some young people struggle with the capacity to inhibit things that are distracting. These young people may find difficulty in concentrating in class, or they may have a problem being able to sit down for long periods. This links to the question of neurodiversity, a topic which will be further discussed in Chapter 7.

Resistance to interference

I have already talked about the capacity to ignore stimuli that are distracting or irrelevant. As I have said, concentration would not be possible without this ability. However, sometimes the distraction is located within the task itself. In this example, the individual has to screen out some aspects of the task in order to find the solution. Reading inhibition, as exemplified in the Stroop test, provides one illustration of this.

The Stroop test was developed as a way of measuring this ability. The task is simple. The individual is shown a picture of the word "RED", and the letters are in red. The task is to name the colour. You may think this is rather easy! However, when the word is "GREEN", but the letters are in red, the task becomes more difficult. The areas of the brain needed to perform the Stroop test keep changing and maturing all through the teenage years (Blakemore, 2019).

The older the adolescent, the better they are at suppressing irrelevant information. In this case, the colour of the lettering is irrelevant information. This is an excellent means of illustrating resistance to interference. A particular area of the frontal cortex plays a key role here, and as a result of scanning we can see how this develops with age. Interestingly, this area continues to mature until the early 20s. Even older teenagers struggle with this task, especially if the demands of the task are increased by giving less and less time to make a decision.

Flexibility

The last of the four elements of executive function is flexibility. Many would argue that this skill is as essential as all the others for learning and memory. Flexibility is needed when we learn new skills. Why? Because in most situations learning requires feedback about how we are getting on. Are we doing something correctly, or have we made an error? If we have made an error, then we need to correct it before we can proceed with our learning.

In essence, this is about feedback. The skill of flexibility is determined by whether the individual is paying attention to feedback from errors or ignoring the feedback and ploughing on (Elkind, 1966). Many studies show that children in primary school have more difficulty taking account of feedback than do those in the older age groups. Of course, feedback can come from many different sources. Thinking about this raises the questions of feedback from teachers and other adults. How is feedback communicated, and with what accompanying message? Does feedback come with praise, criticism or disinterest? The nature of feedback plays a critical role in assisting or hindering learning.

Flexibility has been measured in the laboratory by creating situations where individuals are required to apply rules in problem-solving. For example, the task may be to respond in a certain way following the presentation of a stimulus which is a colour. The individual will then be told whether the response was right or wrong. Once a participant has been responding correctly for a while, the rule can be changed abruptly. The individual has to use the feedback to work out the new rule. Studies show that the skill of flexibility increases with age (Coleman, 2021).

It appears that feedback which indicates that a mistake has been made leads to activation in two brain areas in the frontal cortex connected to purposeful behaviour. Scientists have called this system the "alarm" system, because it becomes active when people make errors. Studies have shown that these areas of the brain are maturing slowly during the teenage years. The learner has to be able to recruit these areas of the brain when solving problems. The ability to recruit only develops slowly, and is affected by maturation in the later teenage years (Galvan, 2017).

Types of learning

It is time now to consider how our understanding of executive function contributes to useful knowledge about young people. As far as working memory is concerned, it will be obvious that this has its limits. This restricts how much information the individual has at their disposal at any one time. This is demonstrated in our everyday life, as for example when we make shopping lists or put a telephone number in our smartphone. We cannot hold more than a certain amount of information in our minds at any one moment. We therefore need to find ways of helping our memory out.

In terms of classroom activity, it is possible to assist students to think about this in order to lighten the load on working memory. Many young people will face difficulties when having to learn new material. One way of dealing with this is to encourage students to articulate the processes they are using to solve problems. This may be through writing things down or by documenting the steps taken to arrive at a solution.

Research has demonstrated how this works in the brain. When students are first introduced to a problem, for example a mathematics problem, they tend to use a range of locations in the frontal cortex. With practice, brain activity alters. As students become more familiar with strategies to reduce the load on working memory, shifts can be detected in the brain. When learning processes become more automatic, activity in the frontal cortex is reduced and relocated to different sites in the brain (Galvan, 2017).

Another question that is important for students is how best to learn new material. This is where we can point to the importance of different modes of learning. For many years, we have known that learning in more than one mode can enhance memory. This is sometimes known as *multi-modal learning*. What does this mean? If learning involves both visual and verbal elements, there is arousal in different regions of the brain. Where more than one region of the brain is involved, there is a clear advantage for students. An additive effect occurs, so that when more than one brain region is engaged, learning is likely to be more successful (Dehaene, 2020).

This leads to a discussion of *visualization*. Studies show that the process of visualizing an object engages nearly as many sites in the brain as happens when we see the object in front of us. As a result, it will be apparent that the use of mental imagery is a powerful tool in any learning activity. The importance of visualization leads to the topic of *vicarious learning*. There has been much discussion in the literature about what are called *mirror neurons* (Crone, 2017). These are neurons that fire when we observe other people doing things rather than doing them ourselves.

The interesting thing about these neurons is that they appear to fire in much the same way as they would if we were actually carrying out the behaviour. This means that learning can occur simply through observation. It also underlines the importance of visualization. Bringing up an image in our minds has a powerful effect, leading to activity not just in the visual cortex but in the frontal areas as well. All this has profound implications for the learner. Attempts to learn material by simply rehearsing it, using what is known as rote learning, will not be as effective as looking for visual or other links to such material.

In the UK, it is rare to find examples of students being taught study skills. We do not have, in our curriculum, information about topics such as visualization and multi-modal learning. In other countries, study skills are routinely taught to students, so that they learn about the topics I have just described. In my own work with secondary school pupils, I find that the majority are using simple rote learning (Coleman, 2021). They have not been introduced to different methods of learning new material. It is clear that the information that I have covered in this chapter could be of great help in schools across the country.

Learning and memory are topics of huge importance for young people and for all who work in education. Our knowledge about the working of the brain when learning takes place has made huge strides in recent years. We now know not just what happens in the brain during the process of learning, but how we can make learning more effective. An important part of this knowledge has to do with executive function. The four aspects of executive function – working memory, inhibition, flexibility and resistance to interference – are all essential for learning.

These have all been illustrated by studies in neuroscience. All four have been shown to be critical elements of cognitive function. They provide the bedrock of skills that underlie new learning during the teenage years. I have also outlined different types of learning, such as visualization and multi-modal learning. Knowledge of these can be used to assist and accelerate the learning process. There is no doubt that one of the major contributions of the science of brain development has been its contribution to knowledge of learning and memory.

> Deep fakes are becoming increasingly problematic in the way images of young girls are being used and exploited. With the age of AI, it leaves behind scars, it destroys their innocence, and causes insecurities to bloom.
>
> (Young woman, aged 17)

Risky thinking

I have referred to risk in previous chapters. There will be a further discussion of risk in Chapter 9 when I consider the peer group and the social context of growing up. Given that this chapter is concerned with cognition, it makes sense at this point to consider risky thinking. For this reason, I am going to include a description of an aspect of thinking that is rarely discussed in the academic literature. Anyone who lives or works with young people will recognize these ideas. I believe it is helpful to be aware of some of the ways young people engage in thinking about themselves that could be described as risky. I would include the following ways of thinking under this category:

Invulnerability. This involves the notion that: "*It won't happen to me*". This type of thinking may be a defence against vulnerability. If you feel that you are superhuman, then the possibility of harm or disaster will not touch you. This could be associated with the previously mentioned personal fable.

Lack of future time perspective. When you are a teenager, the future seems very far away, and it is a notion that is hard to take too seriously. This has links to the difficulty in thinking about consequences, something that is closely associated with risk-taking.

Catastrophic thinking. This refers to a sense of disaster when things go wrong. A lack of perspective leads the young person to feel that, if one thing turns out badly, the rest of life will turn out badly too. This lack of perspective can lead the young person to make risky or unhealthy choices.

Paradoxical thinking. This has to do with the duality of this stage. The young person is both a child and an adult. Thus, it is possible to be mature and sensible at one moment, then needy and childish almost immediately afterwards. This back and forth can be confusing for the teenager, leading to a difficulty in making decisions.

Self-centred thinking. This type of thinking is linked to the egocentrism mentioned earlier. Being self-centred may lead the young person to ignore the needs of others, leading to poor choices and flawed decision-making in social situations.

It would be encouraging to see more research into this aspect of cognition. Nonetheless, I doubt any reader will disagree with this outline. I believe that more discussion of this aspect of young people's thinking could be of help both in the family and in the professional world. A better understanding of this type of thinking will be of assistance to all who seek better relationships with this age group.

> It's quite hard to be a teenager, you've got technology, so lots of social media, and like people on-line, like, editing pictures of themselves to falsify things. I think that's so hard. You are looking at these people who are really not their true selves, but they present themselves to their teenage audience as their true selves. It leads to quite a lot of comparisons. People never feel good enough because these people always seem better than them. That is only because that's what they want other people to see, in a sense.
>
> (Young woman, aged 18)

Moral and political thought

A rather different aspect of thinking and reasoning has to do with the way this is applied to real-world situations. As Eisenberg and Morris (2004) point out, young people's changing notions of justice, morality and ethics are of great interest due to the changes that occur during these years. In terms of moral reasoning, once again it has been Piaget's concepts that have formed the springboard for later thinking about this. Although there have been a number of different theories put forward to explain the moral thinking of young people, there is little doubt that the "cognitive-developmental" approach of Piaget and Kohlberg has been the starting point for most work in this area.

In his work on the moral judgement of the child, Piaget (1932) proposed two stages of moral thinking. The first, which he called "moral realism", refers to a period in which young children make judgements on an objective basis. As an example, when asked which is worst, to break two cups or to break five cups, children are likely to base their reasoning on how much damage has been caused. In other words, to break five cups must be a worse action, regardless of the circumstances. The second stage, applying usually to those between the ages of 8 and 12, has been described as the morality of cooperation, or the morality of reciprocity. During this stage, Piaget believed, decisions concerning morality were usually made on a subjective basis and often depended on an estimate of intention rather than of consequences.

Kohlberg (1981, 1984) has elaborated Piaget's scheme into one which has six different stages. His method has been to present hypothetical situations containing moral dilemmas to young people of different ages, and to classify their responses according to a stage theory of moral development. Hypothetical situations that have been used include taking a decision about whether to hide your sister's wrongdoing from a parent, or whether it is better to cheat or let someone down. Perhaps the best-known dilemma is one which has come to be known as the Heinz dilemma. Although it uses American language and ideas about health care, it has been widely used across other countries. It goes as follows:

> *In Europe a woman was very near to death from a very bad disease, a rare form of cancer. There was one drug that doctors thought might save her. It was a form of radium that a druggist in the same town had recently discovered. The drug was expensive to make, but the druggist was charging ten times what the drug had cost him to make. He paid $200 for the radium, but was charging $2,000 for a small dose of the drug. The sick woman's husband, Heinz, went to everyone he knew to borrow the money, but he could*

only get $1,000. He told the druggist that his wife was dying and asked him to sell it cheaper, or let him pay later. But the druggist said: "No, I discovered the drug, and I am going to make money from it". So, Heinz got desperate, and broke into the man's store to steal the drug for his wife.

Question: Should Heinz have done that?

Kohlberg (1981).

Based on responses to questions like this, Kohlberg has described the following stages of moral development:

Pre-conventional

Stage 1 Punishment-obedience orientation. Behaviours that are punished are perceived as bad.

Stage 2 Instrumental hedonism. Here the individual conforms in order to obtain rewards, have favours returned, etc.

Conventional

Stage 3 Orientation to personal relationships. Good behaviour is what pleases or helps others or is approved by them.

Stage 4 Maintenance of social order. Good behaviour consists of doing one's duty, having respect for authority, and maintaining the social order.

Post-conventional

Stage 5 Social contract or conscience orientation. An increasing shift to internal decision-making.

Stage 6 The universal ethical principle. An example would be the Golden Rule, or Kant's Categorial Imperative.

Broadly speaking, research has supported Kohlberg's notion of a progression through various stages of moral reasoning though adolescence. In a classic study (Kohlberg and Gilligan, 1971), the authors compared three very different cultures: the USA, Mexico and Taiwan. Results showed an almost identical sequence of stages, with variation being shown in the rate of development.

The later, post-conventional stages of reasoning were rarely seen, apart from in groups from the USA.

In a more nuanced study, Walker et al. (2001) explored the actual process of the move from one stage to another. They showed that young people experience periods of consolidation and of transition. Thus, in a period of consolidation there is stability in the type of reasoning, but when in transition there will be some fluidity of reasoning, with adolescents possibly using more than one type of reasoning. Once another period of consolidation is reached, it will be at a higher level of reasoning than that achieved earlier.

Over the years, many questions have been raised about whether this is a valid or reliable way to measure moral reasoning. Some authors (e.g., Eisenberg and Morris, 2004) have suggested other approaches to the measurement of this type of thinking, such as a multiple-choice method. Others have questioned whether moral reasoning has any relation to actual behaviour. Some have suggested that those who engage in anti-social behaviour are likely to evidence lower levels of moral reasoning, and there is some research to support this (Bao et al., 2015). One of the most interesting debates around this issue has to do with gender. One of Kohlberg's former colleagues, Carol Gilligan, has argued that women are more likely to view moral dilemmas from a care perspective, while men might be more likely to make judgements according to a justice framework.

Thinking back to the Heinz dilemma, one can see that using a justice orientation would lead to a very different assessment of morality than if one was using a care perspective. This latter view would argue that looking after a sick person is of a higher order than theft from a greedy pharmacist. Gilligan herself proposed a number of dilemmas that were closer to real-life situations. These are published in her work (Gilligan, 1990) and have been used in a variety of programmes. Finally, there is the question of how the individual is influenced by the context. Is it possible that a behaviour might be considered to be morally acceptable in a group situation, but not when one is alone? This question was explored by Gummerum et al. (2008). These authors showed that the context does matter, and that young people do have different views about what is morally acceptable depending on the situation in which they find themselves. Others, such as Eisenberg et al. (2009), showed that adolescents' moral reasoning can be very advanced, but that does not hinder them from engaging in risky behaviour.

Less is known about the development of political thinking during adolescence than about moral development. Nonetheless, this is a fascinating aspect of the way young people's thinking and reasoning alters with age. The pattern is linked to general cognitive development, but also to the fact that, as they get older, young people are exposed to more political information and ideas

(Flanagan, 2004). The classic studies in the field of political reasoning are those of Adelson and colleagues (Adelson et al., 1969; Adelson and O'Neill, 1966). Their work remains pre-eminent in this field. They approached the issue of the growth of political thinking by posing for young people of different ages the following problem:

> Imagine that a thousand men and women, dissatisfied with the way things were going in their own country, decide to purchase and move to an island in the Pacific. Once there, they must devise laws and modes of Government.

The authors then posed a variety of problems, such as how a government would be formed, whether there would be a need for laws, how to protect minorities and so on. This remains an original and creative way to explore this topic, and it offered rich rewards in terms of the insights provided. These insights have not been challenged since the 1960s. Since that time, there have been real-world examples around the world of groups of people purchasing an island and being faced with similar problems. The island of Eigg off the west coast of Scotland is one good example, where in the early 2000s the inhabitants crowd-funded to purchase the island from the absentee landlord.

The results of the studies by Adelson and colleagues can be discussed under two headings: changes in modes of thinking, and a decline in authoritarianism with age. As far as the first issue is concerned, there was a marked shift in thinking from the concrete to the abstract. This is a finding which ties in with all that has been said previously in this chapter. For example, when asked: "What is the purpose of laws?" one 12-year-old replied: "If we had no laws people would go around killing each other". By contrast a 16-year-old said: "To ensure safety, and to enforce the government". Another replied: "They are basically guide-lines for people, I mean, like this is right and this is wrong. It is to help them understand". (Adelson, 1971).

The second major shift observed was the decline in authoritarian solutions to political problems. The typical young adolescent of 12 or 13 years of age appeared unable to appreciate that problems can have more than one solution, and that individual behaviour or political acts are not necessarily absolutely right or wrong. The concept of moral relativism was not yet available for the making of political judgements. When confronted with law-breaking or even mild forms of misbehaviour, the younger adolescent's solution was, characteristically, to:

> Simply raise the ante: more police, stiffer fines, longer prison sentences, and if need be, executions. To a large and varied set of questions on crime

> and punishment the younger adolescents consistently proposed one form of solution: punish, and if that does not suffice, punish harder. At this age the child will not normally concede that wrong-doing might be a symptom of something deeper; or that it may be inhibited by indirect means. The idea of reform and rehabilitation through humane methods is mentioned only by a small minority at the outset of adolescence.
>
> (Adelson, 1971, page 1023)

By contrast, the 14- or 15-year-old is much more aware of the different sides of any argument and is usually able to take a relativistic point of view. Thinking begins to be more tentative, more critical and more pragmatic.

> Confronting a proposal for a law, or for a change in social policy, he scrutinizes it to determine whether there is more to it than meets the eye. Whose interests are served, and whose are damaged? He now understands that law and policy must accommodate competing interests and values, and that ends must be balanced against means, and that the short-term good must be appraised against latent or long-term or indirect outcomes.
>
> (Adelson, 1971, page 1026)

While Adelson and colleagues did not propose a stage theory relating to growth in political thought, it will be apparent from what has been outlined above that the move from concrete to abstract, and from absolute to relativistic reasoning is consistent with all that has been said about developments in cognition during the early stages of adolescence. Of especial interest is Adelson's finding that in late adolescence a broadly consistent and coherent set of beliefs, akin to an ideology, begins to be expressed that was not apparent at earlier stages. This ideology is "more or less organized in reference to a more encompassing .... set of political principles" (Adelson, 1972, page 121). These principles may concern a wide range of topics. They could include things like civil liberties, freedom of speech and other themes relating to rights and responsibilities of the citizen.

As is the case with moral development, there are likely to be variations between political thinking in hypothetical situations and responses to real-life experiences. The most important influences on behaviour are likely to be discussions with parents and friends, and engagement in these matters in the classroom (see Kim and Stattin, 2019). There is also evidence that young people who themselves have difficult experiences, such as racial harassment or victimization, are likely to show negative attitudes to government and to become more politically active than their peers. In the United States, studies have looked at minority youth, especially those living in poor or deprived neighbourhoods, and this research indicates a greater level of cynicism about politics and the role of government (Steinberg, 2023).

It is also the case that young people's political attitudes change over time. It is undoubtedly the case that social movements such as Black Lives Matter will affect attitudes and beliefs. Other important events, such as the pandemic in 2020 and 2021, and the growing awareness and anxiety about climate change, will also impact on the way young people experience politics and the way it affects their own lives. In the work of Oosterhoff and colleagues (2019), comparisons were drawn between political concerns at different historical moments. Thus, following the banking crisis of 2008, the major concerns of young people were related to economic issues. In the 2020s, one of the priorities for most young people is the warming of the planet. Many adolescents who are interested in politics look to figures such as Greta Thunberg, and see her as an example of how politics should be conducted (Sanson et al., 2019).

Conclusion

In this chapter, a range of topics to do with thinking, reasoning and learning have been covered. There has been a strong emphasis on the value of information now available concerning adolescent brain development. This knowledge has completely changed our understanding of the way learning and memory develop during the adolescent years. The chapter has included an exploration of the shift of thinking during these years and has described how such things as egocentrism come to the fore. Theories of cognitive development, such as that of Piaget, have been outlined, and other approaches, such as information processing, have been discussed. There is an outline of how brain function is linked to various elements of executive function, and types of risky thinking, common in this age group, have been described. The chapter ends with a discussion of social cognition, especially in relation to moral and political thought.

Chapter 5

Self and identity

Introduction

Adolescence is usually thought of as a time of both change and consolidation in respect of self and identity. There are a number of reasons for this. Firstly, the major physical changes that have been documented in Chapter 3 inevitably carry with them an alteration in bodily self-concept. This therefore includes a highly significant element of the overall self-concept. Secondly, intellectual maturation during this stage makes possible a more complex and sophisticated concept of the self. Much of this is related to the possibilities opening up as a result of brain development outlined in Chapter 2.

Thirdly, some development of the self seems likely as a result of changes in social relationships, in particular increasing autonomy, changes in family interactions and the growing influence of peers. Lastly, this is also a time of transition in relation to the social environment experienced by young people. There will be a move from one type of school to another, and in middle and later adolescence it is probable that the individual will experience some aspects of the workplace. In such situations, the young person will be expected to interact with adults in a more mature way, leading to further alterations in the sense of self.

The ways in which young people understand and perceive themselves, their own agency and personality have a powerful effect on their subsequent reactions to various life events. The essential dilemma for an individual young person who wishes to be fully integrated into society is that between "playing appropriate roles" and "selfhood". On the one hand, it is important to play the right roles in a range of social settings and to follow the prescribed rules for these situations. On the other hand, it is equally important to maintain elements of individuality or selfhood. Adolescence is a time when an individual struggles to work out who they are. What are their beliefs? What principles are important to uphold? When should they be guided by the wider peer group?

DOI: 10.4324/9781032640433-5

> Yes, like in Year 10 a lot of stuff happened with friends, and I just wanted to lie low. But I knew then it just wasn't me. But it was hard to build myself back up and find myself again. Yes, identity is a really hard thing to find in this day and age. You can fit into categorizing to be one thing, but I realized that I don't like to be in that category. Even though our generation wants us to be outside of categories, but then you are just fitting into other categories, if you see what I mean.
>
> (Young woman, aged 16)

The adolescent is engaged in a process in which making sense of the social world and finding a comfortable place in it are key to psychological maturation. The adolescent has relative freedom to escape from the rules set by important adults, especially parents, carers and other family members. However, this means making choices about values, social relationships and future goals. This process can be relatively straightforward or fraught with conflict and heartache.

In this chapter, I will cover six aspects of self and identity. These are:

- Self-concept development;
- self-esteem in adolescence;
- Theories of identity development;
- Ethnic identity;
- Gender identity;
- Identity in the virtual world.

Self-concept development

There are many different ways of conceptualizing the self-concept. Indeed, this is a topic with a long history in psychology and related disciplines, and a wide range of theoretical positions can be identified within the literature. For the purposes of this chapter, discussion will remain primarily within the field of psychology, focussing on research and theory relating to the adolescent life stage. The most common way of delineating the self-concept has been to describe a number of dimensions which may be said to constitute the totality of the self.

One good example may be found in the work of Offer and colleagues. Offer is well-known for the development of the Offer Self-Image Questionnaire (Offer, 1969; Offer et al., 1992). In this questionnaire, the adolescent self-image is broken down into five global areas of psychological functioning. These are:

- The psychological self (including impulse control, emotional health and body image);
- The sexual self;
- The social self (including social functioning and vocational attitudes);
- The familial self (including family functioning);
- The coping self (including self-reliance, self-confidence and mental health).

An alternative view may be found in the work of Harter (1990). Harter developed a concept of the self, based on a factor-analytic procedure. As a result of this procedure, she identified eight specific dimensions of the self-concept: scholastic competence, job competence, athletic competence, physical appearance, social acceptance, close friendships, romantic appeal and conduct.

> I think it is a matter of figuring out who I am, and who my friends are. It's been a very difficult process. I struggled a lot with it. Year 9 through to Year 11 I just felt I didn't fit in. I was very shy, very quiet, but I have built up my confidence a bit now. I would have been terrified to do this interview a little while ago.
>
> (Young woman aged 16)

These are not the only examples in the literature, or in the research field, that have been developed to understand the adolescent self-concept. However, they do give an idea of the way social scientists have explored this topic. Such approaches are helpful when one wants to consider the ways in which the self-concept changes and develops during adolescence. Firstly, it can be said that a greater degree of differentiation occurs. Thus, a child will describe herself simply as sad, happy, sporty or something similar. A teenager is more likely to say that they are friendly in such and such a situation, or anxious in other situations.

An adolescent is also likely to be able to include an additional element – who is doing the describing. Thus, a teenager might say: "*My parents see me as ……, but my friends see me as quite the opposite*". This ability to see the self from different points of view is a key feature of the developing cognitive skills that the individual is able to bring to an understanding of the self.

Better organization and integration of the self-concept also develop in addition to differentiation. When asked to describe themselves, children may simply list attributes in no specific order or relationship to each other. As they get older individuals may show evidence of a greater need to organize traits so that they become linked together and form a coherent whole. This is all part of maturation and is a reflection of the cognitive skills that an individual can bring to an understanding of his or her self.

> I'd say it is more of a process. I've never sat and thought I want to be that person. It's more like it takes a gradual time, and that's just how you become. Obviously, it changes slightly over time, but you don't see a drastic change. Like one day I wouldn't just go, right, I want to be this person. It's more of what you've become over time growing up.
>
> (Young woman aged 16)

Commentators in this field have also been interested in two other aspects of self-development: the preoccupation with the self (an element of egocentrism), which I have described in Chapter 4, and the question of how much the self-concept fluctuates during this life stage. In terms of the first of these, there is no doubt that adolescence brings with it a marked increase in introspection. Many well-known writers have explored this notion, including Erikson (1968) and Rosenberg (1979). This shift towards an often painful awareness of the self and how one appears to others is likely to result from a variety of factors. Increased cognitive ability plays its part, together with the physical growth and bodily change associated with puberty.

A changing body will almost certainly lead to a sense that the self is altering, and this in turn can cause intense self-consciousness. The young person becomes increasingly aware of other people and how she or he appears to them. This links to the idea of the "imaginary audience", which I discussed in Chapter 4. Egocentrism and introspection are part of the same process, and are, undoubtedly, one phase in the growing development of a coherent sense of self during these years.

> I think it is more gender based, more what it means to be feminine. It's difficult to come to a clear decision, because through adolescence you come across what it means to look like a woman, like what height is desirable, clothes that make you look attractive, what you should watch and read, people are always trying to fit you into their type of box, and that restricts your growth. These struggles insidiously affect your career too, you can doubt your own abilities, you might want to become a teacher rather than an F1 driver, because it's more of a feminine career.
>
> (Young woman, aged 17)

As far as the stability of the self-concept, this has received less attention in the literature than the stability of self-esteem. Self-esteem will be considered in the next section. Some aspects of the self-concept are bound to fluctuate more than others. Such awareness will not prevent anxiety about the lack of stability. As Harter notes, a young person may ask: "*I really do not understand how I can switch so fast. I mean, how can I be cheerful one minutes, anxious the next, and then be sarcastic*?" (1990, page 363). Now we know more about the brain, we can see that this variability is linked to immaturity of emotion regulation, and to the lack of stability in the hormone balance at this age.

Yeager (2017) has made an interesting point. As a result of his research, he has been able to show that the more stable the young person's self-concept, the better they are able to deal with everyday stresses. This underlines the link between self-concept and overall adjustment. The question then arises, what is it that contributes to the development of the self-concept? What variables will assist the young person to formulate a stable self-concept as she or he moves through adolescence? No doubt both the family and the peer group will play a part. This is a question I will return to in Chapters 8 and 9, when I consider the competing influences of these two major forces operating in the lives of adolescents.

> It was a struggle, definitely a struggle. I didn't know what I wanted to be, who I wanted to be, or anything like that. I used to change a lot. I have worn very different clothes and styles. I went through all kinds of stuff. I cut my hair really short, like a typical boy haircut and stuff. I had a mullet for a while, back to long hair, as you can see. I don't normally dress like this girly, normally I'm just in jeans and T-shirt.
>
> (Young person describing themselves as bisexual, aged 18)

Self-esteem

Self-esteem has received more attention than most other aspects of the self, since it is seen as a barometer of coping and adaptation. The work of Yeager (2017) poses a challenge to this view. Yeager has shown that a number of aspects of the self-concept do contribute to adaptation. However, it remains the case that self-esteem is a favourite topic for research. This is primarily because it has been argued that low self-esteem is a major factor associated with adjustment difficulties. In addition, those with high self-esteem are likely to do better in a range of different domains. To take one classic example, the work of Rosenberg (1965) illustrates this general conclusion. He was able to show that low self-esteem, characteristic of approximately 20–30% of the sample he studied, was linked to depression, anxiety and poor school performance. Those who had higher self-esteem were significantly more likely than those with low self-esteem to value self-confidence, hard work and the wish to make a good impression on others.

Many other social scientists have investigated this complex question. Some have questioned whether Rosenberg's findings would stand up to further scrutiny. One strand of work has considered the relation between self-esteem and school performance. Some believed that high self-esteem would lead to academic success, yet it appears that the opposite is true – success in the classroom leads to higher self-esteem, rather than the other way around (Schmidt and Padilla, 2003).

> I think I went through this period when I stopped being myself because I wanted to fit in, because I didn't want people to, like, make fun of me for not being myself. Then I got to a time when I thought I don't want to do that, it wasn't fun. I'm not being myself anymore. But that's the problem, the pressure. If you didn't have the pressure then you'd be able to be just who you are, free. I guess there's sometimes when you feel you can't truly express who you are, because you know you're going to get comments, right.
>
> (Young woman aged 17)

As for the links between self-esteem and mental health, this is a complicated question, and different studies have provided varying answers. Some studies have shown that low self-esteem is more likely to lead to depression than result from it (Orth et al., 2014). These authors argue that this result comes about because those with low self-esteem are less likely to seek help than those whose self-esteem is higher. Other studies have considered beliefs about popularity (Rieger et al., 2016). They argue that if young people think they are not liked by their peers, self-esteem will be affected, and it is that which leads to poor mental health.

In spite of these studies, it has to he said that the links between cause and effect remain far from clear. Even with the use of sophisticated statistical models, the direction of the effect is not always evident. And perhaps this is not surprising, given the complexity of the variables that contribute both to self-esteem and to mental health. Turning now to the factors that have an impact on self-esteem, most commentators agree that, in early adolescence, it is satisfaction with one's physical appearance that contributes most to self-esteem. Harter (1990, page 367) quotes one young person who says: "*What's really important to me is how I look. If I like the way I look, then I really like the kind of person I am".*

Among young people, especially in the early stages of adolescence, body image satisfaction correlates most highly with global self-esteem, followed by social acceptance by peers. Academic achievement and sporting success contribute, although to a lesser degree. As many authors have shown, there is a marked gender difference in respect of the salience of body image, with this being a more important factor for girls than for boys.

Many studies have reported lower self-esteem among girls than among boys in early adolescence (Bleidorn et al., 2015; Chua and Chang, 2016). It seems most probable that these findings can be explained by the high level of importance attributed to body image satisfaction in global self-esteem. Girls are, perhaps, more sensitive to, and dissatisfied with, their body image during the pubertal years. An important question here is the extent to which social media and AI are contributing to this effect. However, it has to be noted that similar findings were reported well before the arrival of the internet (e.g., Simmons and Blyth, 1987).

> It was difficult to start with, but then I'm learning to live with the changes. It was like, for me, having to go out and buy baggier clothes, so everything happens with your body shape. I buy a lot of jumpers because of how the tight tops go on me. I think people change a lot, especially with girls and mood swings and things like that. Not saying that boys don't go through it too, but I feel girls get it a bit more rougher than boys.
>
> (Young woman, aged 15)

Another important contributor to self-esteem is the opinion of important others. However, which others make the most difference in adolescence? The work of Harter (1990) has been especially significant here. Her research shows that there is a developmental shift, with parents becoming less important as a function of age. Thus, for children, the perceptions of parents play a larger part than any other variable in determining self-esteem. However, with the onset of adolescence, peers become more increasingly salient. In spite of this important conclusion, there is no evidence that parents cease to be influential in respect of adolescent self-esteem.

Parents continue to have an impact, but not to the over-arching degree that was apparent in childhood. I will review evidence in Chapter 8 showing that self-esteem is one of the variables most obviously influenced by parenting styles. Parents and peers both play a part in this important arena, but the balance of influence between the two shifts during the adolescent years in line with the increasing significance of social relationships outside the home.

The second theme which is noteworthy in this context is the stability of self-esteem during adolescence. To what extent does self-esteem fluctuate? What are the reasons for fluctuation, and what impact does this fluctuation have on other aspects of adjustment? Early studies reported contradictory results, but this is not surprising as investigators tended to use different measures. Also, there was no consistency in the samples chosen for study, and all this led to uncertainty about whether any stability was to be expected during this life stage.

> I think being an immigrant child, when you go through teenagerhood, you become stuck in the crossfire of where you belong. You question the uniqueness of your traits and your personality. You wonder what it means to be a woman, your expectations of yourself and not society's expectations. It can affect your dress, how you style your hair, the language you use. Expectations and judgements from people are always lurking behind every decision or thought regarding your identity.
>
> (Young woman, aged 18)

Greater clarity on this question was provided by the research of Hirsch and colleagues (Hirsch and Dubois, 1991). They identified four very different trajectories taken by groups of young people in respect of self-esteem development. The sample they looked at were between the ages of 12 and 14, and their findings indicated that approximately one-third of the group could be classified as being consistently high in self-esteem. A further 15% were consistently low in self-esteem during this stage. However, roughly half the sample showed marked change during the two-year period. Twenty percent showed a steep decline, while nearly one-third showed a small but significant increase in self-esteem during the two years of the study.

This study represented a landmark in the understanding of self-esteem, and subsequently many other studies have explored this topic in other ways. One example is that of Zimmerman et al. (1997). These investigators looked at a wider range of ages than Hirsch and Dubois, including those up to the age of 16. Remarkably, their results were very similar and replicated the trajectories that had already been identified by other researchers.

Zimmerman and colleagues (1997) note that groups with consistently high self-esteem were more likely to resist peer pressure and less likely to engage in anti-social behaviour. They report that it is useful to compare the groups who show improving and declining self-esteem. These two groups often start at much the same point, at age 12, but gradually diverge in respect of scores on most variables. The authors argue that these results have clear implications for intervention programmes. What might work for one group may not have an impact on another group. Being able to track the changes in self-esteem over these years may be of great value for those working with this age group.

Theoretical approaches to identity development

A key figure in any discussion of identity development is Erik Erikson (1968). For those who wish to read of his work in detail, an excellent review can be found in Ferrer-Wreder and Kroger (2020). Erikson viewed life as a series of stages, each having a particular developmental task of a psychological nature associated with it. In infancy, for example, the task is to establish a sense of basic trust and to combat mistrust. The maternal relationship is here considered to be critical in creating a foundation upon which the infant can build future trusting relationships. As far as adolescence is concerned, the task involves the establishment of a coherent identity and the defeat of a sense of identity diffusion.

Erikson believed that the search for identity becomes especially acute at this stage as a result of a number of factors. Erikson laid stress on the rapid biological and social changes that take place during adolescence. He pointed especially to the importance for the individual of having to take decisions at this time in all areas of life. In many of his writings, Erikson either stated or implied that some form of crisis is necessary for the young person to resolve identity issues and to defeat identity diffusion.

According to Erikson, identity diffusion has four major components. Firstly, there is the challenge of intimacy. Here the individual may fear commitment or involvement in close personal relationships because of the possible loss of his or her own identity. This fear may lead to stereo-typed or formalized relationships or to isolation. Another possibility is that the young person may, as Erikson puts it: "*in repeated hectic attempts and repeated failures, seek intimacy with the most improbable partners*" (1968, page 167). In spite of the fact that these words were written so many years ago, readers will no doubt recognize something familiar in descriptions of possible struggles over intimacy and commitment.

Secondly, there is the possibility of diffusion of time perspective. Here the adolescent finds it impossible to plan for the future or retain any sense of time. The problem is thought to be associated with anxieties about change and about becoming adult. It often consists of: "*a decided disbelief in the possibility that time may bring change, and yet also a violent fear that it might*" (1968, page 169). Our more recent knowledge of the challenges inherent in the maturing brain and our awareness of risky thinking (as described in Chapter 3) have clear links to these notions. Although Erikson's ideas are based in psychoanalytic thinking, it is fascinating to see how they are supported by the neuroscience of today.

Next there is the diffusion of industry. Here the young person finds it difficult to harness their resources in a realistic manner in work or study. Both of these activities represent commitment, and as a defence against this, the individual may find it impossible to concentrate. Alternatively, they may frenetically engage in one single task to the exclusion of all others. An adolescent may opt out of taking exams at the last minute or drop out of a course just at the moment when it gets interesting. These are good examples of the adolescent struggle with identity diffusion.

Finally, there is the concept of negative identity. By this, Erikson means that the young person selects an identity which is exactly the opposite of the one preferred by parents or other important adults. Erikson expresses his ideas on this aspect of identity diffusion as follows:

> The loss of a sense of identity is often expressed in a scornful or snobbish hostility towards the role offered as proper and desirable in one's family or immediate community. Any aspect of the required role, or all of it – be it masculinity or femininity, nationality or class membership – can become the main focus of the young person's acid disdain.
>
> (Erikson, 1968, page 172)

These four elements constitute the main features of identity diffusion, although clearly not all will be present in any one individual who experiences an identity crisis. I would emphasize that, whilst these ideas were put forward so many years ago, there is no doubt that they remain both pertinent and perceptive today. Anyone who lives or works with adolescents will recognize elements of Erikson's thinking. This is in spite of the many criticisms that have been expressed concerning Erikson's ideas – criticisms that I will outline shortly.

One other element of Erikson's thinking should be mentioned here. This is the notion of psychosocial moratorium. This means a period during which decisions are left in abeyance. It is argued that society allows, even encourages, a time of life when the young person may delay major identity choices. At this time, they may experiment with roles in order to discover the sort of person they want to be. While such a stage may lead to disorientation or disturbance, it has, according to Erikson, a healthy function. "*Much of this apparent confusion may be considered social play – the true genetic successor to childhood play*" (1968, page 164).

The weakness of Erikson's theory is that he is never specific about the extent of the adolescent identity crisis. His use of terms such as "normative crisis" or "the psychopathology of everyday adolescence" implies that all young people may be expected to undergo such crises, yet nowhere does he acknowledge the broad range of adolescent experience. He prefers instead to deal in the qualitative aspects of identity development. While there is a wealth of insight evident in his thinking, it has been left to others to translate his ideas into a form that can be tested empirically.

The work of Marcia (1966, 1993), also outlined in Ferrer-Wreder and Kroger (2020), is seminal in this respect. Marcia has used Erikson's dimensions of crisis and commitment to define four identity statuses. The four stages, or identity statuses, as they are called, are as follows:

Identity diffusion. Here the individual has not yet experienced an identity crisis, nor have they made any commitment to a vocation or set of beliefs. There is also no indication that they are actively trying to make a commitment.

Identity foreclosure. In this status, the individual has not experienced a crisis but nevertheless is committed to their goals and beliefs, largely as a result of choices made by others.

Moratorium. An individual in this category has not yet resolved the struggle over identity, but is actively searching among alternatives in an attempt to arrive at a choice of identity.

Identity achievement. At this stage, the individual is considered to have experienced a crisis, but to have resolved this on their own terms, and now is firmly committed to an occupation, an ideology and a choice of social roles.

The identity achievement, moratorium, foreclosure and diffusion statuses characterize those attempting to resolve or avoid the identity work of adolescence. Identity achievement and foreclosure individuals share a commitment to adult roles. However, the former have synthesized important childhood identification figures into an original and personal configuration. The latter, on the other hand, have bypassed such development work by adopting identities created for them by others.

By contrast, young people in the moratorium and diffusion stages share a lack of commitment. For the moratorium group that lack is instrumental in acting as a stimulus toward identity synthesis. For those in the diffusion group, it represents an inability to make a commitment to some form of adult identity.

In Marcia's view, these four identity statuses may be seen as a developmental sequence but not necessarily in the sense that one is the prerequisite for others. Only moratorium appears to be essential for identity achievement. The exploration and searching inherent in moratorium must precede a resolution of the identity challenge. In Marcia's original research (1966), he found that as students moved through the four years of college the proportion of those in the identity diffusion category declined, while those in the identity achievement group steadily increased.

Marcia's attempts to operationalize Erikson's original ideas have themselves generated a huge body of research. This body of research is far too substantial for a comprehensive review here. Readers are encouraged to explore this further in Ferrer-Wreder and Kroger (2020). Here I can outline a few of the questions raised by this literature. The first question has to do with association between identity statuses and mental health. Overall, studies have shown that the closer individuals are to identity achievement, the more likely they are to function well in various arenas such as careers and relationships. The second question relates to the developmental sequence of the statuses. Are these statuses linked to specific ages or levels of maturation? Again, research has broadly supported the idea that identity achievement comes at the end of the sequence, and that it is unlikely to occur until late adolescence.

Another major question has concerned the measurement of Marcia's statuses. To this end, a number of measures have been designed and validated. Two of these may be mentioned here. One is these is the paper-and-pencil measure – the Dimensions of Identity Development Scale (DIDS). Work on this scale has been carried out by a number of authors and has been shown to have good internal construct validity and reliability. Another scale is the 13-item Utrecht-Management of Identity Commitments Scale (U-MICS) (Crocetti, 2017). A study by Dimitrova et al. (2015) explored the use of this scale across seven different national contexts, and reported important similarities between different regions and countries.

Finally, it should be noted that the identity status model has not been without its critics. Some writers have questioned whether Marcia's concept of identity statuses does justice to Erikson's original theoretical ideas about identity development. Those working in a psychoanalytic environment are, not unnaturally, concerned that the clinical insights may be lost by translating Erikson's ideas into an empirical framework. Validity of Marcia's statuses have also come into question, and that has led to the development of measures such as those discussed above. It still remains a question as to whether clinical insight and empirical measurement can sit comfortably together. In spite of all this, there is little doubt that identity in adolescence remains a fascinating and critically important subject for discussion and research.

Ethnic identity

In introducing this topic, as well as the next one on gender identity, it may be worth commencing with a note about intersectionality. This idea was first put forward by Kimberley Crenshaw in 1991 to describe how different social categories, such as race, social class and gender, interact to create unique experiences of identity formation. This author also used this term to explore experiences of discrimination and disadvantage (Crenshaw, 1991).

Intersectionality underlines the fact that no one facet or component of identity takes precedence over another. All combine together to reflect the overall sum of identity. Another term also used in this context is identity integration. This stems from Erikson's theoretical approach, and applies to an individual's sense of continuity over time in their ideas about their identity. Intersectionality and identity integration apply to all aspects of identity. However, they are of particular relevance to ideas about ethnic identity and gender identity.

> It's very difficult when you move to another country from a different country. So that was difficult for me. They used to bully me as well. They call you freshly, stuff like that. So now my English is good I say to them: "What you doing? They doing stuff to others like they did to me". And they go: "Shut up, what is with you, you so and so".
>
> (Young man, aged 15)

Early approaches to ethnic identity, such as that of Jean Phinney, were essentially linear in nature. In other words, theories about ethnic identity envisaged a progression from a stage of "unexamined" through to those who were "searchers", and then in the final stage were seen as those who had resolved their identity. Phinney (1993) and others believed that particular experiences, such as witnessing or experiencing racial harassment, acted as spurs to the examination of the individual's ethnic identity.

It was suggested that the position of those from non-mainstream cultures may best be described in terms of two independent dimensions: the retention of their own cultural traditions, and the establishment and maintenance of relationships within the wider society. Phinney herself put forward this argument, as she sets out in her article with her colleague Devich-Navarro (Phinney and Devich-Navarro, 1997). These authors suggest a model in which there are four dimensions, each of which can be classified as either high or low. These are as follows:

Integration. Such individuals would be high on retention of their own cultural traditions, but would also and develop and maintain relationships with the mainstream culture.

Assimilation. Here young people would have a high maintenance of relationships with the mainstream culture, while having a low level of maintenance of their own cultural traditions.

Separation. Those in this group would have high cultural retention, and low identification with the mainstream culture.

Marginalization. Individuals in this group would be low on both dimensions.

As Phinney and Devich-Navarro (1997) note, this model is more useful than a linear one, but it still requires further elaboration to accommodate the variation in ethnic and mainstream involvement among non-mainstream cultural groups.

As discussion and debate has moved on, there is now a recognition that a more sociocultural approach is needed to fully understand the development of identity (Ferrer-Wreder and Kroger, 2020). These authors talk about the ways in which society and culture work to co-construct a person's identity. As they note, the word *co-construct* implies that there is a bi-directional process, and that the individual and the context are essential elements of the formation of the individual's identity.

Many authors have discussed what is known as person–context interaction (Kaplan and Garner, 2017). The problem lies in the complexity of the context for any one individual. Context can include social institutions such as schools, family and cultural activities and rituals, historical times and conditions and so on. If we are to fully understand how the context works to influence the development of ethnic identity, all these factors should be taken into account. Of course, that is easier said than done.

This leads to the measurement of ethnic identity. As a starting point, it is useful to consider what is known as the integrative model for ethnic and racial identity (ERI) development (Umana-Taylor et al., 2014). This approach is based on ideas from earlier theories (Phinney, 1993), as well as from other theories that draw on the African-American experience in the United States. A key figure in this approach is Deborah Rivas-Drake, a professor at the University of Michigan. She and a colleague wrote a book called *Below the Surface: Talking with Teens About Race, Ethnicity and Identity* (Rivas-Drake and Umana-Taylor, 2019). This book provides an outstanding introduction to this topic for adults and young people.

In many writings about the study of identity, Rivas-Drake outlines the challenges inherent in this type of work. She is quoted in Ferrer-Wreder and Kroger (2020) as saying:

> It is definitely hard because you have to go beyond self-reports. You definitely have to have a multi-disciplinary view. Because something like a school context – it's multi-level, multi-layered, there's pedagogy, there's climate, there's curriculum, there are just so many ways to understand the school context, that if you really want to understand how it informs identity .... You have to get into all of that ....
>
> (page 128)

The integrative model includes a description of how ERI should normally change from childhood to early adulthood. While concepts of race and ethnicity may be relatively concrete in childhood, the development of perspective-taking and awareness of others in adolescence will lead to a more nuanced awareness of identity. In addition, a wider range of personal experiences will also shape the individual's notions of identity.

Many of the ideas in Marcia's approach to identity status, referring to identity exploration and commitment, will be pertinent here too. These processes work together with such things as collective verification, where the individual makes comparisons with others who are seen as belonging to the same group. A whole range of experiences and explorations will take place as the individual moves through adolescence. These include the salience of experiences, in the sense of working out how much these are relevant to the individual's sense of self. Power dynamics between social groups will be relevant, as the individual manages peer relationships and selects particular friendships.

Turning now to the measurement of ethnic identity, there are many options available. Ferrer-Wreder and Kroger (2020) highlight two particular measures. The first is the Multi-Group Ethnic Identity Measure (MEIM), which has been widely used in many research studies. This measure was developed by Jean Phinney, already mentioned earlier in the chapter. Phinney's theory of ethnic identity development, itself based very much on Erikson's theory, has led to the widespread use of the MEIM. Different editions of this measure are available and range from 6 to 20 items. It is relatively brief, and its reliability has led to its use in many large-scale studies of youth. It is not limited to the study of one particular ethnic or racial group and can therefore be used in many parts of the world.

The Ethnic Identity Scale (EIS) is one other quantitative measure that has been widely used in research. Developed originally by Douglass and Umana-Taylor (2015), like the MEIM, it has many versions. It contains scale scores for ethnic identity exploration, resolution and affirmation. These two are not the only approaches being used for the measurement of ethnic identity. There are examples of what are known as mixed method approaches, where surveys and interviews with young people are combined with quantitative methods such as the EIS scale (e.g., Rivas-Drake et al., 2017). This is an expanding field, with many examples of studies across regions and cultural settings.

One study worth noting here is the work of Hammack (2006, 2014). This author studied Israeli and Palestinian adolescents using a mixture of fieldwork, life story interviews, participant observation and the setting up of a peer group encounter for both groups in the USA. Much rich material emerged from this study. The authors discussed the idea of a master narrative. Results showed how experiences of close contact with the "out group" could shift ideas of identity, only for those ideas to be altered when there was further contact with the "in-group". The study highlights how Palestinian young people's efforts to create a coherent life story and to make meaning out of their lives can run up against national master narratives.

> By the end of the camp, I was ready to make peace with them. But when I went home, I just realized that this is wrong .... you can't be making friends with them. They are killing you! The whole thing is wrong.
>
> (Hammack, 2006, page 358)

Finally in this section, it is important to recognize studies that have underlined the positive features of identification with a particular culture. Daha's (2011) study of Iranian young people in schools in the United States illustrates this well. Two quotes from young people in this investigation highlight their experiences.

> Being an Iranian among all the kids at school shows that I am an individual. (My culture) is related to my authenticity here in America.
>
> (Ferrer-Wreder and Kroger, 2020, page 137)

> Culture is very important to me. I feel like it gives a little bit of perspective to me. I view things from 2 angles. I feel like I have a sort of self-identity that is deeper. More layers to it. I think culture has given me that aspect.
> (Ferrer-Wreder and Kroger, 2020, page 137)

In this section, I have explored the history of research on ethnic identity. As I have noted, this is a fast-growing field, and a number of measures have been developed for use in this particular area. As immigration continues to be a major issue for the Western world, and as more young people are able to move from one culture to another, the study of ethnic identity will only become more relevant. It will become increasingly important for those countries with growing immigrant populations to recognize the value of research on ethnic identity.

Gender and gender identity

As culture and ethnicity have become key themes for identity research, the same can be said for gender. Questions surrounding gender are controversial, and this is reflected in the literature on this topic. As I have noted in the previous section, the idea of intersectionality is a good place to start. In practice, this means recognizing all the dimensions – such as class, sexual choice, ethnicity – which may be part of any one individual's identity. As Ferrer-Wreder and Kroger (2020) say:

> Intersectionality is a framework to guide research. It encourages researchers to attend to social and power structures as well as a person's total identity package across a variety of personally salient domains and areas.
> (page 157)

Definitions of terms such as sex and gender are contested by many commentators, and their use has led to numerous debates and controversies. As social structures and values change, the use of these terms can be seen to alter. Sex is mostly used to describe the individual's status, as male or female, based on biological characteristics present at birth. However, this idea is seen as controversial by some who believe that biology is not necessarily a determining factor in one's identity.

A second concept is gender identity. This represents a person's sense of self along a continuum between female and male. This identity may change over time, and in recent years there has been a great variation in the ways in which gender identity is perceived. For many, the idea of a binary choice between male and female is overly simple. Statuses such as transgender or non-binary are becoming more common, and I will discuss how these ideas are being translated into research later in the chapter.

A third concept here is sexual orientation. This refers to the individual's experience of being attracted to people who are of the same sex, other sex or both. Again, these ideas are complex, and many people experience different orientations in relation to sexual behaviour during their adolescent years. I will discuss sexual orientation in Chapter 6.

There are a wealth of disciplines and frameworks through which gender identity has been studied. These include feminist psychology, queer theory, life course theory and social identity theory. Marcia's identity status model (discussed earlier in the chapter) can also be applied to this subject. One good example of a helpful approach is contained in the work of Bussey (2011). This author suggests that individual, behavioural and environmental factors all contribute to the way gender identity is understood and experienced. These factors are defined as follows:

Individual factors. These include how people understand their physical sex and gender, and characteristics such as agency, self-regulation and personality.

Behavioural factors. These include what people do in their relationships and in the settings and activities they choose.

Environmental factors. Here are included the way others react to a person's choice of identity, and the social and structural factors that impact on any particular gender option displayed by the individual.

In Bussey's model, these three factors are thought to interact and mutually influence each other. In this approach, developmental change in gender identity is considered to be ongoing and continuous. For our purposes, it is important to note that adolescence is a hugely significant time of life when identity questions are being addressed. This will be true of all aspects of identity, with gender identity often being at the forefront of this search for a stable identity.

There has been some discussion in the literature about the notion of synthesis (Dillon et al., 2011). By this is meant a way in which the personal and social aspects of gender identity can be combined to bring a sense of stability for the individual in this domain. For many young people, this will provide a significant challenge during adolescence. The pressure from friends and the wider peer group to behave in certain ways that are seen as acceptable in relation to gender identity and sexual behaviour will be a major factor affecting one's sense of self and self-esteem. The more the young person finds themselves in the identity diffusion or moratorium statuses (as described by Marcia, 1966, 1993), the more likely they are to be questioning gender identity.

In recent years, there has been an increasing interest and focus on diversity and multi-dimensionality. There is greater awareness of the range of possible ways in which young people may describe themselves in relation to gender identity. There is debate in the public sphere concerning the rights of individuals who describe themselves as non-binary or trans, and questions on this issue clearly feature in many an adolescent's search for identity.

> Honestly the idea of being a guy, kind of was just not me. I like my pretty floral dresses and some makeup occasionally and whatever. When I was younger, I was absolutely against the idea of being with any girls when people were saying: "Oh you're a lesbian", and stuff like that. I was, like, taking it as an insult, right? But now I've grown up a bit, I kind of knew what I was, and I started to look a bit more, you know?
>
> (Young person, describing themselves as pansexual, aged 18)

This is reflected in the literature, as seen in work by Bussey (2011). There is undoubtedly an enhanced recognition of the variety of ways in which gender identity may be described and experienced by young people. One good example of this may be found in the work of White and colleagues (White et al., 2018). This study included nearly 20,000 young people with an average age of 16. Recruitment used a variety of methods, including through social media and using celebrity figures such as Lady Gaga to encourage students to engage with the study.

Responses were on-line, and participants were asked to self-identify their gender and sexual identity. Terms such as female, male, trans male and trans female were provided, but the participants were also given the opportunity to write in their own labels. In the section on sexual identity, labels were provided, such as heterosexual, lesbian, gay and so on, but there was also the option of self-description.

Results were fascinating, in that approximately 65% used the given labels, but the rest used a wide variety of descriptions to convey their ideas about gender and sexual identity. For gender identity, write-in labels included: gender fluid, non-binary, unsure, questioning and other similar words illustrating uncertainty. As for sexual identity, words such as asexual, unsure, demi-sexual, pan-sexual, queer and questioning were all used. This study is a good example of both the variety of notions about sexuality, as well as the uncertainty and exploration among young people in regard to their gender identity and sexual orientation.

> This is going to sound weird, but I used to want to be a boy. I don't want to be a boy, girl into boy. I wanted to be born as a boy and experience it like that. That's always what I wanted to be, like, you know? I wish I was a boy. I think it would be so cool. I think I would have a lot more confidence if I was a boy.
>
> (Young person describing themselves as bisexual, aged 18)

Another example of a series of studies in this area is that of Diamond and colleagues (Diamond, 2005, 2008; Diamond and Butterworth, 2008). These investigators were responsible for a longitudinal study lasting 10 years. Participants were late adolescents who were known to have questioned their sexual orientation. Having a number of time points allowed the study to explore the stability or otherwise of gender identity and sexual orientation.

While some of the individuals showed variability in sexual attraction and behaviour over time, others were relatively stable over this 10-year period. Among this group, some experienced or described experiences in which they believed they were or might be transgender. A few reported a significant change in gender identity during this stage of their lives. This series of studies is important in that it is a rare example of a longitudinal approach to gender identity. It also reflects the need to identify different trajectories in gender identity formation and the importance of taking intersectionality into account when studying this topic.

Masculinity

In a consideration of gender identity, a word about masculinity is in order. In recent years, the concept of "toxic masculinity" has been much publicized and debated, and there are now discussions taking place concerning what is known as the "manosphere" (Over et al., 2025). This concept refers to the notion that males have to be "strong and dominant" to be real men, including the idea that males can and should impose their ideas and wishes on sexual relationships. These ideas may include the possibility of violence or abuse towards their female partners.

> So, for girls I think it is difficult, with that comparison, I think girls probably compare themselves more than boys do. Then obviously there's a lot of hegemonic masculinity and stuff like that. I think for example, Andrew Tate.

> I think boys are more easily influenced, and that might be hard on them, because they feel they have to be, not particularly nice to certain genders, because they have to fit in.
>
> (Young woman, aged 18)

Understandably this leads to a sense of anxiety about how to bring up boys with attitudes that are more tolerant and sensitive to the needs of the opposite gender. This poses a real challenge for parents and for schools, a challenge for which there are no easy answers. The role of the internet is also highly significant here, and there is potential for social media platforms to influence attitudes to gender and to gendered behaviour. This can be achieved through the role of influencers, through the publicizing of certain norms relating to gendered behaviour, or through the sharing of experiences on group chats or sites that focus on content relating to gender and sexual behaviour.

> Boys have to face bullying from their friends, if they are not in a particular way, sort of strong and tough. And, like, having to act like a man, and having to follow standards and style stuff. The internet, they get a lot of pressure I think – how to be manly. Who cares? But they do.
>
> (Young woman, aged 17)

Virtual identity

I will conclude this chapter with a look at the role of social media and AI in the formation of identity. I will include a further discussion of these topics in Chapter 9. For the moment, it is important to recognize here the role that the internet is playing in allowing identity exploration in adolescence. As I mentioned earlier in the chapter, Erik Erikson wrote about a stage of psychosocial moratorium, a stage when young people could experiment with what he called "social play". By this he meant a period when it was possible to try out alternative selves and explore a variety of identities.

> It's when you get Instagram, you get famous people on Instagram, who you want to look like. Like people compare and be like, why don't I look like that person? And, I think it can get to them.
>
> (Young man aged 15)

The opportunities provided by the on-line or virtual world offer exactly what Erikson envisaged all those years ago when he was writing in the 1960s. In this space, adolescents have the perfect opportunity to try out all manner of identities, through a variety of media. Davies and Eynon (2013) wrote a chapter in their book, specifically on the development of identity in the on-line world.

They make the point that new technologies have facilitated a more transient, flexible and global set of choices for young people. These choices are less rigid than those available in the off-line world. They provide a wider range of identities and a wider range of channels though which identity can be explored (Maheux et al., 2025).

Davies and Eynon suggest that in many ways the lives of young people are regulated, either in school, by parents and carers or in their own communities. Thus, the virtual world offers a greater degree of freedom, away from the constraints of the real world. Many studies (e.g., Talmud and Mesch, 2020) have noted that being on-line can offer emotional support, the maintenance of relations, and openings into spaces that are simply not available in the off-line world. However, it is important to note that, while technology is not radically transforming identity, it is having a very significant effect, and it does allow for a freedom that is not available elsewhere.

I will pick out three aspects of the virtual world that have a direct impact on identity exploration. The first of these is the extension of personal space. The on-line world provides opportunities to cross boundaries of time and geography, making it possible to envisage aspects of one's identity in entirely other worlds. The second element is what has been called the performative aspect of identity. The perfect example of a site that has enabled this is, of course, TikTok. Here anyone can upload whatever aspect of their interests and skills they like, allowing new aspects of identity to be shown to the world.

Thirdly there is the question of popularity. Most sites provide a function for showing "likes". Thus, the individual can monitor how images, photos or other personal details are evaluated by others. For young people, especially those in the younger age groups, how one is perceived and assessed by others is extremely significant. Indeed, it could be argued that during the early years of adolescence this information constitutes a major element of one's identity. I will explore this in greater detail in Chapter 9. Many commentators have pointed out that the sites used by young people alter as they move through adolescence. Where profiles are uploaded will be a statement about identity, with sites altering as technology alters and as sites gain or lose attractiveness for particular groups.

While considering these questions, the roles of AI and of virtual reality should be taken into account. These features of the internet have introduced new dimensions into the notion of identity. They have made possible different types of exploration, with opportunities to invent new personalities and create a variety of alternative realities. For some, these new versions of reality provide exciting new fields of exploration, while for others these opportunities present potentially dangerous experiences.

An example of a positive opportunity might be through Google Character – an app which allows the individual to play with and invent a huge variety of new personalities and avatars. While such apps may appear to offer new and positive experiences, some may worry about other aspects of AI. One example here would be what are known as "beauty rating" apps such as Beauty Scanner or Face Score. These allow the young person to upload a photo of themselves, following which AI determines facial symmetry and the proportions of the individual's features. The adolescent then receives a "prettiness" score. For young people who are filled with anxiety about their appearance and popularity, apps like this can have a powerful negative impact on mental health.

It is worth noting that the virtual world has provided endless opportunities for identity exploration. Yet, it would wrong to assume that the real, or off-line, world is no longer important. Studies have shown that the two worlds interact (e.g., Maheux et al., 2025), so that people still spend significant amounts of time in actual, real world, relationships with peers. Not everyone is stuck in their bedrooms all the time, staring at a screen. Identities on-line and off-line feed each other. While the virtual world has provided new dimensions for identity exploration, it is certainly not the only space where adolescent identity is formed.

Conclusion

This chapter has explored identity in all its aspects. I have included a review of notions of the self-concept, as well as an outline of research on self-esteem in adolescence. Theories of identity development have been described, starting with those of Erik Erikson and continuing with Marcia and other more recent authors. The chapter covers both ethnic and gender identity, and includes reference to some of the controversies surrounding these concepts. The chapter ends with a discussion of identity in the virtual sphere, and includes a mention of new developments stemming from the availability of AI and opportunities in the worlds of altered reality.

Chapter 6

Sexual health and development

Introduction

Sexual health and development is a central strand in all adolescent development. Underlying this is the biological maturation which starts at the outset of puberty. However, sexual development involves not only biological change but also maturation in the social and emotional worlds of the adolescent. In this chapter, some of these changes will be documented, and consideration will be given to how the experiences of young people interact with, and are affected by, the context in which they grow up.

> I feel like this stuff is really heavy for my generation. It was like a trend, like a phase. When you're younger you see stuff on-line and you're, like, "Oh yes, I want to do that!" Like when I was in Year 7, Year 6, like anybody from my school will tell you that half of our year was questioning their sexuality, not because they wanted to, just because they were, like, yeah, everybody's doing it now.
>
> (Young woman, aged 17)

Adolescent sexuality is influenced by a range of factors. These may be internal, as for example the rate of pubertal maturation. Alternatively, these factors may be external, such as the type of family and neighbourhood or the impact of social media and the on-line world. The developing sexuality of the young person may be a source of considerable anxiety, both to the teenager themselves and to the adults who are responsible for their care and education. This is especially so for adults when adolescents appear to be involved in risky sexual behaviour. In the course of this chapter, consideration will be given to safe sexual practices, as well as to the changing patterns of sexual behaviour. I will also cover romance and intimacy, sexual orientation, teenage pregnancy, the role of the internet and effective sex and relationships education.

DOI: 10.4324/9781032640433-6

Changing patterns of sexual behaviour

The era of the 1960s is usually held up as the height of sexual permissiveness, but in fact patterns continue to alter and evolve. Up until the early 2000s, the anxiety of adults centred around the fact that young people were becoming sexually active at a younger and younger age. With my colleague Fiona Brooks, I documented this trend, showing how sexual activity had changed between the years between 1964 and 2002 (Coleman and Brooks, 2009). Since then, there have been further changes. More recent data appear to show that the trend to earlier sex has either reached a plateau or been reversed (Li and Davis, 2020; Temple-Smith et al., 2016).

> Now is a good time to start being in a relationship with other people. I always used to think that people were in them far too young, especially in middle school, like it was far too young to be like "I have a boyfriend". I always thought it was just like to brag about it, like to impress people. But now, also, I think it can be more difficult with social media, like, you can see things and they are like: "what's on your phone? what are they posting?"
>
> (Young woman, aged 17)

Data on this topic are not always easy to find, and depend on large surveys which are expensive to carry out. Steinberg states: "... *national surveys indicate that fewer adolescents are sexually active today than in previous decades*" (2023, page 296). This author bases his statement on reports from the Centre for Disease Control and Prevention in the United States. In the UK, the National Survey of Sexual Attitudes and Lifestyles (NATSAL) studies (Tanton et al., 2015) summarized three waves of research on young people's age of sexual initiation. This programme has included a fourth wave which was carried out in 2022. However, this study focussed mainly on the impact of Covid on the sexual behaviour of adults, so there is little here about adolescence.

In this area, as in so many others, there are significant individual differences. The evidence shows that the age of sexual initiation will depend on many variables, including culture, location and a wide range of background circumstances. Many authors (e.g., Temple-Smith et al., 2016) report earlier sexual activity among some groups than others. They find that sexual activity is likely to occur earlier in Western countries than in non-Western countries. In the United States, there is evidence that African-American young people may become sexually active earlier than their White American peers (Steinberg, 2023). Having said this, it is important to note that cultural norms and the age of consent vary significantly from country to country (Pearce, 2017). In some non-Western countries, the age of consent is lower than 16, which in turn has an impact on the age of marriage in such countries.

> I think each generation is more mature than the last. Like my little sister, she acts like as if she is the same age as me now! She's very much: "I need a boyfriend, I need a boyfriend". You're 13 years old and you need a boyfriend. Really?
>
> (Young woman, aged 17)

The question of the validity of data on sexual behaviour is a key feature of research in this area. Many authors have set out the difficulties of investigating sex in young people. In the first place, there is the problem of defining sex. What does "having sex" mean to different people? Most agree that intercourse involving vaginal penetration is sex, but what about other activities? Should mutual masturbation or anal and oral sex be included here? Clear definitions are essential, and researchers have to be careful to be inclusive and to cover the range of sexual behaviour. This is especially pertinent as gender and sexual orientation will affect sexual behaviour, as discussed in this and the previous chapter.

Another problem is that of recall. Since very little research in this area is done with anyone under the age of 16, it is frequently the case that participants are being asked to remember past events. A number of studies show that young people do not report their sexual behaviour in a reliable manner. This may be due to embarrassment, shyness or the wish to keep this information private. Although dated now, a good study on this was that of Upchurch and colleagues (2002). They reported that only 22% of young people aged 16 to 18 who were sexually active were consistent in their reporting. The great majority changed the date of their first sex when re-interviewed at a later date.

The context and timing of adolescent sexual behaviour

Adolescents are not isolated from what is happening in the adult world, and nowhere is this more pertinent than in sexual behaviour. Young people are intensely aware of how adults behave in this sphere. From early childhood, sex is a topic of enormous fascination, and much learning takes place before the individual becomes an adolescent. Sex is everywhere in our society and is evident in all forms of media, including television, films and of course the internet. Equally important is the fact that young people know about the adults around them and their sexual relationships, whether in the extended family or in the neighbourhood. Not surprisingly, they are influenced by such experiences.

> In the movies and stuff, like you have romance and relationships, and I think it is really romanticized. Like me, from a young age, watching like Disney with all the princesses and stuff like that, I was always, like, I need to find my prince! I think movies and TV shows have had a big impact because there's always this thing around relationships, even on YouTube, kind of asking my crush out, talking to my crush, and for me that was like, cool. I felt I should be in a relationship now!
>
> (Young woman, aged 17)

Of the range of factors impacting on the sexuality of young people, most readers will be thinking of social media. In recent times, there has been a high degree of concern regarding the type of sex that is viewed online, and how that impacts actual sexual behaviour. As far as the family is concerned, parents and carers will have attitudes to sexuality, and this will play out in a variety of ways. Attitudes to the body, to nudity and to intimacy will all be elements of the learning that takes place as the child grows up and becomes more aware of their sexuality.

The behaviour of significant adults will also play a significant role here. Adults act as role models in this sphere as in many others. The way the two parents act towards each other, the way they treat each other, and the way they behave sexually will act as powerful influences, even if these influences are covert or unacknowledged. One obvious example of this is the substantial body of research showing that young people in families where parents have divorced or separated are likely to become sexually active at an earlier age than those living in intact families. A number of studies have compared the effects of living with a single parent with other variables such as pubertal timing, school performance and economic circumstances. Studies show that, of all the variables, the most influential is parental status (Nicholson et al., 2014). A variety of explanations have been put forward for this result, including exposure to permissive sexual norms, as well as more limited parental monitoring and supervision.

> I think because my parents got married when they were 18, they had my brother when they were 18, and now my brother had a baby when he was 18. And now they're like: "Oh! You're so weird, why don't you want this?" Like, I respect what you've done, but I'm sure I don't want that for myself. I think it's weird wanting a relationship right now, because I feel, like, now is

> the moment to be selfish, so you need to put yourself first. You're constantly worrying about other people and I feel like you miss a lot. If you're not in a relationship you are free to do whatever, you can live your life happily, and then you can worry about that later, when you've lived your life quite fully.
>
> (Young woman, aged 19)

There are further ways in which parents and carers can be influential. In some circumstances, adults can be the most effective sex educators, especially if they are open without being intrusive. As with all communication, parents and carers are more likely to be able to offer support if they are willing to deal with the young person's agenda, rather than with their own (Coleman, 2019). As noted previously, adults can provide monitoring and supervision, assisting adolescents to delay involvement in sexual activity. Alternatively, they may leave young people to set their own boundaries and make their own decisions about the pace of their sexual development. I will have more to say about parenting strategies in Chapter 8.

Many studies have looked at the role of communication about sex between adults in the family and young people. Steinberg (2023) reviews a number of studies indicating that it is not so much the discussion that matters, but rather it is the attitudes and values that are communicated within the discussion that are crucial. If the values and attitudes are congruent with those of the young person, then there is a greater likelihood that communication between adult and teenager will have an impact on behaviour (see also Temple-Smith et al., 2016).

Some authors have noted that much depends on what is understood by communication. While the two generations may subscribe to the idea of openness and honesty, they may well come at this from different points of view. For parents and carers, openness and honesty may mean having more information about what young people are doing. On the other hand, for young people, withholding certain information, especially when it is to do with something as important as sex, means that they gain privacy and a sense of control over their own choices.

> I think the last relationship I was in, it was like a proper thing but one-sided. Because it was always him wanting to talk to me, calling me at random times, and then he would get annoyed if I didn't answer him. And it was, like, I felt a bit controlled. And then it was, like, on and off for a year, and then I sat down and I was like, I don't want to be in a relationship with someone that controls me every time.
>
> (Young woman, aged 16)

In today's world, when the internet is having such a powerful influence on attitudes to sex and on the norms associated with sexual behaviour, it is probable that wider gaps are opening up between adults and young people in their beliefs and experiences of sex. The use of social media for the exploration of sex, the use of sexting and other messaging to send content about sex, and the ubiquity of dating sites are all examples of ways in which the internet is having an impact on young people's experiences of sex. While there is much written about this by commentators in mainstream media such as newspapers and magazines, there is as yet very little academic research investigating exactly how attitudes to sex differ between the generations as a result of social media and AI.

> I think there's a big challenge, like if my boyfriend doesn't do this right, like what right? What kind of things are people posting when they are, like, my boyfriend hasn't done this, hasn't done that. Like I was watching this video, it's like my boyfriend has gone out with this girl's family friend. This boy has opened the door for a girl I don't know, so should I ask him about it? Do I confront him and be like: "What have you done this, what have you done that?"
>
> (Young woman, aged 15)

Romance and intimacy

Falling in love is an integral part of the adolescent experience. Yet for many it is hard to work out exactly what this means and how to distinguish between love and sexual arousal. Erikson (1968) argued that falling in love is part of the search for identity. For Erikson, the resolution of the identity crisis depends partly on the ability to experience intimacy. According to Erikson, intimacy involves openness, sharing, trust and commitment. Thus, an experience of intimacy contributes to the development of identity and maturity through opportunities for self-exploration.

> I think maybe my first boyfriend, knowing that someone liked me. I think it was that validation that made me realize my own self-worth, and that's the thing for me. I needed that confirmation from someone else to be able to tell me I'm doing good. I can feel, like, I'm doing well. To have someone be interested in me like that was a big boost of my confidence.
>
> (Young woman, aged 17)

The intimate relationship enables the young person to hold up a mirror to themselves, even if it is a distorted one, as well as to experience a sense of extraordinary closeness with another. This must in some way echo the contact between mother and child in infancy. It is perhaps for this reason that falling in love in adolescence has an intensity that is different from that experienced in adulthood.

Since the 1990s, there has been an expansion of research in this area. Brown (1999) was responsible for early writing on this topic. He identified four stages in the development of romantic or intimate relationships during adolescence. These stages are as follows:

- *Infatuation*. In this stage, the young person is in love with "being in love". There is as much focus on the self as on the other person, and any actual romantic relationships tend to be short-lived.
- *Status*. Here the young person is looking at the romantic relationship from the point of view of how it will affect their status in the peer group. There is much concern with dating "the wrong person", and this is a period when relationships are as much about reputation as they are about closeness and intimacy.
- *Intimacy*. It is in this stage that close relationships begin to be formed. These are founded on mutual interests and feelings for each other. Although young people are still learning about themselves, they are developing the ability to share emotions, to develop trust, and to explore their needs in the context of intimacy.
- *Bonding*. Here concerns about commitment come to the fore. How long is the relationship going to last? Where is it going well, and where not so well? At this stage, care and loyalty are of equal importance as pleasure and passion.

This is helpful as a framework for the understanding of romance, but as a commentator writing about this schema some years later, it is noticeable that sex is hardly mentioned. Passion only comes into the discussion when bonding is mentioned. More recent discussions of the topic of intimacy (e.g., Temple-Smith et al., 2016) view this stage as much as a place for the exploration of sex as an integral part of experiencing closeness to another. However, these experiences vary hugely depending on gender, personality, the peer group and individual circumstances.

> Like, I discovered I was pansexual. You know what? I don't see what the big deal is. Absolutely. I actually don't care if I'm interested in someone, and I

really don't think gender is such a big thing. Great if they make me happy, so if they make me happy, perfect!

(Young person, aged 18)

One example of this is the experiences of LGBTQ+ young people, who do not always have the freedom to publicly express romantic and sexual interests. It is harder for adolescents who question their sexual orientation to engage in many of the social activities of their heterosexual peers. This means that, for these groups, dating and the exploration of sexuality have to take place in a less open manner.

One study which considered dating patterns among 15-year-olds across six European countries (Kolto et al., 2018) showed remarkable similarity across these countries in patterns of dating behaviour. Very similar numbers reported dating with the same gender, with the opposite gender and with both genders. Among these groups, around 30% reported never having dated at this age.

Romantic relationships have the potential to provide positive experiences about the self, and can lead to affirmation of positive characteristics. The experience of being close to another person, and exploring questions about identity together can contribute to a process of maturation and personal growth. Alternatively, it is entirely possible that early experiences of romantic attachments can prove upsetting and problematic. The break-up of a relationship can be painful, especially in the stage when so much other change is happening. Break-ups can lead to intense questioning about personal limitations. Relationships that go wrong can have a big impact on self-esteem. These may cause the young person to feel inadequate, lacking in the capacity to experience what others in the peer group are experiencing.

I wouldn't say it is the rules, but sometimes you just don't answer. They could get in a bad mood. It's not because I'm being rude, I just want my own space. There's no need to be constantly like, knowing where you are, or, like constantly communicating, because then when we see each other, what are we going to speak about? Like, there's only so much you can talk about. Like, there's no need to keep a conversation going, I'll see you the next day, yeah, speak to you another time.

(Young man, aged 17)

In the literature, there are a number of studies that have linked romantic break-ups with depression (e.g. Soller, 2014). However, break-ups are a common feature of early adolescence, and there are many variables that may contribute to emotional struggles, low mood and in some cases suicidal thoughts or behaviour. Studies show that other factors will also play their part, including family support, friendship patterns and the reason for the break-up. Many authors, such as Temple-Smith et al. (2016), point out that the degree of hurt is usually related to previous experiences of depression and to whether the break-up was self-initiated or not. A break-up that is initiated by the partner is usually much more painful than if it is either mutual or self-initiated.

Young people and safe sex

In previous decades, the problem of HIV/AIDS loomed large in any discussion of safe sex. In the 2020s, this virus is seen primarily as a problem for the Global South rather than for Western countries. While it is still the case that certain groups, such as intravenous drug users, are at risk from HIV/AIDS, this is something that affects a very small minority. It is now the case that chlamydia and herpes are much more common as sexually transmitted infections (STIs). Chlamydia in particular is a key indicator of poor sexual health, with potentially serious long-term health consequences, especially for young women.

The incidence of chlamydia infection among girls and young women has more than doubled over the last two decades (Kang et al., 2026). Of all the STIs, chlamydia is the most prevalent for those in the age ranges 15–19 and 20–24. Looking at the distribution of STIs across the age ranges, it is clear that the group with the highest levels of these infections is those in the 20–24 group. However, those in the 15–19 group come a close second. Importantly, the increase in chlamydia and other STIs does not apply only to the UK or other European countries. Research in Australia shows very similar trends, with a significant increase in chlamydia and herpes over the last decades (Moore and Rosenthal, 2006; Temple-Smith et al., 2016).

In trying to understand the increase in STIs among young people, one spotlight needs to focus on contraceptive use. Research over the years has shown that there has been a steady increase in the use of contraception at first intercourse. The high profile of HIV/AIDS, as well as a focus on better sex education, have both had an effect (Kang et al., 2026). This has emphasized the importance of using a condom, and today condoms are used more than any other method by young people at the start of a sexual relationship. Nonetheless, there are many barriers to effective contraceptive use among young people.

In the first place, condoms have to be purchased and to be available at the right moment. Next, it has to be acceptable to both partners to admit that one partner has planned to have sex. It is also probably necessary to be able to discuss the use of a contraceptive. In addition, it also assumes that one partner is sober and rational at the beginning of the encounter. When you are young, at the beginning of a relationship, and not at all sure of the other person, it is hardly surprising that often the use of contraception is not always easy to negotiate.

Another factor is the very nature of early sexual activity in adolescence. It is frequently sporadic, rather than a regular part of a relationship. Sex for young people is likely to be irregular and may be marked by times of abstinence. This makes the planning of contraceptive use problematic (Hadley, 2023). Furthermore, there may be many questions about what contraception is best. Many individuals do not like the idea of condoms, believing that they limit arousal or enjoyment. There may be concerns about the long-term impact of the use of the contraceptive pill or other intra-uterine devices (IUDs). Gender also plays a part, as questions of agency and control will influence how decision-making takes place in the context of first sexual relationships. All these factors contribute to the possibility that early sexual activity will be in the form of unprotected sex, with the consequent risk of infection.

Sexual orientation

In Chapter 5, I referred to sexual orientation as one aspect of identity development. I also pointed out that there are different terms for sexuality, sometimes used in different ways by different commentators. Sexual orientation is considered to apply to the way individuals choose people of a particular gender to have sex with, or with whom to engage in a long-term, intimate relationship. In the past, terms such as gay or lesbian were used to describe individuals who chose same-sex partners. Today the preference is to use the term LGBTQ+ to describe the range of possible choices that are made about sexuality and to apply to anyone who is not heterosexual.

Much has been written about the process of establishing a person's sexual orientation. This is not an easy process, and for many individuals this takes a long period of time. Adolescence is, of course, a critical stage in this process, since as we have seen, this is a time during which hugely important decisions about identity are taken. Troiden (1989) suggested that there are four stages in the sexual identity development process. Firstly, there is the stage of "sensitization". During this stage, the young person begins to be aware that they may be different from others. They may have different interests and may begin to recognize sexual feelings that are not the same as those experienced by others of the same gender.

> Yes, I'm straight. I've put that I am, and I'd say that I am, but like I was always unsure. Because everyone else would be like: "Yeah, I've got, like, butterflies in this guy, and I'd never get that, and I'll be like, wait, what? And like, you know, I'd really question myself, about everything, so it has been a struggle".
>
> (Young woman aged 16)

The second stage is that of "identity confusion". Here the individual experiences an altered awareness of the self. Sexual arousal may be associated with those of the same gender. There is a growing consciousness of the fact that being a member of the LGBTQ+ group may carry consequences in terms of other people's attitudes to this choice. The third stage is known as "identity assumption". Here the young person begins to take on an identity that is aligned with those in the LGBTQ+ community and is able to express that identity to close friends and family. Lastly, there is the stage of "commitment". At this point, the individual can make a commitment to an intimate relationship with someone of a similar orientation.

Although this stage notion is helpful in identifying a process of development, it has obvious limitations. As with all stage concepts, it cannot be assumed that everyone goes through the same stages in the same manner. It will be evident that there is great variability in the way that young people come to the realization that they are part of the LGBTQ+ community. Some may know from an early age, while some remain confused and uncertain throughout adolescence and beyond. It is sensible to consider these stages as examples of the tasks and issues faced by young people who may be questioning their sexual orientation rather than seeing them as a fixed sequence. As an illustration, I will use some words gathered in an earlier study of mine (Coleman, 2001).

> I suppose I started having sexual feelings – I didn't characterize them in any way – from the age of 11, and these feelings carried on until I was 14 or 15. It was only then, through watching television and talking to friends, that I would characterize them, not all of them, as gay thoughts. At first, I just thought they were ordinary sexual feelings, which in fact they were.
>
> (Coleman, 2001, page 124)

Numerous studies have explored the question of how many individuals make these choices during their adolescent years. Steinberg (2023) reports that in the USA about 85% of students say that they are heterosexual, with 9% as bisexual, and a much smaller number saying that they are gay or lesbian. Similar numbers are reported in Australia, with 83% of boys and 76% of girls saying that they are heterosexual (Mitchell et al., 2014). It is possible that these numbers are an under-representation, since the results will depend on the way the data are collected, and the willingness of students to report accurately their sexual orientation.

It is not unusual for young people to go through a phase of temporary same-sex attraction. This is especially the case in boarding schools and other institutions where opportunities for mixed socializing are restricted. However, for others a gradual realization of their sexual orientation is part of a long process of acceptance of a particular identity. As the individual gradually comes to recognize the nature of their sexual orientation, they then manage the process of what is known as "coming out". This involves "coming out" to the family, and then the same process is needed for friends and the peer group.

In both cases, the young person has to manage the possibility of rejection or homophobia. Generations of young people who have questioned their sexual orientation have faced these problems. Some have found acceptance, while others have had to deal with a wide range of responses that are unhelpful or damaging.

In a report by Temple Smith et al. (2016) they note various responses from parents on learning that their child is not heterosexual.

> No, you can't be gay. It's too hard a lifestyle to live in. Just be straight, it's a lot easier. You're just going through a phase.
>
> (page 176)

> Basically, what they said was they were not happy, but they wouldn't kick me out of the house. But that didn't seem very accepting to me. They would tolerate it, but they didn't really like me in the house.
>
> (page 177)

On the other hand, there are families who are accepting, and who do their best to support their children in this situation. This is one mother's report of what happened in her family.

> So, he sat down and said: "I've got something to tell you and it's important". I knew that it may be his thought about being gay. I said: "What makes you think that?" And he said: "I just know". So, I said "OK, you know, that's OK". And I could see the relief on his face, his absolute relief in his whole body. And I just went up to him, and he burst into tears.
>
> (Coleman, 2001, page 145)

As attitudes towards sexual orientation have changed over time, it is probably easier in some cultures for young people to be open about their identities. There is no doubt that the internet has provided support, as well as access to others of similar orientation through chat groups and sites dedicated to particular identities. There are also many initiatives that seek to recognize the positive aspects of a wide range of sexual orientations. This is sometimes known as sex positivity (Neves, 2025). Here great efforts are made to show acceptance and provide support for all types of sexual orientation, including those who are gender fluid or transgender This is a very helpful change in society, making choices about sexual orientation less problematic for many adolescents.

Pornography

Exposure to pornography is widespread, as well as being high on the list of anxieties experienced by parents, carers and professional adults. Many studies have sought to explore the amount of exposure among adolescents (see especially Behun and Owens, 2020). While some exploration of pornography is intentional by the individual adolescent, there are many reports of unintended exposure, when images and other material appear unwanted on the individual's phone. As an example, one study of 16-year-olds found that three-quarters of young men had seen pornography, with just over 50% of young women also having seen this type of material (Behun and Owens, 2020). The average age of first exposure was 14 years of age. Most participants in the study reported watching pornography on their own rather than with others.

Content analysis of popular and free-to-view pornography shows that almost all scenes and images contain some violence, with many also including verbal aggression. Perpetrators are almost all male and targets of aggression usually female. Much content includes risky sexual practices, and there is almost no evidence of the use of safe methods of sex in pornography (Temple-Smith et al., 2016).

A key concern is the possible harm resulting from the viewing of pornography. In the first place, it is suggested that pornography has an effect on body image. Both men and women in pornographic material are shown as being of a particular body type. This then reinforces stereotypes, creating anxiety among those who believe they do not fit this stereotype. Another feature of pornography is the likelihood that it leads to altered expectations about what is appropriate in a sexual relationship. Is it the case that seeing violence in sex leads to expectations about what is "normal"? Examples of such practices include choking, hitting and other sadistic behaviours. Many have expressed concern that such behaviours then become an expectation, with women feeling that they have to submit to such practices (Pirrone et al., 2022).

Research in this area is restricted, for obvious reasons. One study in the UK (Marston and Lewis, 2014) showed that high levels of exposure to pornography altered sexual practices among a sample of 16–18-year-olds. Those who had watched more pornography reported engaging a wider range of sexual practices, including those that involved violence. Some studies report that viewing pornography leads to earlier sexual behaviour, with those watching more pornography being more likely to start having sex at an earlier age (Pathmendra et al., 2023).

There are also reports of addiction to watching pornography, and of those who watch a high level of pornography having poor mental health and having feelings of guilt and shame. Finally, some commentators have discussed the impact of pornography on gender inequality. In pornography, it is almost always the case that the male is the dominant partner, dictating what is going to happen. Consent is not an element of pornography.

There is no doubt that the existence of pornography poses a challenge for families of adolescents, as well as for educators. Pornography is not going to disappear, and so it is important that sexual experiences are seen in a broader context, and as an experience that is pleasurable and consensual. I will discuss this below in the section on sex education.

Abuse, exploitation and violence

Sexual abuse occurs when a person is forced or coerced into a sexual act against their will or without their consent. For various reasons, sexual abuse is under-reported, especially when this occurs within the family environment. There is evidence that most sexual abuse is committed by someone known to the victim, and many cases involve incest or rape carried out by a trusted adult. It is often the case that those who are sexually abused within the family feel that there is no one they can talk to about the abuse. The abuse may be accompanied by feelings of shame or guilt, and if the victim is a child, then there can be a sense of confusion and incomprehension about the meaning of what is happening. Another common experience for children or young people is the feeling that they will not be believed, making it even harder to report such experiences.

Research examining the effects of sexual abuse which starts in childhood suggests that this is likely to have a very damaging impact on the individual's mental health. Many studies have reported long-term impacts which may lead to alcohol and substance addiction, or to continuing guilt and shame linked to a sense of helplessness about the events over which the individual had no control. Some of these studies are reviewed in the book by Temple-Smith and colleagues (2016) and by Wroe and Pearce (2022).

Another aspect of abuse that has been much discussed is that of sexual exploitation. Here the young person is coerced or groomed, either in person or on the internet, into having sex with an exploitative partner, usually an adult, but sometimes another young person. Authors who have written about this include Pearce (2019) and Holmes (2022). These authors set out three types of influence that might create routes into sexual exploitation. These are:

- *Individual.* Here the young person is likely to have low self-esteem and to be highly vulnerable to the influence of an older adult. In this situation, it is the young person's own fragility and their individual needs that play the largest part in leading to them being sexually abused.
- *Family.* In this case, it is the family situation which plays the largest part, either because of domestic violence, sexual abuse or intolerable family circumstances which cause the young person to run away from home and end up on the street.
- *Environmental.* It is not uncommon that environmental factors add to the other risk factors, such as poverty or deprivation, interrupted schooling, placement into care and limited access to family support services. All these contribute to making a young person vulnerable and therefore open to exploitation.

Violence is closely linked to sexual exploitation, with many young people reporting violence closely aligned to coercion and control. Children and young people experiencing poverty and deprivation and those living in gang-affected neighbourhoods are more likely to be impacted by extra-familial harm, including sexual exploitation.

This is not the only situation in which violence plays a part. In recent years, there has also been a focus on violence in dating relationships. This topic was first investigated in the UK by Christine Barter and others (2009). They found that in a sample of young people aged between 16 and 18, 10% of young women and 4% of young men reported being the victim of serious violence in an intimate relationship. These authors argued that experiencing violence in a dating relationship was closely linked to experiences of domestic violence in the family.

A later study (van Lawick, 2014) reported that alcohol use was a common feature of violence in sex. It was often the case that the perpetrator had being drinking heavily before an assault, or that the victim had been coerced into using alcohol by the perpetrator. These authors reported that self-blame was a common feature of the victim's thinking, and that because of shame it was often the case that the victim had difficulty reporting the incident.

Teenage pregnancy and early parenthood

Discussion of this topic is often hindered by stereotypes about young parents. It is therefore important not to talk of pregnancy and early parenthood as one subject but to recognize that there are many different experiences and situations which fall under this heading. Parenthood for an 18-year-old which is planned and thought through in the context of a stable relationship is completely different from parenthood for a 14-year-old that results from a failure to use contraception or from abuse or coercion.

One of the key challenges is to disentangle the various factors that play a part in determining whether a young woman becomes pregnant following a sexual encounter. As Hadley (2025) shows, explanations for early pregnancy fall into two categories. One is historical, while the other is related to future orientations. Those in the historical category include those women living with a mother who was herself a young mother, those with a poor level of knowledge about sex or those who were having regular sex at an early age (Wellings et al., 2013). Those who fall into the second category may wish to have an object for their affection, they may wish to demonstrate fertility or they may have a need to cement a relationship. Of course, these two categories may overlap, and it is not always clear which factor plays the major part.

When considering this topic, it is usual to think about the impact of early parenthood on the mother, on the father and on the child. Much of the literature has highlighted poorer outcomes for young mothers when compared with their older counterparts. However, there is considerable evidence that this is an over-simplification. Research by Hawkes (2010) showed that it was not age itself but many other factors that contribute to the outcome for young mothers. These factors include relative poverty, a lack of support from partners or other family members and a poor housing environment. These variables are cumulative, and so the more risk factors there are for young mothers, the greater the impact on the young woman and her parenting ability.

Turning now to young fathers, there is limited research in this area, as noted by Hadley (2025). However, Berrington et al. (2005) were able to show that young men who became fathers under the age of 20 were more likely, in comparison with older fathers, to be unemployed and to have separated from the mothers of their children. It is also the case that data on the children of young mothers do show poorer outcomes in terms of health and education. The results, however, indicate that it is not the age of the mother but other factors such as poverty and deprivation that are the key causes here. Also limited access to maternity services, linked to low income and difficulties with travel and practical day-to-day management issues all contribute to the difficulties experienced by young mothers.

This takes us to the stereotyping that I mentioned at the beginning of this section. Given good support and adequate financial resources, it is probable that young mothers will be able to parent just as effectively as older mothers. However, it is so often the case that the cards are stacked against young parents, and this leads to poorer outcomes. More needs to be done to provide good support for those adolescents who, for whatever reason, become parents at an early age. It is to be hoped that Hadley's (2025) work can be heeded, leading to a better understanding of early parenthood.

Health and sex education

In Chapter 3, I covered health literacy and the role of health-promoting schools. Here I will explore these topics as they relate to sexual health. In this realm, it will be obvious that communication between young people and adults may not be as open and straightforward as might be hoped. Sex is of course a difficult topic to discuss, and when it comes to sharing ideas about this, many factors get in the way. Shame, embarrassment and uncertainty all play their part. In addition, there are often large gaps in the experiences of the different generations when it comes to sexual relationships. In today's world, with the increasing influence of the online world, this is of even greater importance (Goodyear and Armour, 2019).

> I think a lot of people, guys and girls, go a little bit crazy with that feed, those features on Snapchat where you can see where your boyfriend's location is. It's weird because some girls, they go: "Oh my god, he was here like 10 minutes ago and he still hasn't replied to my message. He was lost being active five minutes ago and what now?" Yeah! Calm down. Like he'll get to it when he gets to it, he can't be replying to your message every two minutes. A lot more relationships don't last, they don't really know each other, they just want that label.
>
> (Young woman, aged 17)

Even though communication may be problematic, it is obvious that adolescents need as much information as possible. Indeed, all the evidence is clear that there is a huge need for young people to be as informed as possible about topics such as contraception, pregnancy and sexually transmitted infections. In recent years, there has also been a greater focus on harassment and predatory behaviour, by both strangers and by those in power. This focus has given rise to positive actions such as the *"MeToo"* movement, and in schools to the "*Everyone is invited*" programme. These movements have raised public awareness of gender equality, and they have meant that in sex and relationships education, greater attention is being paid to introducing young people to the concept of consent (Foulkes, 2024).

While parents are going to play a major part in any education to do with sexual development, there is no doubt that the school has a major role to play. More young people can be reached in this than in any other setting, and there is the likelihood of well-trained professionals being available. However, those who are disaffected or who are absent from school may miss out, and without adequate training teachers are not always the best people to deliver teaching on sensitive topics of this nature (Hadley, 2025).

Some have argued that young people are more likely to listen to messages delivered by those of their own age than to messages put across by adults. This has led to a growing interest in peer mentoring or peer-led health education. There are some obvious advantages to be gained from this approach to sex education. These include:

- Peer education makes use of existing social connections and networks;
- Young people may be seen as credible sources of information;
- Peer educators may be seen as less likely to break confidences;
- The experience itself may lead to the acquisition of new skills among peer educators.

Peer mentoring will only work if time and resources can be given to appropriate training of peer mentors. It is also important to ensure that the goals of adults are in tune with those of the peer educators. Conflict between the two groups will undermine any health promotion activity. Many commentators (e.g. Goodyear and Armour, 2019) have written about the key features of health and sex education which contribute to its effectiveness. These are:

- That it is communicative rather than moralistic or didactic;

- That it is empowering;
- That it is participative.

In the best of circumstances, there three elements that will all work together. Health promotion should have the intention of imparting information in an objective and easily accessible manner. How this is done will have a significant impact on the way the information is received. Topics to do with sex have the potential to be highly value laden. Sex education progammes, if they are to be effective, will seek to avoid any underlying or unspoken messages. Sex and relationship education poses many challenges. A wide range of elements will all play their part in facilitating the very best education in this sphere. As Temple-Smith and colleagues note, all these influences will impact on young people:

> Local contextual factors, including school policies, norms about how and in what ways students and teachers relate to each one another, and the neighbourhood in which schools were located were essential components of how students made meaning of sexuality, gender and relationships.
>
> (Temple-Smith et al., 2016, page 109)

One key conclusion is that sex and relationships education cannot be seen as a subject on its own in the school environment. Nor should it be seen as a strategy isolated from families or sexual health services in the community. To be effective, education in this sphere has to be seen in a holistic framework, incorporated into a "healthy living" curriculum in schools and in broader society. It should also, as outlined by Goodyear and Armour (2019), be integrated with messages coming from social media and other virtual platforms which carry health-related messages.

> It's so bad. Like people, guys and girls, like everyone will go on Snapchat, they'll add about six guys, and they'll start talking to them all the time. But talking isn't like it was in the old days, like calling and stuff. It's more like: "what do you look like? what's your age? where do you live? and so on." And then you move on to, you know, like, now, let's get in a relationship, but you don't know them pretty well. Like I think people start relationships too quickly, and like, it is luck, it's not even a thing they want to be with, it's just because they want a boyfriend, right?
>
> (Young woman, aged 17)

If there is one lesson to be learnt from research in this field, it is that young people need relevant and unbiased information, together with the tools to manage the internet in a resilient and informed manner. Sexual health is a key element of what we, as a society, will want to achieve for adolescents as they grow through this phase of their lives. As attitudes and behaviours change with the times, it is essential that all adults – parents, carers and professional educators – take this responsibility very seriously indeed.

Conclusion

In this chapter, there is coverage of a range of topics relating to sexual health and relationships. The challenges in collecting data on sexual behaviour among adolescents were discussed, and there was a consideration of the context and timing of sex among this age group. I discussed ideas about romance and intimacy, and then I went on to outline communication around sex and relationships. This topic was linked with ideas about safe sex. I included a section on sexual orientation. The chapter then went on to review pornography, as well as violence and abuse in relationships. The chapter has a section on teenage pregnancy and parenthood, and the chapter concluded with a discussion of health education and health literacy.

Chapter 7

Mental health

Introduction

The very term mental health has different meanings for different people. For some, this term refers to good health, and sometimes emotional health and well-being. On the other hand, mental health can also be used to describe disorder or illness. It is essential to keep these two meanings apart; otherwise, there is considerable confusion. In this chapter, attention will be paid to both meanings. A significant number of those who struggle during the adolescent stage of development are affected by mental illness or distress, and thus it is essential to understand something of this topic to make sense of these difficulties.

As was noted in Chapter 1, early theories of adolescence suggested that the stage itself could be considered a troubled time, and the term "*storm and stress*" was used to describe this period of life. As I have pointed out, this concept is no longer believed to be an accurate portrayal of adolescence. The majority cope well with this period in their lives, yet it is clear that a minority of young people do struggle with mental ill-health. This is a topic much debated in recent years. A central question here is whether the mental health of young people is getting worse.

> I think it is getting worse. I mean, like, if you go back 50 years, mental health may have been exactly the same, but we have more awareness of it now. We have the internet, we have social media and stuff. We have ways of getting more information and, like, talking it about it more, which is amazing, but there's a lot more awareness of it all now, isn't there?
>
> (Young woman, aged 18)

I discussed the notion of what is known as the "*snowflake generation*" in Chapter 1. This notion is reflected in a book by Joseph Haidt entitled *The Anxious Generation* (2024). In this, Haidt argues that the mental health of adolescents

DOI: 10.4324/9781032640433-7

has deteriorated over the last decade or so, and that this is happening across the world. He argues that rates of depression, anxiety and suicide have risen substantially since 2010, and he puts this down to the increasing use of smartphones and the internet by young people.

I have serious concerns about this argument, concerns which I will outline in this chapter and which I have set out in Coleman (2024). However, I highlight Haidt's book, as this argument is widely shared and discussed by worried adults in all spheres, and thus it is important to examine this claim as closely as we can. In this chapter, I will look at the data on mental health in adolescence over the past 30 years and consider the validity of the idea of the "*snowflake generation*". I will then look at the variety of mental ill-health conditions, including suicide and self-harm, anxiety and depression. I will consider psychosis and neurodiversity. The impact of Covid and the climate emergency will be reviewed, and I will consider the relation between social media and mental health. The chapter will conclude with a look at mental health literacy.

Incidence of mental ill-health among adolescents

Understanding exactly what the rate of mental ill-health is among adolescents is not easy. There are many factors to take into account, and measurement itself poses many challenges. If an assessment is to be carried out by a qualified professional, and if it is to include a large enough sample, such a process will prove extremely expensive. Any other approach is going to rely on self-reports, or reports by parents and teachers. Because of this, studies vary in the data they report, and this will always be a difficult subject to write about with clarity.

I will start by considering what we know about the incidence of mental health problems. For obvious reasons, there is going to be a time lag in the reporting of data on this matter. I should note that in England and Wales there have been three major studies over the last 25 years. The first was in 1999, the second in 2004 and the third in 2017. These three studies represent the very highest level of credibility, using a range of measures including individual interviews carried out by mental health professionals. Results reported from the 2017 study showed 14% of boys and 15% of girls between the ages of 11 and 15 to have a mental disorder (Hagell and Shah, 2019). The gender balance appeared to have shifted for those between 17 and 19 years of age, with 24% of young women having a mental disorder, while 10% of young men fell into this category. This is a worrying trend, and one which is reflected in further research reviewed in this chapter.

I will now turn to time trends in mental ill-health. Is it true that mental health is getting worse? And if so, why would this be? Looking first at the major studies just mentioned, there is little evidence that between 1999 and 2017 there was much of a deterioration in the mental ill-health of young people in England and Wales. Data show that, overall, for 11–15-year-olds, the change was marginal, with little increase in incidence of mental disorders (Hagell and Shah, 2019). In terms of depression and anxiety among 16–24-year-olds, there was some increase among young women, with the incidence going from 20% to 24% (Kang et al., 2026). There appeared to be little change for young men.

One other study may be mentioned (Armitage et al., 2025). In this study, the authors looked again at the results from the 1999, 2004 and 2017 studies, and although they did not highlight any major changes in the incidence of mental ill-health in young people, they did show that, for those who have mental ill-health, their problems appear to have got worse. As they note, if one compares all three time points, young people with a disorder in 2017 experienced more severe difficulties, and a greater impact on functioning in home and at school. Again, this is a worrying finding, and the authors put it down to increased levels of poverty and disadvantage among the most vulnerable families in England and Wales.

> I think there is a lot more awareness of mental health, right? So, Ofsted came into school last week, and we all did a survey, and one of the questions was: how much does your school advocate for physical health? And how much do you see about mental health? And I stopped to think about it, it's weird how much mental health is now talked about so much more than physical health. I think it is good in a way, but I think the awareness is almost turning into a bad thing, with everyone else seems to be, like, self-diagnosing themselves or think that they should have a mental health illness. If you keep telling yourself, I have anxiety, I have depression, that's going to happen to you, like you're going to create that for yourself, and I don't think that's great.
>
> (Young woman, aged 17)

I should note that these data relate only to England and Wales. In other countries, different measures are used, and of course different approaches are taken to the design of studies. From one paper (Azzopardi et al., 2019), which notes comparisons across different regions in the world, it would appear that rates of mental ill-health, at least in Western countries, are much the same as in Great Britain.

It can be misleading to consider only the incidence of disorder when coming to conclusions about time trends. There are many factors that will influence levels of mental ill-health, as I have argued in other writing (Coleman (2024). In the first place, it is important to consider broader economic and political factors that may influence the lives of young people. In the UK, the period of austerity from 2010 onwards will have had a significant impact on the provision of services for this age group. A variety of types of support for vulnerable young people were withdrawn, and this led to longer waiting times for treatment and therefore a greater level of distress.

Peter Wilson (2016) argues that the medical model may not be the best or only model if we want to fully understand mental health. To understand mental ill-health only in the context of the medical model restricts the type of interventions possible, and allows only one way of making sense of distress or disorder. There are, of course, many ways to understand mental ill-health. This is graphically illustrated if we consider the link between poverty, social disadvantage and mental ill-health. As I note later, higher rates of mental ill-health occur in circumstances where there is poverty and disadvantage (Pickett and Wilkinson, 2024). If this is the case, then the medical model cannot fully account for problems in the mental health field.

It is also the case that there has been a cultural shift in the recognition and understanding of mental ill-health (Putwain, 2025). There is now a much greater awareness of mental health issues, with young people being encouraged to talk openly about their anxieties and worries. As Foulkes (2022) has argued, the very teaching of mental health in schools may lead to higher levels of anxiety among those who are already vulnerable. Guzman-Holst et al. (2025) make the same point. A greater focus on mental health issues has, inevitably, had an impact on the way adolescents understand mental health. In addition, there is the influence of social media and the digital world. It is now possible to self-diagnose by simply going online and using AI or other social media platforms which are openly discussing mental health. It is not possible to compare how young people understood and reported mental health issues in 1999 with the way they do in the 2020s.

> The awareness around it, it's good because people are realizing that people do have mental health illnesses. But then also, I feel like people, they start to feel pressure to have a mental illness so that they can talk about it. Or, like, they should have a mental illness because they're a teenager and they're growing up, and they're experiencing all this. But you don't necessarily have a mental illness. Yeah, it's almost like creating one for yourself.
>
> (Young woman, aged 17)

Covid-19

I have mentioned the incidence of mental ill-health up to 2017. Since that time, two factors have spurred further research. The first is the pandemic of 2020/2022, and the second is the continuing debate about the effect of the internet on mental health. Looking at Covid first, there have been many studies of the way in which this has impacted on young people. It is beyond the scope of this book to review all the literature on this topic. I will select one or two representative studies. The first is a study reporting a systematic review of many studies considering the changes in mental health of children and young people during and after the pandemic (Kauhannen and Yunus, 2023). The review concluded that the majority of this population experienced the period of Covid-19 without a deterioration in mental health. However, outcomes depended on a variety of factors, including previous mental health problems, poverty and economic disadvantage and family circumstances. For a child or young person in any of these categories, it was more likely that their mental health would be affected by their experiences during the pandemic.

The impact of social circumstances is brought sharply into focus in an article by Pickett and Wilkinson (2024), as I have noted earlier. In this article, the authors consider evidence on the impact of income inequality on child mental health across the globe. These authors review a number of studies, all of which highlight the way in which economic inequality has a profound effect on the mental health of children and young people. As they note, the pathways though which inequality affects children and adolescents are indirect, as they act through the effects of inequality on parents and care-givers. These impacts include, among other things, longer working hours, quality of housing, higher levels of household debt and the mental health of key adults.

Other studies explore similar issues, as for example, the mental health of those in Black and minority families in the USA during Covid (Rusk et al., 2024). From this study, it is clear that young people in populations experiencing higher levels of disadvantage were more likely than their advantaged peers to show a greater level of mental ill-health as a result of the pandemic. One reason for this is that it is more difficult for these groups to access services, and this was especially the case during the period of the pandemic. The same finding applied to the UK, as it became clear that where access to services was restricted, it was more likely that the mental health of children and adolescents would deteriorate.

It is hard to understand how the pandemic contributed to mental health issues without recognizing that a key element of the experience for young people had to do with school closures. This experience was, of course, different for different individuals. For some, not going to school was a great relief, and a positive experience. They were able to sleep later in the morning, spend quality time with parents and siblings and be relieved of the pressures of the school experience. For others, it was quite the opposite. They missed the social life of the school, and if housing was poor or restricted, then staying at home was hard. As with so many other issues, so much depends on the particular circumstances of the individual. School closures were clearly a negative experience for some, while for others it came as a great relief. For this group, it made it harder to return to school, resulting in a serious problem of school absence in the years after the pandemic.

The last point to make on this topic has to do with the types of mental health problems seen during this period. One of the striking findings relating to mental health during the pandemic was the increase in eating disorders. Among girls and young women in particular, this problem was seen to increase greatly during period of the pandemic. Rates of eating disorders among these groups doubled at this time (Nicholls, 2023). Nicholls explores why this should have been the case, and argues that many factors may have contributed to this situation. Anxiety about body image, fear of obesity, and wanting or needing to have some aspect of life over which one has control all may have contributed to this phenomenon.

Social media

One of the topics exercising the minds of adults, and one that is attracting more research focus than almost any other, is the impact of social media on the mental health of young people. There have been literally dozens and dozens of studies on this topic, with greatly varying results. One of the striking things about this cultural phenomenon is the speed of change in this field. What is written today is likely to be out of date in a year or so, making any commentary problematic.

Long gone is the time when it was possible to say something like: "*Screen time rots the brain*". Yet in many ways this notion is still very much with us, as adults think about ways to protect young people from the harms of social media and access to the internet. As I write this, there are movements across the world considering how to ban smartphones for those under the age of 16. Indeed, the book by Haidt, which I have already mentioned (*The Anxious Generation*; 2024), addresses exactly this question. Another popular book at the moment is entitled *Stolen Focus* by Johann Hari (2022). This sets out why our preoccupation with social media has impacted on our ability to pay attention. This author directs his primary concern to the consequences of this effect on young people.

There are many reasons why questions concerning the relation between mental health and social media will never be answered in a satisfactory manner. In the first place, so much depends on what the individual is actually doing when accessing the internet. There are such a wide variety of uses that it is almost impossible to generalize about this. The second issue has to do with the time spent on the smartphone or other device, and indeed what part of the day the individual spends most time on-line. Then there is also the particular personality and mental health status of the individual. Those with a predisposition to anxiety or depression will be affected in a different way from those without such dispositions.

> I feel like, especially being on my phone, that's the really tough part, because I think I'm addicted. I spend quite a lot of time on my phone. I'm trying to stop, that's why I am picking up reading, so I can take time off my phone. I think it's very stressful, you're on-line as a teenager, like, you take a lot of opinions from on-line and you input that into your day-to-day life. I think what I try to do is to get off my phone, that is a bad bit about being a teenager, is that you're so obsessed with everyone else's life. You forget to live yours, you really do.
>
> (Young woman, aged 16)

As many writers and commentators have pointed out, there are both positives and negatives about social media platforms and the opportunities of the online world (Talmud and Mesch, 2020). It is understandable that adults take fright when they see young people being groomed or influenced in damaging ways by interactions on-line. However, it is questionable as to whether the genie can be put back in the bottle. For many, the answer lies in helping young people develop a greater understanding of the ways in which the internet works, and greater resilience in managing the potential harms that exist on-line. In addition, of course, the way adults use the internet also has an impact. I will say more about this later in Chapter 8 when I consider families and how they function.

Looking now at some of the research reports, it is noticeable that most of them take a nuanced approach to this subject. A good example here is a paper entitled: "*Adolescent social media is not a monolith: towards the study of specific components and individual differences*" (Maheux et al., 2025). As these authors note, in understanding the impact of social media on mental health it is essential to consider, first of all, individual differences in the adolescent. Furthermore, social media platforms are different in content, in their features, and in their functions. All these elements may impact the health of the individual user.

To give some examples of findings from a variety of studies, one research report highlighted a difference between on-line interactions with real-life and virtual friends. This study found that on-line interactions with actual friends leads to better well-being, while on-line interactions with virtual friendship networks leads to poorer mental health (Anthony et al., 2023). Another study (Murray et al., 2023) showed that body image satisfaction mediated experiences of online interactions. Those with lower body appearance satisfaction tended to experience higher levels of depression following on-line interactions. These studies illustrate how important it is to understand background factors in looking at the impact of online experiences on the mental health of young people.

I will conclude this section by considering what can be done to limit or mitigate any harms that result from the use of social media. One approach has been to investigate ways to moderate the content of social media platforms (Zhang et al., 2024). These authors argue that attempts to censor content may not always lead to the intended results. Censoring mental health content may lead to the creation of isolated and polarized communities that use various strategies to avoid such censorship. An alternative view is that social media content relating to mental health can have positive benefits, such as facilitation of help-seeking behaviour and providing support for the most vulnerable.

Another approach is for psychologists and other social scientists to work directly with tech companies, helping them to identify characteristics of the algorithms which have the greatest impact on the mental health of young people (Maheux et al., 2025). In a similar vein, some authors (Livingstone et al., 2023) have put forward the case for academics to collaborate with game designers and other tech companies to seek ways to improve young people's mental health. In this approach, it is not so much about avoiding harm as about encouraging tech companies to be players in enhancing mental health.

What can be done to give greater protection to the mental health of young people in the on-line world? There are, of course, many actors in this space. Governments can enact legislation such as the Online Harms Bill going through the Westminster Parliament in the UK at present. There are initiatives that tech companies themselves can take, such as the Teen Account on Instagram, and then there are actions that schools, parents and carers can take to enhance knowledge and coping skills. This is a subject that is beyond the scope of this chapter. We can be sure that this is a worldwide challenge for all concerned with the mental health of children and young people. Nothing will be achieved without a recognition of the multi-faceted nature of the internet and the complexity of the reactions to it. These reactions will depend on a huge variety of variables, and these will need to be fully understood before progress can be made to keep young people safe online.

Internalizing and externalizing conditions

The terms *internalizing* and *externalizing conditions* are useful descriptors of the most common conditions concerning mental ill-health. The concept behind these terms is a distinction between conditions in which the behaviour or emotion is either turned outwards or turned inwards. Internalizing conditions generally refer to anxiety or depression, while externalizing conditions cover such things as aggression, offending behaviour, oppositional behaviour and substance abuse.

As far as internalizing conditions are concerned, these are most often seen in girls and young women, although it is not unknown for boys and young men to experience these conditions. For a review of the evidence on internalizing conditions, see Keyes and Platt (2024). I will consider anxiety first. Within this category there are many different types of anxiety. Some of the most common forms of anxiety include phobias, obsessive compulsive disorder (OCD) and post-traumatic stress disorder (PTSD). A full description of these types of anxiety will be found in Ogden and Hagen (2019). Risk factors for these conditions include temperament, genetic factors and family history. There is also the possibility of what are known as contextual factors, such as stress at school, bullying and parental conflict or disharmony.

> I'm kind of, like, always stressed, and I'm always worried. I'm always scared of doing stuff, even though there's nothing to be scared of. I think people will know I'm always stressed, because I'm always: "Oh! My god, I can't do this, it's too stressful". But then I know it's just in my head, and I kind of go, the time will pass, you don't have to do amazing, just go through it. But yes, stress comes like a freaking brick to me.
>
> (Young woman, aged 17)

In recent years, two particular types of anxiety have come into focus – these include health anxiety and climate anxiety. Health anxiety, sometimes known as hypochondriasis, has been known about for a long time, but has received more attention recently because of Covid-19. In a helpful review (Rask et al., 2024), the authors outline how health anxiety can lead to impairment, distress and increased use of health care services. They also point out that in many cases there is an inter-generational effect, with young people who show health anxiety having family members also showing high levels of anxiety.

The link between this type of anxiety and Covid-19 is less clear (Sonuga-Barke and Fearon, 2021). They argue that health anxiety during this period is likely to be closely linked to levels of anxiety which existed among young people pre-pandemic. They also make an important link between the role of public health information and levels of anxiety during the early months of the pandemic. The greater the fear that is generated by public information, the greater the possibility of health anxiety among those who are already vulnerable.

Climate anxiety is another topic that is receiving more attention at this time (Sanson and Dubicka, 2022). Many have stated that this is a rational response to an actual emergency, rather than a mental illness. However, for some young people this is a very real experience, sometimes known as "eco-anxiety". This type of anxiety may be demonstrated through sleep problems, low motivation for everyday tasks and a general sense of unease and anxiety about the future. In an interesting study, researchers looked at engagement in climate-related behaviour and its links with climate anxiety. They found that even high levels of anxiety do not inhibit young people from engaging in environmental activism (Becht et al., 2024). While this activity does not mitigate the impact of climate on the mental health of adolescents, it does show that positive responses are possible for those struggling with the effects of climate change.

As for depression, many believe that feelings of depression are an integral part of the adolescent experience. It is possible that at times a young person may feel a sense of loss for the safety and security of childhood. The unknown future may appear scary, and this can lead to a feeling of gloom and despondency for what lies ahead. It is also true that emotions of sadness and low mood are part of everyone's experience. Depression usually refers to something more serious, when the individual loses motivation and may show physical symptoms such as loss of appetite, difficulty in sleeping and low energy. There are some indications that rates of depression among young people have been increasing over the last decades, and indeed that gender differences have become more pronounced (Keyes and Platt, 2024).

> I mean every teenager gets these grumpy spells, yeah, lack of sleep etc., but my teenage years were a lot of stress for me, my parents, all my family in general, even my friends. So, during my teenage years, say from 14 to 16, I found myself having high rates of depression, like, I was flipping through suicidal force, I was an inpatient for a few days, I was placed on many different anti-depressants. Most of them didn't work, or made me feel worse

> actually, so there was a lot of trial and error to find the correct medication, a lot of what they called talking therapy, art therapy, basically any type of therapy they do, right? I even had pet therapy, with ponies, like I didn't even know that was a thing.
>
> (Young person, aged 17)

There are many reasons as to why an adolescent may experience depression, including grief over the loss of a family member or even a pet, a break-up with a partner, difficulties with friends or family and traumatic experiences. In extreme circumstances, depression may lead to suicide and self-harm, and I will turn to these topics shortly. Symptoms of depression can also include cognitive distortions, where thinking is affected by low mood. The young person may experience a loss of motivation and feel hopeless about the future. Low self-esteem is also often part of the picture, with the adolescent believing that they are worthless and unable to achieve much.

With young people who are either anxious or depressed, it is hard to draw a line between what is normal adolescent worry and gloom on the one hand, and genuine pathology on the other. Young people who struggle with these problems may come across as angry, awkward or closed off. If the symptoms of anxiety or depression persist over time, or seem to reflect a change in the personality of the individual, then it is important to seek professional help.

Now I will turn to externalizing conditions. These are behaviours that are outward-directed and involve negative actions towards other people or towards aspects of the environment. As I have noted, these behaviours can include aggression and violence, vandalism and a variety of acts that transgress social norms. These behaviours are sometimes referred to as anti-social behaviour, or as problem behaviours, and I will be dealing with this topic in greater detail in Chapter 10. A distinction is usually made between behaviours that are manifested in the community, and those that are manifested in the home. Anti-social behaviour occurs in the community, while other types of externalizing behaviours occur in the home. These behaviours would include defiance, stealing, and general oppositional behaviour, as well as adolescent-to-parent abuse (Holt, 2025). I will discuss this topic in Chapter 8.

There are marked gender differences in the incidence of these behaviours. Externalizing conditions are seen at a significantly higher level among boys and young men than they are among girls and young women. This is not to say that there is some evidence of externalizing conditions among females, but this is more likely to be covert and focussed largely on relationships. There is no one single explanation for the existence of externalizing problems. There are a range of possible risk factors, including family background, the school environment, the role of the peer group as well as personality and temperament. I will discuss this in greater detail when I explore anti-social behaviour in Chapter 10.

Suicide

Of all the mental health problems faced by families and by professionals, the likelihood that a young person is harming themselves or that they may be considering taking their life are two of the most challenging things anyone has to face. This is a topic about which there are so many inhibitions. One young person put it to me as follows: "*Nobody knows anything about death, suicide …. Suicide is probably the most frightening thing. If you mention it to somebody they don't want to talk about it. That's it, they close up. They don't want to know because it is too scary …*" (Coleman, 2011, page 122).

Rates of suicide fluctuate but, contrary to popular assumption, in recent years there does not appear to have been any significant rise in rates. Data comparing 2009 with 2019 in the UK show that young men between the ages of 15 and 19 have a rate of around 7 per 100,000 (Association of Young People's Health. *www.ayph.org.uk 2024*). This rate has varied to a small extent, but during this decade there was no significant increase. For young women, this rate was around 3 per 100,000. Again, there was relatively little variation in this rate.

In terms of the impact of Covid, we now have data comparing the years 2021, 2022 and 2033. While it could be argued that this is too early to definitely identify consequences of the pandemic, it does illustrate the same finding – relatively little change over time. For those in England in the 15-to-19-year age range, there were 198 suicides in 2021, 168 in 2022 and 177 in 2023. As will be apparent, the rates vary to some extent but are broadly similar across three years (Ching et al., 2025).

In terms of risk factors for suicide, there is a view that these can be divided into primary and secondary risk factors. The primary risk factors for suicide in young people are as follows:

- Psychiatric disorder;
- A previous suicide attempt;
- A sense of hopelessness about the future;
- Drug or alcohol abuse.

There are a range of secondary risk factors, and these include a family history of suicide, an experience of someone close taking their own life, a recent loss and a significant blow to self-esteem leading to guilt or shame. In addition to these primary and secondary risk factors, there are also populations in which there are higher suicide rates than would be expected by chance. These populations include those in custody, those who are care-experienced, those living in isolated rural communities and those in the LGBTQ+ groups. In considering these groups, it is important to understand that it is not the characteristics of the individuals involved but rather the circumstances in which they are placed that leads to enhanced risk of suicide (Berk, 2022).

These circumstances include being isolated from the family, placed in an environment where there is a loss of control, and experiencing depression and hopelessness about the future. For those in the LGBTQ+ community, it is not their sexual orientation that makes them vulnerable, but the isolation and difficulty in obtaining emotional support that leads to the possibility of hopelessness and despair.

In addition to these factors, there is also the question of why more young men than young women are likely to take their own lives. This is a topic that has been much debated, and there is no clear answer. Possible causes include the difficulty boys and young men find in seeking help, their greater involvement in violence and access to weapons and other means of suicide. Rates of self-harm show the opposite gender distribution, with significantly more females than males being involved in such things as self-poisoning and cutting.

Self-harm

One of the first issues to be considered here is the definitions used to describe this behaviour. It is perhaps most helpful to think about self-harm as a continuum from actions which have a strong suicidal intent (e.g., some types of self-poisoning) to those which are intended to help the individual stay alive (e.g., self-mutilation or cutting). There is a problem with the term "*deliberate self-harm*" since it has an implication of intention about it. This may be unhelpful to the young person if they believe they have little control over their behaviour. It is also the case that "*attempted suicide*" may be unhelpful since some young people take an overdose with little suicidal intent.

In terms of the incidence of self-harm, it will be apparent that data are not easy to collate, due to the varying locations that self-harm takes place and the difficulties of assessment. However, it is clear that the gender balance is almost exactly the opposite of that for actual suicide. In a study by Townsend et al. (2022), the evidence from 5,000 patients in the UK showed that 75% of those who self-harmed over a period from the year 2000 to 2013 were female with an average of 16. These authors also make the point that the most frequently reported problems by those in this population were family difficulties.

> You also got peer pressure, and then some, like, they have anxiety, they have their own mental issues, mental issues they don't want to speak to anyone about. So, they keep it to themselves and some of them cut themselves, and they just do so because it's a way to control their emotions, they know how to control their emotions or how they feel, and that's their way to use it or take it out.
>
> (Young man, aged 15)

One of the key challenges faced by anyone helping a young person involved in self-poisoning is to be able to assess the degree of suicidal intent. A variety of criteria may be used, but some of the most helpful include:

- The length of time the attempt was planned. The longer the planning period, the greater the risk;
- The severity of depression in the young person;
- A sense of hopelessness;
- Whether the young person was alone at the time of the incident. If the young person knows that they are not alone, a lower degree of risk is indicated.

An act of self-harm can have many meanings. Where self-poisoning is concerned, it can represent a serious attempt to die. Alternatively, it can represent a wish to escape from an intolerable situation without knowing any other means to do so. The young person may feel helpless to change their circumstances and yet also feel that things are too difficult to cope with (Mason et al., 2025).

Some professionals believe it is most helpful to think about self-poisoning as a form of communication. To concentrate on the meaning of the communication may be a way to avoid or help prevent a repetition of the act. It is frequently the case that troubled relationships, either with parents, carers or with a close friend, lie at the heart of the episode of self-poisoning. For this reason, it is especially important that, following such an episode, the young person has the opportunity to talk with a caring adult and to give expression to some of the painful emotions caused by the relationship difficulties (Witt et al., 2025).

Where cutting and other forms of self-mutilation are concerned, the motivation may be quite similar, in that cutting can be seen as a form of communication about the degree of pain the individual is experiencing. Cutting is at the opposite end of the continuum where suicidal intent is concerned. By and large, those who self-harm by cutting do not intend to die. Indeed, for some cutting is a way of staying alive rather than the opposite (Townsend et al., 2022).

Cutting may be a strategy to seek attention, and to indicate how much pain the person is experiencing. For some, it is a way to create a sense of reality. As one young person put it to me: "*In a way a part of me does it for attention, you know .... It is like crying out 'Look at me, I am hurting'. At other times it is because I feel totally out of touch with reality, and I think it is a short sharp shock if you cut yourself, it snaps you back into reality*" (Coleman, 2011, page 124).

It is clear that many who cut themselves are the victims of various types of abuse. For these individuals, cutting often reflects the degree of pain and damage that has been caused to them as a result of abuse. In these situations, self-mutilation can represent an attempt to relieve emotional tension or distress, or it may be a method of redirecting the intense anger and hatred which is felt towards the abuser but which cannot be expressed to that individual.

To conclude, self-harm refers to a wide range of behaviours which lie along a continuum from high to low suicidal intent. Broadly speaking, those who cut themselves are likely to have low suicidal intent, while those who take an overdose may, depending on the circumstances, have greater suicidal intent. Assessment is critical, and should always be carried out by a mental health professional. Risk factors are similar to those I identified for suicide, but also include abuse, exploitation, anxiety, low self-esteem and relationship difficulties.

Psychosis and psychotic experiences

Psychosis in adolescence is considered to exist on a spectrum from early onset psychosis to psychotic experiences, such as hearing voices when no one is speaking. Psychotic experiences differ from full-blown psychosis in that young people who report symptoms usually have some degree of insight, realizing that the voices they hear are inside their head rather than from outside. Both psychosis and psychotic experiences are rare in the general population, but are more common in those with other diagnosed disorders, such as severe anxiety or depression (Sunshine and McClennan, 2023).

Early onset psychosis may include disorganized thinking, hallucinations, delusions and elements of paranoia. In essence, this illness involves a loss of contact with reality, and it is this feature that differentiates it from psychotic experiences. As I have noted, these lie along a continuum to do with insight. The majority who experience psychotic experiences, such as hearing voices, do have some awareness of reality and a sense that the voices may come from themselves rather than from some outside force.

A good review of this phenomenon may be found in Kelleher (2025). This author outlines a range of studies which have investigated this condition. In terms of risk factors, Kelleher makes the point that these are similar to other psychiatric conditions and include family history and early childhood difficulties.

Kelleher points out that psychotic experiences are strongly associated with suicidal behaviour and with substance abuse. Indeed, one of the most studied links are those between cannabis use and psychosis or psychotic experiences. The more cannabis is used, the greater the likelihood of psychotic experiences. Those who use cannabis on a daily basis have a 43-fold increased risk for psychotic experiences. It should also be noted that cannabis use before the age of 15 may be especially risky for psychosis or psychotic experiences.

> Yes, it happened to me on a massive scale. So, last year I spent about six months in a psychiatric hospital. Because, yes, basically I just went through a bit of a rocky patch, because nobody would listen to me. It kind of just escalated, and then I ended up in, like, the worst place I could be. It kind of felt like one size fits all, it didn't feel very tailored to me, right? It was kind of, like, a holding cell sort of thing. I only got better when I got out of the hospital, and I was able to do things on my own.
>
> (Young person, aged 17)

It is apparent from research that psychotic experiences do not necessarily lead to full-blown psychotic illness. Less than 1 in 10 of those who hear voices or have other psychotic experiences go on to have a psychotic illness (Kelleher, 2025). This can be reassuring for parents and other care-givers. It is suggested that these experiences may be related to the changes in the brain that occur during early and mid-adolescence, associated with the re-wiring caused by pruning (see Chapter 2). Unusual perceptual experiences are more common than people realize, and for the majority these experiences are transient. Early onset psychosis (usually considered to occur before the age of 18) is much less common and may be associated with other mental health disorders.

Neurodiversity

The term *neurodiversity* is now used to describe those with attention-deficit hyperactivity disorder (ADHD) and those on the autistic spectrum. It is important to note that this term has played an important part in shifting the emphasis in our understanding of these conditions. For many years, autism was seen as an illness, something that was included in a catalogue of psychiatric disorders. The shift has enabled these conditions to be understood as part of a range of different ways in which the human brain works. This shift has also enabled individuals with these conditions to play a greater part in society and to have their achievements recognized and valued.

This shift in attitude is perfectly described in Steve Silberman's book *Neurotribes* (2015). Here the author outlines the history of autism, reaching back to the work of Leo Kanner and Hans Asperger in the 1940s. It is a fascinating story, and one that charts in detail how attitudes to neurodiversity have changed over the years since the work of these early pioneers. As Baron-Cohen (2017) argues, neurodiversity is a revolutionary concept for autism and psychiatry. The author questions the concept of disorder, arguing that this is clearly a false way to understand these conditions.

Baron-Cohen concludes that there are several messages that arise from the concept of neurodiversity. Firstly, there is no single way for the brain to be normal. There are many ways in which the brain can be wired and can reach adulthood. Secondly, it is essential to avoid stigmatizing those with ADHD and those who are on the autism spectrum. Thirdly, we need a framework that does not focus on the pathology and the things the individual cannot do, but rather focusses on the things the individual can do, and on their achievements rather than on their failures.

ADHD

I will consider the two conditions included in the category of neurodiversity separately, and I will turn first to ADHD. This condition is generally considered to include the following three symptoms: impulsivity, hyperactivity and inattentiveness. In recent years, rates of ADHD have increased significantly in young people (Sibley et al., 2025). There has been much discussion as to whether this condition is being over-diagnosed. Many are questioning whether aspects of behaviour that were once considered within the normal range are now seen as a mental health condition. Timimi's book (2025), entitled *Searching for Normal: A New Approach to Understanding Distress and Neurodiversity*, explores this idea, arguing that we have lost a sense of what behaviours are within the normal range, and what should be considered to fall into the category of needing professional help.

Another problem with ADHD is that the symptoms do not demonstrate one consistent picture but may occur in isolation from each other (Hinshaw et al.,

2018). It is possible for an individual to be impulsive, or to be inattentive without any of the other symptoms. Do they cohere into one condition? There is also an argument that this label may be used as a convenient diagnosis for young people with a range of behavioural challenges, some of which may be part of the developmental pattern associated with adolescence.

In many of the reviews of this condition, there is consideration of how ADHD is associated with other conditions. It is believed that those who are diagnosed with this condition are more likely to struggle with a misuse of digital media, to have low self-esteem and to have difficulties with the use of drugs and alcohol. ADHD is traditionally seen as being more prevalent in boys than in girls. However, recent reviews have suggested that many females with ADHD have been missed or been unrecognized in the past. Hinshaw et al. (2022) review studies indicating that boys are more likely to show hyperactivity and impulsivity, while girls may demonstrate higher levels of inattention. There is a view that girls and young women may indeed experience ADHD to a greater extent than was previously realized, and that more attention should be paid to this condition in females.

Finally, what about the long-term outcomes for those diagnosed with ADHD? The evidence appears to show that girls and young women are more likely than boys and young men to continue to show symptoms of ADHD into adulthood. Interestingly the ratio of the condition in adolescence is in the range of 2–2.5 times higher in boys than in girls. However, in adulthood the ratio becomes closer to equality (Hinshaw et al., 2022). It should be noted that there has been relatively little research into adult ADHD, and this is an area in need of further investigation.

Autism

Autism is an enormously complex condition. It is usually understood to be include a continuum of symptoms, ranging from severe handicap to relatively minor difficulties. There is debate about the description, with most clinicians using the term *autistic spectrum disorder* (ASD). However, there has been a pushback against this, as many believe it is wrong to consider this to be a disorder, thus the term *autistic spectrum condition* (ASC) is preferred. I have already mentioned the book *Neurotribes* (Silberman, 2015), which puts the case for a much wider understanding of autism. The author gives many examples of individuals with what is known as "high-functioning" autism who have demonstrated remarkable achievements in art, mathematics and other fields.

What exactly is autism? Most agree that it is characterized by difficulties in social communication and by the presence of restricted and repetitive behaviours and interests. Those with this condition often experience sensory overload, so that it may be necessary to assist the individual in reducing sensory input. It is often the case that this condition is associated with other difficulties, such as social anxiety, oppositional behaviour and obsessive-compulsive disorders (Ghirardi et al., 2021). Because of the wide range of behaviours and different levels of handicap associated with autism spectrum condition, it is hard to be too specific about the causes and the outcomes for those with this condition.

In spite of this, there have, over the years, been many attempts to identify the causes of autism. In the early years, the idea of "toxic parenting" was put forward by commentators. It was only in the 1990s that this notion was finally laid to rest (Silberman, 2015). More recently there has been an intensive focus on the possible genetics of autism. However, there remain many questions about the genetic links with autism. Most evidence demonstrates links between genotypes and a range of psychiatric and neurodevelopmental disorders, so that it is hard to be specific about the genetics of autism (Ghirardi et al., 2021).

An alternative view is put forward by Franke and colleagues (2021). These authors believe that ASC heritability is high, yet they also point out that environmental factors play their part. In their editorial, they suggest that obstetric and other familial variables are part of the overall picture. They also discuss the expanding field of research looking at brain biomarkers, identifying early indicators of autism and raising the possibility of early intervention.

In terms of understanding the incidence of ASC, this too has its problems. Edwards et al. (2024) report that in clinical samples, the ratio is four males to every female having this condition. In community samples, however, the ratio is less extreme, with more females reporting the condition. Some have argued that girls and young women are better at masking their difficulties, although this is debatable. It is perhaps more likely that autism spectrum condition is manifested differently in girls and young women, with females having more restricted and repetitive interests linked to dolls and animals, which are gender-appropriate (Edwards et al., 2024).

To conclude, autism is one condition within the wide spectrum of neurodiversity. The move towards identifying those with autism as being part of the neurodiverse community has been enormously helpful. To be neurodiverse is not to be ill or to have a faulty brain. All our brains are wired differently, and this recognition has led to many changes in treatments and in opportunities for those who are neurodiverse. As all commentators have noted, our understanding and our responses to this condition are changing all the time. While the challenges associated with neurodiversity should not be underestimated, greater recognition of this condition represents progress for all concerned.

Trauma and adverse childhood experiences (ACEs)

The concept of trauma and its use in clinical practice have become widespread in European countries. There are many different ways of understanding and defining trauma. One possible approach is that described by Forster (2021) when she says: "trauma is the term used to describe the impact of early, repeated adverse childhood experiences that happen within a child's important relationships" (page 195). This sets up a link with the concept of ACEs, or adverse childhood experiences, a concept which is outlined in an article by Lansen and Leitjen (2025).

These authors make the point that there are a variety of possible adverse experiences, ranging from child maltreatment (including physical, sexual or emotional abuse) to deprivation, significant loss, peer victimization and other threats within the family or in the community. There is a significant literature which uses ACEs as the main variable, looking at the outcomes for children and young people who have experienced these adverse childhood events. The problem lies in the fact that not all adverse experiences are the same or have the same impact later in life.

> I think there's, like, a lot of trauma gets passed down through families, because I think of older generations, it never got dealt with, and it just kept passing down, and there's a lot more pressures now. And as much as social media can be amazing, it can also be really detrimental, so I think it has got a lot more common now to be mentally ill.
>
> (Young person, aged 17)

The increased focus on this subject has led to many services recognizing the impact of trauma and developing what has become known as "trauma informed practice". An example of such practice is described by Robertson et al. (2025). These authors emphasize the need to create safe spaces for those affected by trauma, and to avoid replicating in any way the conditions under which earlier trauma was experienced. Trauma-informed practice recognizes the significance of power relationships, and the difficulty that those who have experienced trauma will have in trusting others and feeling safe in situations where there is a power imbalance.

The focus on trauma has led to many different initiatives and research endeavours. One example is the investigations that have been carried out on the effect of child maltreatment on brain development in adolescence (Golm and Kreppner, 2021; McCrory et al., 2017). These studies show that there may well be significant effects, including elevated threat sensitivity, an impact on memory function and a reduction in reward responsiveness.

Another strand of work that has originated from the focus on trauma is that relating to post-traumatic stress disorder, otherwise known as PTSD (Christie, 2021). This condition applies to the after-effects of the experience of traumatic events, such as natural disasters, major accidents, war-related experiences and other similar occurrences. Much effort has gone into the development of treatments for post-traumatic stress disorder, and these are outlined in Ogden and Hagen (2019).

Interventions in mental health

To conclude this chapter, a brief mention should be made of interventions and treatments that are available in the mental health field. Clearly there is a wide range of literature on this subject, and only the shortest note will be possible here. Useful introductions will be found in the book by Fonagy and colleagues entitled *What Works for Whom?* (2015). Other useful coverage of this topic may be found in Ogden and Hagen (2019) and in Laver-Bradbury et al. (2021). Reviews in this field distinguish between the following elements of interventions:

- Whether the intervention is medical or non-medical, and in particular whether psychiatric medication is used;
- The theoretical basis of the intervention, i.e., whether it is cognitive-behavioural or psychodynamic;
- The location of the intervention, e.g., whether it is based in the clinic, the school or the community.

Since there are such a variety of conditions that may require treatment, it is inevitable that there are many different approaches which are available. Decisions about the choice of approach will depend on the severity of the condition, the professional background of the therapist, the referral process and the interventions available in the young person's environment. Here again I can note the point made by Peter Wilson (2016) about the use of medical or non-medical models in understanding mental ill-health. As this author makes clear, mental health is a continuum. While the medical model for interventions may have credibility in the health service, there will be many situations in which other, non-medical, approaches may prove more effective.

> Like, my friend, he was going through social anxiety, and he started crying a bit. I started doing that too, and I had to calm myself down. And I've got, like, a drawer and in there I've got a bucket and it's filled with squishies and stuff. So, all I do is get them and start squishing them, and they actually calm me down, they really do and I feel more relaxed this year.
>
> (Young man, aged 14)

I will end this section with a note on mental health literacy. Due to the greatly increased focus on mental health in young people, there have been a range of initiatives within the school setting which set out to provide a greater level of information and understanding on mental health. These initiatives aim to help young people recognize mental health difficulties in themselves and in their peers, to reduce stigma concerning mental health disorders and to encourage help-seeking.

As Yan Ma and others (2023) point out, there is a distinct lack of standardization of the curriculum being used in different settings. There is also a dearth of research investigating whether these mental health literacy programmes have the effects that that are claimed for them. Goodfellow and colleagues (2023) provide some evidence that, in Scottish schools, mental health literacy programmes do increase help-seeking, as long as the curriculum includes information about treatment efficacy.

> I don't get anxiety, really, panic attacks and things. But my best friend, she really used to struggle with them, like, really mad. So, I learnt a lot of techniques, so I could help her through it. Like, deep breathing, like exercises that you can do, like smell, taste and stuff like that. Like take yourself out of it when you're in that kind of headspace, kind of distract a bit.
>
> (Young woman, aged 17)

While these advantages are attractive, research has also shown that there are pitfalls which should not be ignored (Foulkes, 2024; Guzman-Holst et al., 2025). These authors raise the possibility that information about mental health may increase anxiety among those who are vulnerable rather than reducing it. Such programmes could also lead to pressure for self-diagnosis and to a greater use of the internet for this purpose. It is not clear that the use of chatbots and AI in this context will always be helpful, and this is a development which will need to be watched in future.

Conclusion

In this chapter, I have covered a wide range of topics relating to mental health in young people. It is believed that the incidence of mental health problems in the young is increasing, and here I have explored the evidence for such a conclusion. This is a subject of great importance to families and schools and in public policy. I have looked at the impact of Covid-19 and of other factors that may impact on mental health in adolescence. I have discussed neurodiversity, suicide and self-harm, psychotic illness, trauma and a range of other conditions. I concluded the chapter with a very brief word about treatment and interventions and a note about mental health literacy.

Chapter 8

The family

Introduction

In the first chapter, I referred to the fact that, for many parents and carers, this stage is one of challenge and conflict. What are the reasons for this? Is it the behaviour of young people that leads to these generational difficulties? Alternatively, is it more to do with the fact that adults have to let go and accept that their sons and daughters are no longer pliant and amenable to adult direction? In this chapter, I will explore these questions and outline what the research tells us about the family during the adolescent years. A mother I once interviewed put it like this: *"It's very difficult to be a parent of a teenager. It's the most underrated job in the world. It's easier to be a brain surgeon than to be a parent of a teenager"*.

I know from my own experience that this is a common view. Why should this be so? In my own work, I have been heavily involved in developing and delivering parenting workshops for parents of young people, and I will include some of this work here. I mentioned the STAGE framework in Chapter 1, and I will come back to this and give more detail about the framework in this chapter. I will also look at questions of developing autonomy, conflict and the so-called generation gap, parenting styles, divorce and family breakdown, culture and ethnicity, fathers and siblings, and finally I will consider what can be done to support parents of adolescents.

> Parents are just like a massive safety net.
>
> (Young man, aged 17)

The family is changing

Over the last few decades, the family has altered in many ways. Marriage is not always understood or experienced as a lifetime commitment, and divorce and family breakdown are not uncommon experiences for children and adolescents.

DOI: 10.4324/9781032640433-8

There are many more family types to be recognized, so that single parents, step-families, blended families, same-sex parents and non-married parents are all possible arrangements that are experienced by young people. Some young people are living in foster care or extended family care. It is also important to note that there has been an increase in the number of families where both parents are working. There has been a significant growth in the number of women in the workforce, and this impacts on how parenting works in practice.

Another important change relates to the length of time young adults remain living in the family home. This is true across Europe, as well as in North America. The fact that the ability to set up home independently is being postponed in Western societies is related to the phenomenon of emerging adulthood. This pattern of delayed independence has significant implications for the achievement of full autonomy, as well as for various aspects of family life. Among other things, parents are likely to remain financially responsible for their older adolescents for longer, space in the home for the young adult will be needed and parents will stay involved with the lives of their sons and daughters for a longer period than was the case in previous generations.

> I mean, now that I am 18, there's less rules. They are trying to stop worrying about me a bit less now. They want to give me that independence. Like, I've got a car now, so I can drive around. They don't really restrict me now, it's more relaxed.
>
> (Young woman, aged 18)

An interesting trend identified in reviews of parenting is the fact that parental monitoring and supervision has increased over time (Gardner et al., 2012). These authors report that in the 1980s, oversight of young people's behaviour was related to social disadvantage. The greater the level of disadvantage, the lower the level of monitoring. This difference had disappeared by the 2010s in the UK. In addition, the overall level of monitoring has increased over the years by a substantial amount. These authors put this down to greater fears about safety in public spaces and of course the advent of social media.

In the world of research there has been a greater recognition of what is known as directionality. In other words, scientists are recognizing that influences between parents and adolescents go both ways. It is insufficient to look only at the impact of parents on their adolescents. Adolescents have an influence on their parents and carers, and their behaviour affects the way that parents and carers respond and the parenting styles they adopt. This notion is congruent with the ideas outlined in Chapter 1 regarding the focal model and the impact of young people as constructors of their own development. It also fits with concepts of agency and individuality. As will be suggested in this chapter, this is manifested best in work on monitoring and supervision which underlines the two-way nature of influence in family functioning.

The development of autonomy

It could be argued that for many young people, the development of independence, or autonomy, is one of the key tasks they face. To be free from parental constraint, and to achieve control over one's life, is the goal of many young people. However, this is not a straightforward journey, and over the last few decades it has become even more problematic as economic and social circumstances alter. To some extent, the way in which autonomy is achieved will depend on the particular family, on ethnicity, and on the cultural, social and economic factors operating in the environment. There is significant variety in the values of each family, and it is important to note that in some cultures it is expected that a greater degree of closeness with parents is maintained into adulthood.

In terms of our understanding of this feature of adolescent development, there have been some significant shifts over the past several decades. In early writings, it was assumed that emotional disengagement by adolescents from parents was a fundamental element of the move towards maturity. It was believed that, unless separation and detachment occurred, it was not possible to become fully adult. This view was very much influenced by psychoanalytic theory. More recently, however, empirical research has cast a different light on the matter.

In the first place, from the 1960s onwards, investigators were reporting more positive relationships between parents and young people than had been expected. The work of Douvan and Adelson (1966) is a good example of such a landmark study. In more recent times, these conclusions have been supported by the work of Abela and Walker (2014) and by Meeus (2019).

> I guess they're there to support you, but not in an overwhelming way. Like, letting you explore some freedoms, using your own agency to make some decisions and becoming more responsible. They kind of view it as becoming more responsible, but still within the parameters that are appropriate for someone my age.
>
> (Young woman, aged 17)

As a result of this work, commentators came to believe that it is possible to develop autonomy without the separation and disengagement that had been envisaged in earlier writings. Youniss and Smollar (1985), for example, talked of interdependence, a stage during which both parent and adolescent work together to redefine their relationship. In this situation, close ties are maintained without the young person's growing independence being threatened. One of the most frequently quoted papers from that time is that of Grotevant and Cooper (1986). They put forward the notion of connectedness. In this view the young person can move towards a state of individuation while remaining connected to the family.

> Like I'm trying to make a decision. I might be unsure on what I'm doing. Whether it's with school, or whether I go out or something, they've got more experience with everything. Even though you might feel all the time, like, I'm right, I'm not always right. If I'm trying to make a decision I might ask my Dad: "Is it safe?" Or ask my Mum: "Is that a good decision?" It gives me more of an outlook, other than me just going and doing something.
>
> (Young man, aged 17)

How this happens will depend on both actors playing their part. Writers in this field have pointed out that there is a big difference between separating from one's parents in a way that maintains emotional closeness and in a way that involves alienation and conflict. An important contribution to this field was made by Steinberg and Silverberg, where they attempted to measure autonomy and to separate out various elements of this complex phenomenon. They developed the Emotional Autonomy Scale (EAS), and this has been widely used in research ever since (Steinberg and Silverberg, 1986). This scale measures four aspects of emotional autonomy.

1. De-idealization – i.e., the extent to which the young person sees the parent as fallible and human;
2. Non-dependency – i.e., the absence of childish dependence on the parents;
3. Individuation – i.e., the perceived lack of parental knowledge and understanding about the young person and their life;
4. "Parents as people" – i.e., the realization that parents are ordinary people who have separate lives, existing in a world not known to the young person.

Results from research studies show a steady increase with age in all aspects of autonomy, but it is also the case that high scores of various elements of this scale were linked to less positive behavioural outcomes (Steinberg, 2023). Research also shows that those who have higher scores on separation experience greater degrees of parental rejection and report higher degrees of conflict in the family. This has led to a question of whether this scale is measuring adaptive autonomy, or whether it is tapping into something more dysfunctional. This debate is summarized in a review by Goossens (2006).

One sensible conclusion may be that there are many different routes to separation. Some will be able to manage the route to individuation without too much conflict. This will, of course, depend on the inter-relationships within the family, and the role of both parent and adolescent. Others will struggle to find their own course to become independent and will find it hard to pull themselves away from an intense relationship with their parents.

Another approach to the topic of autonomy is to distinguish between different types of autonomy, with the most common distinction being between emotional autonomy, behavioural autonomy and value autonomy. Emotional autonomy refers to the de-idealization of the parents, together with a more mature conception of parents as individuals who may be fallible and who have a life of their own. On the other hand, behavioural autonomy refers to the degree of independent decision-making that is allowed, together with the ability to make choices about leisure, friendships and social activities. Finally, value autonomy refers to the development of one's own system of values and morals (Goossens, 2006).

These ideas have also been developed by Smetana and colleagues, who have developed the social domain theory of parental authority (Smetana, 2002). This theory states that parents and adolescents will hold different opinions on who has the final say regarding different aspects of family life. Thus, we might imagine that an adolescent believes that they have the final say about which friends they choose or whether their bedroom is tidy or untidy. However, they may agree that parents have the right to be involved in decisions regarding health matters or education. However, parents may take a different view, believing that they should have a say in what happens in the young person's bedroom.

The social domain theory has generated a considerable amount of useful research. One of the most interesting aspects of this is the exploration of what happens when there are "violations" of the parent's or adolescent's view of the social domain (Smetana, 2002). In this view, if the parents believe they should have a say regarding the state of the young person's bedroom, and the young person takes a contrary view, this will generate conflict. How will this be resolved? And will this violation lead to further conflict over other issues?

There has been some useful cross-cultural work on this topic, especially in Asia. Research indicates that very similar issues occur in families in China, Hong Kong and Japan (Smetana and Villalobos, 2009; Yau and Smetana, 2003). This is a good place to include a blog I wrote after running groups for parents of young people in China in 2022.

Blog "Parents of teenagers in China"

In 2021, I was contacted by a parenting organization in Beijing to tell me that they had arranged for my book *Why Won't My Teenager Talk to Me?* to be translated into Chinese. I was delighted, and not a little surprised. They asked if I would like a copy, and before long this indeed arrived through the post. Following this I then received an email asking if I would be willing to offer them some help with their parenting courses. I had no idea that such a thing was happening in China, but since it is now possible to work with people in any part of the world without leaving one's desk, I said yes.

There followed a fascinating period of work with parents of teenagers across China. The enthusiasm for my input was striking, and of course very rewarding. Here is an example of one parent's comments to me:

> Thank you for your efforts all the time dear teacher. In fact, when I study the course and read your book, I also heal myself. I love my children very much, and I hope they can grow up happier and happier. So, I am looking forward to seeing what I can do better with your help.

How can I offer help to parents in such a different culture? This is a question I have been asked numerous times by colleagues here in the UK. The remarkable thing is that the majority of the concerns of parents are almost identical to those in Western countries.

> "Dilly-dallying on homework"
>
> "Do some people's adolescent traits persist into adulthood?"
>
> "I would like to ask how to cultivate children's gratefulness?"
>
> "There are lots of worries and anxious of negative peer influence".
>
> "How to limit and monitor screen time? It seems we compete with the screen to win our children back, but for lots of time, our teenagers choose screen more than us".

So where are the differences? The most striking fact has to do with the pressure on young people from the education system. Many questions focussed on homework and how parents can support their young people with the pressures they experience. Typical questions ran like this:

> "The school is very intensive. The teacher put a lot of pressure on the students. Often using physical punishment, scold students".
>
> "It is difficult to change the environment of intense learning competition. How can I help my child relieve stress, relax and face it?"

In subsequent discussions with the Chinese facilitators, they told me that academic performance is critical for future job prospects. Unless students perform well at school, future opportunities are severely limited. This leads to high levels of anxiety for both parents and young people.

This work has now concluded, although I remain in contact with colleagues in China. As one put it: "*I hope you will be able to use our examples in your next book!*" The most striking conclusion for me has to be the similarity of parental concerns about the teenage years. Whether you are a parent in London or Beijing, you still worry about the changes that take place as children move into the teenage years.

A second conclusion relates to the fact that there is so little support for this group of parents in Asia. I was struck by the high level of need that was constantly expressed to me. My book has become a best-seller – to my utter amazement. That my knowledge about adolescence can be so useful in such a different culture is truly extraordinary. In the webinars that I ran for parents, we were getting over 1,000 participants. Remarkable.

All in all, it proved to be a fascinating and rewarding project. It is clear that, no matter where you live, parents of teenagers struggle to make sense of this stage of life. If anything can be done to help families across the globe, it is evident that more knowledge about adolescent development could play a useful part.

27.06.23

Family environment and adolescent development

In thinking about family environments and their effects on young people, it is important to look first at the role of parents, and in particular at their parenting styles. When considering this topic, it is essential to acknowledge the work of

Diana Baumrind and Eleanor Maccoby. It can be argued that their writing has had a profound effect on our understanding of parenting behaviour. There are few studies of parenting that have not been influenced by the work of these two eminent psychologists. In the early 1970s, Baumrind (1971) first put forward her view that there are two dimensions of parenting behaviour which need to be distinguished.

These are parental responsiveness and parental demandingness. Baumrind believed that parents vary on both these dimensions, and also that the dimensions are more or less independent of each other. This made it possible to look at various combinations of the characteristics of parenting behaviour, and numerous studies have provided evidence of the validity and usefulness of this concept. According to the scheme developed by Maccoby and Martin (1983), parental behaviour can be classified as:

- Authoritarian;
- Authoritative;
- Indulgent;
- Indifferent.

Authoritarian parents place a high value on obedience and conformity. They are more likely to punish for misbehaviour and tend not to encourage autonomy. Authoritative parents are warm but firm. They set standards and hold to boundaries but are more likely than other parents to give explanations and to reason with the young person rather than to be punitive. Indulgent (or permissive) parents behave in a benign, accepting but essentially passive manner. They are unlikely to set standards or to have high expectations for their children, and do not see punishment as important. Finally, indifferent parents are often also called neglectful. This group of parents takes little interest in the lives of their children and is likely to spend the minimum amount of time on child care activities.

Readers will note that these four styles of parenting can be classified according to the original idea of responsiveness and demandingness. As an example, indifferent parents are low on both these dimensions. On the other hand, authoritative parents will be high on both dimensions. It is this classification that has acted as the basis underpinning the four parenting styles (Coleman, 2014, 2019).

> And if your parents are good parents, they should always be there to understand what you are trying to tell them. And they should always be there to

support you. It's just a lot of kids don't have that trust with their parents, because they're like: "Oh! My parents are not going to understand this, yeah! Why not punish me for this, like?"

(Young man, aged 17)

As I have noted, this typology has inspired an enormous range of studies and provided numerous valuable insights into family functioning. The results of these studies are fairly consistent. They show that in almost all cases, children and young people brought up in families where parents use an authoritative parenting style do better on a range of outcome measures. These include having higher self-esteem, being more advanced on such skills as perspective-taking and having a greater likelihood of avoiding problem behaviours.

These results are summarized, for example, in Lila et al. (2006) and in Steinberg (2023). Young people who are brought up by indulgent parents are often less mature, more irresponsible and more likely to conform to peer group pressure. Those who grow up with indifferent parents are those who are most at risk, as might be expected. They are more likely than others to be impulsive and to get involved in high-risk behaviours.

The finding that authoritative parenting leads to such positive outcomes has, not surprisingly, led many to question what it is about this style of parenting that makes such a difference. Steinberg (2023) is one of the writers who has put forward a convincing explanation for these results. He notes that there are three components of authoritative parenting style. Firstly, there is warmth, leading to a young person feeling loved and nurtured. A second element is structure, which is especially important for adolescents, as they begin to push the boundaries and challenge parental authority. The provision of a clear structure means that young people have an understanding of the rules and an awareness of the consequences when these rules are broken. For adolescents to understand that there is a structure allows them to feel safe and valued by their parents.

I think they will always be there for you, no matter if you don't want them to be. You can always go to them about everything, even if you don't want to. They'll sit there and listen to you, even if you're in the wrong, they'll still help you through it. They'll give you advice how to get through it. Like me, like with learning disabilities, like, my dyslexia, you need extra help seeing you're struggling, they'll be there with you.

(Young woman, aged 15)

Lastly, authoritative parents give autonomy support, in that they accept and encourage the adolescent's individuality and the young person's gradual moves towards taking greater control over their lives. All these things are critical in providing a family environment in which independence is valued, while parents also set limits, provide support and acceptance and endorse achievement. These ideas are inherent in the development of the STAGE framework, which will be discussed later in the chapter.

It may be thought that this description of parenting is too good to be true! Studies have shown that, while this may be the ideal, few parents manage to hold to this parenting style all the time. Indeed, many studies have shown that parenting styles may vary depending on the circumstances and indeed on the behaviour of the child or young person (Mounts, 2002, 2004). It is all very well to imagine a benign style of parenting with a happy, responsive and well-balanced young person. However, when faced with stress, tension and constant arguments, even the most resilient parent will be forgiven for slipping into authoritarian or even indifferent parenting.

This leads on to the question of directionality. While for many years there has been an awareness of the fact that influence between parents and young people goes both ways, it has proved difficult to incorporate this insight into research designs, as set out by Schaffer (2006). All too often commentators slip back into assuming that influence goes one way, i.e., that certain types of parental behaviour result in certain types of outcomes in children and young people.

Research in the field of monitoring and supervision has made this point. Work by the team of Margaret Kerr and Hakan Stattin has shown how the behaviour of parents is directly affected by the behaviour of the adolescent. While it was believed that low levels of monitoring and supervision resulted in higher levels of antisocial behaviour, Kerr and Stattin demonstrated that something different happens in families. Based on their research, they were able to show that parental monitoring and supervision was affected by the young person's willingness to disclose their activities. In other words, parental behaviour is influenced by how the adolescent behaves, rather than the other way around (Kerr and Stattin, 2000; Stattin and Kerr, 2000).

One interesting notion that has been introduced into the discussion about parents and young people is the that of information management. Implicit in this is the concept of reciprocal relationships between the generations. However, this goes further, in that it argues that young people are taking an active role in managing the flow of information between themselves and their parents. This is of course a good example of how the adolescent goes about constructing their own pathway through this stage.

The first paper to be published on this illustrated how young people made use of a sophisticated set of categories into which they place different types of information (Marshall et al., 2005). Thus, an adolescent might decide not to disclose something because they believed it is none of the parents' business, or alternatively they may take the view that they will not tell their parents because the information may be hurtful to the adult. Marshall and colleagues set out a distinction between five categories, including "*Ask me no questions*", where this information is not going to be disclosed, and "*Tell or else*" – a category where the information needs to be passed on to the parent for safety or other reasons.

Further studies on information management have appeared in Daddis and Randolph (2010), where they looked at information management in the context of romantic relationships. This study highlighted the finding that trust between parent and young person made a difference to disclosure, but so did the adolescent's estimate of the impact of disclosure. If the young person believed that sharing information with the parent would have a positive outcome, they would be more likely to disclose. This finding reinforces the notion of active management by the young person depending on their awareness and assessment of the result of disclosure.

> It's quite hard to talk to them, because we've got such different views on things. It's harder to talk to them about really important things because I just know they are going to go against what I believe in. I try to avoid talking about, like, politics and things, because we have such different opinions, and they're quite traditional, like they think we're kids, so should be taught by their parents and believe what their parents believe. That's how I got to where I am right now, with believing what I believe in. And they're like always: "You'll see one day". And I'm like: "I've already seen, I've already seen".
>
> (Young woman, aged 17)

In another study (Tilton-Weaver et al., 2010), a longitudinal design was used, and in this study the authors were able to show that parents' response to disclosure at Time 1 influenced the young person's management of information at Time 2. In other words, whether the parent responded positively or negatively in the first place had an impact on the future disclosure patterns of the young person. Findings such as these provide graphic support for the idea that adolescents are actively shaping their environment and that they are constructing their own development. Further studies have explored these elements of parental behaviour and provided additional support for the idea that the responses of parents have an impact on later disclosure by the young person (Dotterer and Day, 2019).

Culture, ethnicity and globalization

As the world becomes more multi-cultural, and as there is greater movement of peoples across different regions of the world, it is important to recognize that there are cultural differences in the way families approach the parenting of young people. These differences will be influenced by a range of factors, including cultural beliefs and economic factors. There is less research available on these topics than on others relating to families and adolescents.

One subject that has been the focus of attention has to do with the time spent in the family setting and variations in the emotional closeness of parents and adolescents in different cultures. One example is the work of Hendry (2015). He looked at family relationships in Scotland and in Argentina. The comparison was illuminating, as he found that the great majority of young people in Argentina reported having meals with their parents, in contrast to only 35% of adolescents doing so in Scotland. A general picture emerged of warm and positive relationships with both parents in this South American country, similar to studies of family life in countries such as Spain and Italy. Here parents and young people are close, and young adults remain in the family home until they are in their 20s. However, as already noted, this trend is now being seen in all Western countries, which is a good example of economic factors influencing family life.

It may be helpful to draw a distinction between "individualistic" and "collectivist" cultures. This is a distinction well-known to commentators on culture and values, but it has particular relevance to any consideration of family life for adolescents. Essentially, in a collectivist culture it is believed that the young person's behaviour and aspirations should centre around the family and community. In contrast, in an individualist culture the opposite value system obtains. Here it is expected that the young person will seek to identify his or her own personal goals. It is accepted that, in most cases, the adolescent will be encouraged to find ways of reaching these goals without undue regard to the needs and wishes of the family.

> I definitely worry about my parents, right? Because they work so hard, to bring us here, because we lived in Italy, and then they used to live in Nigeria, so they went from Nigeria to Italy, and they brought us over here so we can have, like, a good future. And they've done so much for us, and I just worry because they are working so hard.
>
> (Young man, aged 16)

Webster (2009) makes the point that, in the British context, there is a complex situation with many different cultural groups whose value systems vary according to their particular backgrounds and experiences of immigration. It is sometimes suggested that first-generation immigrants assimilate relatively easily, as they wish to conform and accept the values of the mainstream culture. On the other hand, their children make take the opposite position. In this situation, young people find assimilation hard to cope with, and end up rejecting some or all aspects of the mainstream culture. This creates a vicious circle, so that some become marginalized and believe they are excluded from all that the mainstream culture has to offer. This may be based on experiences of racism and harassment in the school and in the workplace.

Because of the multi-ethnic nature of society in the United States, there have been a wide range of studies on parenting practices in this country. One major focus has been the variation in parenting styles across ethnic groups (Deater-Deckard et al., 2018). One key finding is that there is less evidence of authoritative parenting (as defined in the previous section) in African-American, Asian-American and Hispanic-American families than there is among White American families (Smetana and Chuang, 2001). This finding no doubt reflects differences in values and beliefs across different cultures.

It should be noted that adolescents in non-mainstream cultures do appear to benefit just as much from authoritative parenting as do those from White American families. However, it should be added that authoritarian parenting (where there is a greater focus on demandingness and control) is more common in families from minority communities. Secondly, young people from European-American backgrounds are more adversely affected by authoritarian parenting than are minority young people (Ruiz et al., 2002). One possible explanation for this finding may be that higher levels of parental control are more adaptive in communities where violence and risk are prevalent (Zhang et al., 2017). On the other hand, it may be that these dimensions of parenting style have less meaning in non-European countries (Chao, 2001).

Finally in this section I should note the impact of globalization. This topic is explored by Melinda Mills (2014). She notes that there is a wide range of implications for families, and inevitably these have repercussions for the parenting of adolescents and for the life expectations of these young people. In particular, Mills points out four major implications of globalization for families. These are:

- The declining importance of national boundaries;
- The increasing connectedness and communication across regions;

- The changing nature of economic reality as countries adapt to austerity and economic pressures;
- The changing nature of work and of barriers to entry into employment.

All these factors may seem a far cry from parenting practices, but as Mills points out, they impact parents, their behaviour and expectations and therefore what happens in the family.

Divorce and family breakdown

The very notion of family has undergone a profound alteration over the past decades. It is usual to distinguish between four family types – couple families, single-parent families, step-families and blended families (Abela and Walker, 2014). While it was the case that, for a long time, research tended to focus on divorce as a topic for investigation, it is now recognized that there are many other factors to be taken into account. Family breakdowns occur for many different reasons. Indeed, some single-parent families exist not as a result of divorce but as a result of parental choice. It is also recognized that divorce is only one event. The process, including the family circumstances both before and after divorce, may be more important than the divorce itself.

> I mean, my parents are divorced, and it happened when I was very young, and that caused a lot of struggle for me growing up. Because I was going from one house to the other, and it was right round the corner, so I could just walk around. But the struggles with my Dad, I had a very challenging relationship with him. Like, me growing up, I did not like him at all, and it's not anything he did wrong. He lives in another country now, and he comes over every month, and I get on better with him now. Now again, because I'm older, and more able to manage the relationship. And my Mum got married, so her husband, me and him, I also had a very challenging relationship with him. But as I've got older, I've become more mature, it's just gotten easier to just get along, we don't need to be all hugs, but it's just easier to coexist.
>
> (Young woman, aged 17)

Other factors that need to be taken into account include the economic hardship which may occur as a result of relationship breakdown, and the differences between ethnic groups in their response to family change. It is also the case that, in considering families following divorce, the role of the non-biological parent is critical. It used to be the case that there was much focus on the non-residential parent, usually the father, but now we are attuned to other factors in considering post-divorce adjustment.

Many writers have grappled with the question of why relationships end (Pryor, 2014). The variables that have been explored include age at marriage, the educational levels of both partners and employment. Most reviews come to the conclusion that these relations are complex, with no clear pattern emerging. However, the one variable that does appear to show a clear link is that of intergenerational transmission. For children of divorce, there is a higher risk that their own marriages will break down. Of course, this is only a risk factor, and there are many marriages which do not follow this pattern.

A primary consideration here has to do with the advantages and disadvantages for young people growing up in intact married-couple families and those growing up in other family types. Work by Scott (2007) and others suggests that there are undoubtedly disadvantages in living in reconstituted families, but that these disadvantages are as much about economic factors as they are about stress in relationships. The evidence is clear that parents who bring up children on their own are significantly more likely to be living in poverty. This in turn has an impact on a wide variety of aspects of family life, including housing, health and opportunities for further education and employment for young people.

In order to understand the impact of family change and reorganization, it is essential to recognize that divorce or family breakdown is a process rather than an event. This is a truism, but it highlights a key element of the picture relating to divorce. Events taking place before the breakdown, as well as what happens subsequently, play a larger role than the event itself. For example, reports indicate that a high level of family conflict before the breakdown is a significant factor in determining the adjustment of the children and young people post-divorce (Pryor, 2014).

Some studies have compared intact and step-families in respect of children's problem behaviour (e.g. Jenkins et al., 2005). This study showed that marital conflict about children increased children's problem behaviour, but that children's problem behaviour predicted marital conflict, especially in step-families. However, siblings differed in their exposure to conflict, and thus the long-term impact is not the same for all children and young people. This study is a classic, in that it demonstrates how inter-related parents' relationships are with the behaviour of the younger members of the family.

Research also shows that what happens after family breakdown is closely related to young people's adjustment to this event. The phrase "caught in the middle" will be familiar to readers. This notion has a long history in research on family breakdown and was first used by Buchanan et al. (1996). Following research in California in the 1990s, these writers identified the damaging effect on young people of continuing conflict between parents over access and other arrangements. More recent research into family conflict reflects the complexity of family relationships.

It has been shown that conflict can occur between different members of reconstituted families, and that some types of conflict are more damaging than others. Thus, conflict between mother and non-resident father is more likely to lead to poor adjustment than other types of conflict. It has also been noted that it is the young person's involvement in the conflict rather than the frequency of conflict that makes the difference to adjustment. Finally, Pryor (2014) makes the point that where young people experience conflict in more than one family environment, e.g., at home and in a step-family, the impact is likely to be especially detrimental in terms of adjustment.

Turning now to protective factors, it has been noted that divorce and family reorganization can actually mitigate harm, as young people are relieved of having to witness domestic violence or chronic conflict between parents (Holt, 2025; Scott, 2007). Another potentially positive experience that may stem from family reorganization is the opportunity for the adolescent to take on new roles within the family. For some young people, growing up with a single parent or in a reconstituted family may allow easier movement to a more mature status in the family. Thus, the adolescent may be able to play more of a role in decision-making than was the case in the family of origin with both parents present.

One final protective factor not yet mentioned is the potential role of both siblings and friends. On siblings, Sisler and Ittel (2015) illustrate the powerful role of other children in families where there is conflict or disruption. These authors make the point that having others close in age within the family environment allows a sharing of experiences and has the potential to reduce the trauma and damage that arises as a result of parental conflict.

Friends also play important roles where there is family breakdown. In studies that look at young people's communication patterns and the role of confidants at times of family difficulty, the findings are clear. Friends can play a key role. Those who lose friends because of moving house or changing school have a harder time adjusting to family change than those who remain with the same friendship group (Steinberg, 2023).

In conclusion, it is clear that it is not the family breakdown itself that is the damaging factor but rather the circumstances that surround such an event. Serious conflict between parents, both before and after separation, is one of the key risk variables determining the outcome for young people. Being removed from violence or hatred between parents and being able to keep the same group of friends can help to mitigate some of the more damaging effects of family breakdown.

Fathers, siblings and grandparents

I wish to include this section of the chapter since these figures play a major part in family life, yet are rarely recognized in the academic or research literature. Starting with fathers, the classic book on this topic is one published many years ago by Shmuel and Seiffge-Krenke (1997), entitled *Fathers and Adolescents: Developmental and Clinical Perspectives*. In this book, the authors explore the role that fathers can play with sons and daughters, as well as in step-families and blended families. In an especially important chapter, they discuss the importance of the non-custodial father, recognizing how difficult, and yet how important, this role can be.

> My Dad, he's quite old, he's 60 now, well, old compared to everyone else's parents. So, I often have worries, like, if he's not going to be in my life anymore soon, things like that. Like, he's quite healthy, but I often worry about it. But it motivates me to be less angry with him, and to spend more time with him.
>
> (Young woman, aged 18)

Shmuel and Seiffge-Krenke (1997) emphasize the significance of the father, pointing out that, with some exceptions, outcomes for young people following family breakdown are strongly related to father involvement. These exceptions relate to situations where there has been past abuse or domestic violence. In general, however, the more fathers remain involved in the life of the adolescent, the better the outcome is likely to be. Not surprisingly these authors bemoan the lack of interest in fathering in the academic and research literature, especially in the context of adolescence.

Gavazzi (2011) quotes fathers as "*the forgotten contributors to child development*". He outlines so many ways in which fathers are central to the development of the family during the years in which parents provide support and nurture for young people. Many commentators have looked at the low level of father involvement in parenting programmes (e.g., Coleman, 2014). These authors ask what can be done to improve the engagement of fathers, and offer a range of suggestions, including the labelling of programmes to include fathers, the greater use of on-line programmes and the inclusion of content that speaks directly to men.

As far as siblings are concerned, again there has been far too little attention paid to their role in the life of the family. One exception to this is the book, mentioned previously, by Sissler and Ittel (2015). As much as anything, this book is a call to action. The authors outline ways in which research on the role of siblings could be developed. Their approach is based on systems and ecological theories, and they explore a variety of research designs that could incorporate the place of siblings in longitudinal studies of the family.

> My brother, I know it's different because he's a boy, but he was allowed to go out with his friends, and I'm not allowed to do that. I don't know if it's just my family, but he had less expectations of, like, to help around the house, and he didn't have to babysit my little siblings. He's never had that responsibility. I have to miss out on things, but he's never had that, right?
>
> (Young woman, aged 17)

The authors outline some of the ways in which siblings play a role in both enhancing and interfering with the development of the adolescent. They highlight the difficulty of exploring this topic as family composition is so varied, and of course the age of siblings makes such a substantial difference to outcomes. However, their argument is that we will be missing so much in any understanding of family dynamics if the place of siblings is ignored. In one important chapter, they review interventions that have been designed to reduce sibling conflict, including a variety of parent training programmes. As they point out, the majority of these are aimed at parents of younger children, but there are a few that tackle adolescent–sibling conflict.

Lastly in this section I will mention grandparents. If siblings get little mention, this applies to an even greater extent to grandparents. Yet, as people live longer and have active lives into their 70s and 80s, there are more and more individuals playing an active role as grandparents. I personally know of many examples of young people turning to their grandparents for advice when the young person feels unable or unwilling to share problems with parents. This point links back to information management. Adolescents have a variety of ways of managing the flow of information to parents, and it is here that grandparents can play such a key role.

In my experience, however, grandparents often feel disempowered in their relations with young people. Older people think they do not understand "this generation" and believe that they may not be able to offer sensible advice. Of course, grandparents can play a significant role in families where there are young people. There is a real place for more information and support for the grandparent generation, so that they can play their part in reducing conflict and smoothing the path of young people during this stage.

Parenting teenagers

In the first chapter, I referred to the fact that the adolescent stage is one that creates anxiety, even dread, among parents. All the old certainties seem to disappear, and a range of challenges occur that were not evident in the earlier years. One important difference between parents and carers of teenagers and parents and carers of younger children has to do with uncertainty about the parenting role. For parents of young children, there is relatively little difficulty in defining roles and responsibilities. Yet this is not the case for parents and carers of teenagers, particularly in the face of so much change in attitudes, values and opportunities for young people. Part of this has to do with the changing nature of power and authority in the family. It is hard for adults to be clear what is expected of them in relation to monitoring and supervision, or in setting boundaries and limits for a 14-year-old or in regulating homework or screen time.

In fact, there is much in the literature that can act as a guide and that can assist parents and carers in day-to-day living with young people. I have discussed family environment and parenting styles earlier in this chapter, where ideas directly relevant to parenting are explored. In addition, I believe the STAGE framework is pertinent too. I referred to this framework in Chapter 1, and here is a good place for me to say more about it. I was once in front of an audience of parents, when one parent raised a hand and asked: "*What exactly is good parenting for a teenager?*"

It was this question that prompted me to develop the STAGE framework. My answer at that time was that we do know what is good parenting. I wanted to set out a simple framework that would be easy to remember, would be based in reputable research and would cover most of the key features of positive parenting for this age group.

I have set out this framework in more detail in my book *Why Won't My Teenager Talk to Me?* (Coleman, 2019). I also mentioned the framework in Chapter 1 when I described theories and models of adolescence. I called this framework STAGE because I wanted to emphasize that this is a stage in the life course. It is important for adults to recognize that things will not stay the same. The young person is going through a process of change, and this change will be going on all the time, even if it is not apparent at the time. I also called it STAGE as each letter stands for a key element of parenting.

S – represents significance. This is about the significance of parents. Parents of teenagers have an essential role to play and are as important as parents of younger children; they are just important in a different way.

T – stands for two-way communication. This emphasizes that communication goes both ways. Listening is as important as talking.

A – refers to authority. This has to be exercised in a different way for teenagers as it is in childhood.

G – stands for the generation gap. Parents and young people will have different values and attitudes. These should be recognized and accepted. Parents must be careful not to judge their young people based on their own experiences of growing up in a different era.

E – represents emotion. The emotions of both adults and young people can be very powerful and may interfere with good relationships. It is important to recognize this and to ensure that the emotions of both young people and parents are acknowledged and understood.

More details about the framework can be found in Coleman (2019, 2024). I can also recommend Hill's (2025) book, which outlines the Take 3 approach to supporting parents of young people. There is more about this later in this section.

There is much in the literature that can be used to guide parents. The subject of parenting styles has already been mentioned in this chapter, as has the topic of monitoring and supervision. As one further example, Grolnick et al. (2008) underline the importance of reciprocity in parent–adolescent relationships. They argue, just as I have, that for parents to understand the two-way nature of relationships is key to better parenting. They also identify three areas of importance – the type of control used, the importance of involvement and the provision of structure.

As far as control is concerned, they draw a distinction between behavioural and psychological control. They go on to argue that both these types of control can be either positive or negative, but this will depend on other factors. As they note, control can be helpful if it aims to create rules that are seen as fair and reasonable, and if it does not involve too much intrusion into the life of an adolescent. However, there is evidence that behavioural control leads to better outcomes than psychological control. This is because psychological control may take the form of withdrawal of love or care, or threats of this outcome if the young person does not do as they are told (Coleman, 2014). This can undermine a relationship. While it may seem like a useful tool for a parent at a time of conflict, it rarely achieves the aim of harmony in relationships and is likely to have long-term effects. This is well described in Kerr, Stattin and Engels' book *What Can Parents Do?* (2008).

Control is also very much age-dependent, so that what might be appropriate for a 13-year-old will not be appropriate for a 15-year-old. Parental involvement also has an important part to play. Parental involvement refers to the extent that parents are interested in, knowledgeable about and active in various elements of their teenagers' lives. However, the opposite side of the coin is over-involvement, or intrusiveness, which can be counter-productive and lead to constant tension between parent and young person.

The question of structure is an important one for any parent, and Grolnick et al. (2008) have set out a useful classification of six dimensions of structure that may underlie effective parenting for this age group. These are:

- Clear and consistent communication of expectations;
- Opportunities for young people to meet or exceed expectations;
- Predictability in parental behaviour;
- Feedback of information to young people;
- The provision of explanations and a rationale for any rules;
- Parental authority should be coupled with the taking of leadership roles in the home.

It is these ideas that underlie many of the parenting programmes that have been developed over the years as interest in support for parents of teenagers has grown. Together with colleagues, I reviewed parenting programmes in the early years of the 2000s (Roker and Coleman, 2007). A more recent review of parenting programmes may be found in Laver-Bradbury (2021). In this review, the author outlines some key decisions that need to be made before any programme can be introduced. These include the theoretical underpinning of the programme, any evaluation that has been carried out, the location and context of the delivery of the programme and the needs of the particular group of parents who may be the focus of the delivery.

Laver-Bradbury (2021) mentions many programmes – too numerous to catalogue here – that have been designed for various groups of parents. I want to highlight one programme that had its origins in my own work setting. This is the Take 3 programme created by Rosie Hill (2025). In this programme, Rosie helps parents of teenagers focus on their own behaviour and feelings as much as they do on the behaviour and feelings of the young person.

It is my belief that one of the most helpful approaches for parents of young people is to give them an understanding of brain development in this age group. Over the years, since 2014, I and my colleagues have developed a programme entitled "*My Teen Brain*" which we have run for literally dozens of groups of parents in Hertfordshire in the UK. This programme is described in my book *The Teacher and the Teenage Brain* (Coleman, 2021). Chapter 11 is entitled: "*The Teenage Brain for Parents: Engaging Families in New Knowledge*".

I have argued that this information can have a profound effect on parents' attitudes. Many parents say that this is completely new knowledge for them. As one example, they are not aware of the extent of the changes in the brain during the adolescent years. Furthermore, they have no knowledge of the impact of pruning and of the effect of the various hormones that impact on emotion regulation. They describe hearing about all this as a "light bulb" moment. As a result, many report that they will respond to their son or daughter in a different way now that they understand what is going on in the brain. This approach has enormous potential in the field of parent support. I am hopeful that it will become part of parenting programmes for parents of teenagers in the future.

Conclusion

In this chapter, I have covered a variety of topics concerned with adolescents and their families. I have outlined the ways in which families are changing, and I have described how these changes affect young people. The chapter covers ideas about autonomy, parenting styles and divorce and family breakdown. There is a discussion of culture and ethnicity, and the importance of these factors for the parenting of adolescents. I have added a blog I wrote about my work with parents of young people in China. There is a section on the roles of fathers, siblings and grandparents, and the chapter ends with a discussion of programmes which offer support and information for parents of this age group.

Chapter 9

The peer group

Introduction

Peer groups are not unique to adolescence, nor do they first appear in these years. However, they do have a special place in adolescence, and in this period of the lifespan they do receive a lot of attention from the adult world. This is partly because there is a sense of threat when groups of young people gather together, and partly because much of the negative stereotyping of adolescents is linked to behaviour in peer groups.

In this chapter, various aspects of friendship and the peer group will be considered, together with other social networks and settings in which young people meet and interact. The use of digital technologies has become an integral part of the social world of adolescence, and so this will be an important feature of this chapter.

> They're like my main social circle. If I want to talk about anything to anyone, it's going to be my friends before my family, right? It's like debating, but we have a lot of different opinions. And I think, like talking them through and sort of seeing the other side, sometimes it's quite good as well.
>
> (Young woman, aged 17)

In one of the classics of the literature on adolescence, Dunphy (1972) first wrote about peer groups following his study of Australian youth. He suggested that youth groups form in society when families or kinship groups – groups we have little choice in joining – cannot provide the adolescent with the social skills or the roles they need in order to function in the wider society.

Dunphy maintained that participation in youth groups was necessary in order for the young person to become self-regulating and for the construction of an adult identity. In this way, adolescents become embedded in a complex network of relationships which includes best friends, close friends, acquaintances, peer

DOI: 10.4324/9781032640433-9

groups and crowds. These groups all allow the young person some degree of choice in whether to join or not. In this chapter, I will start with a section on the social brain. Then there will be sections on the genesis of adolescent social relationships, the dynamics of friendship and of peer groups, the interactions between families and friends, the role of the virtual world and finally the problem of isolation and rejection.

The social brain

In Chapter 2, where I discussed the brain and its development during adolescence, I did not refer to the social brain. At the outset of the chapter on friendship and the peer group, this seems a good place to outline some of the key features of the social brain. A good review may be found in Galvan (2017, chapter 7). As Galvan notes, this is not simply one site in the brain, but many sites which network together. These include parts of the prefrontal cortex, as well as areas that control emotion processing and vision.

Emotion recognition is an essential skill necessary to manage social relationships. Recognition of emotion in the human face may at first sight appear to be a very basic skill. However, it is an important aspect of the ability to stay safe in social situations, to manage conflict and to respond appropriately when with other people. Knowing when someone is angry from the expression on their face is a good example of such a skill. To be able to do this successfully often determines the outcome of an interaction.

Research has highlighted three key findings concerning the recognition of emotion. The first is that there is a specific area in the brain dedicated to facial recognition. This is known as the fusiform face area. This is in the temporal lobe of the cortex, located at the back of the brain with close links to the visual cortex. We know that this area plays a vital role in face recognition, since when it is damaged the individual has great difficulty in recognizing faces. The fusiform face area also has links to other areas which play a role in the interpretation of faces. All these areas can be shown to mature as the adolescent grows older.

The second finding is that the recognition of emotion becomes progressively more sophisticated. While some emotions such as happiness and sadness can be recognized by children as young as three or four, the recognition of more complex emotions only becomes possible during the teenage years. Emotions which show in the face such as surprise or fear are harder to interpret. The ability to recognize these complex emotions only develops slowly with age.

The third finding is that, in young people, the amygdala plays a key role in emotion recognition. A number of studies have shown that in adolescents the amygdala is much more engaged in facial recognition than it is in adults. As a result, young people are much more likely to be influenced by their own emotions when recognizing emotions in others. This, of course, may lead to confusion or error in recognition. Some writers have called the amygdala "*the agent of change in adolescent neural networks*" (Galvan, 2017). This means that the amygdala is playing a greater role in the development of social skills, allowing emotion to be more influential in young people than in adults.

Perspective-taking

Perspective-taking is an important social skill. We cannot form or maintain social relationships without being able to see situations from another person's point of view. Crone (2017) makes the point that perspective-taking is an essential skill for the development of autonomy. Autonomy involves the ability to think for oneself and to behave independently. This requires awareness of different beliefs and attitudes and the ability to choose between them.

In Chapter 4, I referred to mentalizing. This is the process where we think about the thoughts of other people. While children are able to recognize the thoughts of others at a simple level, more complex perspective-taking only begins to be available during adolescence. As an example, social perspective-taking involves not only being able to ascribe complex emotions to other people, but it also involves being able to see things from a third person perspective. A good example would be the realization that the behaviour of one friend may impact the feelings of another friend, even when one's own feelings are different from both these individuals (Blakemore, 2019).

Social evaluation

The term *social evaluation* is used to describe the way people judge or evaluate themselves as they interact with others in social situations. This process has links with the notion of *adolescent egocentrism*, which I discussed in Chapter 4. Young people slowly begin to be able to think about what others think about them. At the same time, they begin to be concerned with questions of identity and appearance. This leads to intense self-consciousness, and what has been called *preoccupation with the self*.

Research has tackled the question of self-consciousness in many different ways. One example used brain imaging. In this study, young people were told that, while they were in the scanner, they would be observed via a video link by other young people. These young people reported more embarrassment and greater activation in areas of the brain involved with anxiety than adult participants.

Another similar study placed young people and adults behind a one-way screen. On the other side of the screen was a corridor where people were constantly walking by. The participants knew that the onlookers could see them, but they could not see the onlookers. An area of the brain close to the area related to physical pain was activated in such situations. For this reason, embarrassment has been called "social pain". Interestingly the adults adjusted to the situation, and activation in these brain regions calmed down. For adolescents, however, this activation reached high levels and continued for much longer (Blakemore, 2019).

From what I have said, it can be seen that the maturation of the social brain leads to greater skills in such things as emotion recognition, perspective-taking and so on. These skills are what underpins the ability to create friendships and to manage the larger peer group. It should also be noted that, for a time, these skills also lead to some challenges. To have a constant concern about how you look to others can be inhibiting and can lead to obstacles in social relationships.

The genesis of adolescent social relationships

Two theoretical notions can be helpful in understanding the genesis of social relationships in adolescence. These are attachment theory and social identity theory. Both of these theories give some insight into why friendship and the peer group assume greater significance in adolescence than in childhood. As far as attachment theory is concerned, psychoanalysts have argued for nearly a century that adolescence is a time of gradual separation from parents and a turning towards the wider social environment. While parents gradually fulfil less of the individual's emotional needs, friends step forward to fill the gap. As part of this process, the attachment patterns learnt very early in childhood will be transferred to the close friends and intimate relationships formed during adolescence (Gale, 2021).

> Like my really close friend, we really get into it. We're sitting down, just the two of us, and we're talking about different practices, like, what makes us happy, what makes us sad, and then what we enjoy, like, really talking and opening up.
>
> (Young woman, aged 17)

Attachment theorists believe that people have mental models of relationships, models that are learnt in the earliest contact between the mother and the infant.

These are known as attachment representations, and as Carlson and colleagues (2004) note: "These representations carry forward previous social experience and provide structure for subsequent encounters with the world" (page 67). The behaviour of adolescents with their friends illustrates this process. The key elements of such contacts include security and stability. Another is proximity-seeking, illustrated by the need of young people to remain in constant contact with their friends, made even easier through the internet. Attachment theory argues that the shape and texture of young people's relationships with their friends are based on earlier attachment experiences (Cotterell, 2007).

Turning now to social identity theory, this arose initially as a result of research into prejudice and stereotyping. Brown and Larson (2009), as well as other commentators, have talked of a group identity, and of the interpersonal benefits that may be derived from a shared world view and a shared set of attitudes and opinions. This is especially true when individuals are experiencing major transitions, where they feel vulnerable in respect of their identity, or where they feel under threat from other groups.

In the case of adolescence, this threat may be perceived as coming from adults or from other groups of young people. It has been suggested that the value of belonging to a group is dependent on its status relative to other groups (Cotterell, 2007). Those who are vulnerable for one reason or another make distinctions between in-groups and out-groups. They then denigrate the out-group or find fault with the out-group, thus boosting their own status. These notions have a long history in the sociology of groups, and it is not difficult to see how these ideas can be applied to adolescent social relationships.

> We'll go up out, like, we play football, and then come back to someone's house, watch the football in the evening. Then we'll have a few drinks, play darts and stuff like that. So, or often we'll be watching other sporting events, like boxing, ok? Or Formula 1. Usually, like, there'll be girls around, like our girlfriends and stuff, we're all quite quiet, ok?
>
> (Young man, aged 17)

In terms of the process of friendship formation, it is usually during early to mid-adolescence that personal needs and social pressures direct young people toward at least one friendship group. Research shows that 75% of 13-year-olds are likely to belong to a friendship group, with a small number having only one friend, and about 15% having no friends at all (Brown and Larson, 2009). Although friends typically live in the same neighbourhood, and are similar in socio-economic background, friendships sometimes cross boundaries in terms of gender, race and age. Friendships frequently begin in school, while time outside school can strengthen those bonds. Some individuals find it difficult to establish out-of-school friendships because they lack confidence or the necessary social skills.

> Something that I really enjoy right now is spending time at my local youth club. I came to know about them through CAMHS, and ever since then, like, taking time to meet new people, and make new friends, and dive into activities has become part of my life, which I cherish sincerely. I think I have really grown in confidence, and become more determined, thanks to the tireless encouragement of the staff here. It makes me realize how important youth clubs are to our community.
>
> (Young woman, aged 17)

The dynamics of friendship and the peer group

The manner in which social relationships operate through the adolescent age range is of great interest. Before looking more closely at this, it is important to distinguish between friendships and relationships with the wider age cohort. One distinction that is widely used is that between crowds and cliques. This distinction is outlined in Brown and Larson (2009) and in Steinberg (2023). Cliques are small groups – usually between 3 and 10 people – defined by activities and shared interests. Crowds on the other hand are larger groups, defined by age and class in school or neighbourhood. These groupings are also known as peer groups.

> Yes, tight, quite tight. There are three of us in this small circle. But the wider circle, about 10 or 15 I suppose, but they serve different purposes. With the inner circle I will walk up to them, talk about anything, have lunch with them. The others not so much. Like, I was with a couple of girls of the outer circle groups, and they were, like, "Isabel, knock on the teacher's door and run away, and then go up to the teacher and say something really funny". And I'm, like, no thanks, I'll leave that to you.
>
> (Young woman, aged 16)

Of course, this picture is too simple, since within the peer group there will be sub-groups, often given particular names which shift with the context. The distinction between the small intimate group and the larger crowd is useful, and here I will first consider friendship, and then move on to look at the dynamics of the larger group.

There has been much discussion in the literature friends during adolescence. A useful starting point is the work of Mendelson and Aboud (1999), who identified six dimensions of friendship. These are:

- Companionship;
- A reliable alliance;
- Help;
- Intimacy;
- Self-validation;
- Emotional security.

As noted by Cotterell (2007), these attributes describe key elements of friendship, such as being available, providing someone to share things with, being loyal and trustworthy and offering support in times of difficulty. Cotterell argues that there are two factors which underlie any categorization of the functions of friendship. These are, firstly, that relationships with those of the same age offer a route for integration into a social network, and secondly that they offer reassurance of worth through validation by one's age cohort. These ideas can be subsumed under a general notion of belongingness, since they describe social processes that include "fitting in" and "feeling accepted". They also include social identification and well-being.

> I've had some struggle with making friends in the past. I was trying hard to be friends with these people, it was, like, in Year 7 and Year 8, and then I had some other friends, and they were getting into trouble, and I didn't really want to be friends with them. And then, like, Year 10, I found these guys, and it's been a very positive experience.
>
> (Young man, aged 15)

Many studies have shown that those who become friends share common interests. Steinberg (2023) points out that motivation towards school, interest in a particular sport of hobby, orientation towards teenage culture or involvement in anti-social behaviour are all dimensions which might differentiate friendship groups. Today it is also the case that involvement in particular online groups or interests in gaming or other on-line activities may well be factors that influence friendship choice.

Popularity is, of course, highly valued by everyone, but it is of particular significance during adolescence. Having a friendship group and being accepted within that group are factors which relate to self-esteem and to the development of a coherent identity. The chief determinant of popularity is whether the individual is socially skilled or not. Those who are popular act appropriately in the eyes of their peers, are able to recognize the needs of others and are confident without being conceited (Steinberg, 2023). However, these are generalities, and there are many routes to popularity. Most studies highlight the fact that there are differences between boys and girls in the attributes that contribute to popularity, and within any one gender there are a number of factors that play their part. I discuss the impact of social media and the on-line world in a section later in this chapter.

> Social media, that poses an issue for people. Because they're behind a screen they'll say more than they would in person. So, in person someone might say something that's hurtful, but it's to their face. So, I'd say it's more people saying it behind their backs, and then nattering at school to each other, but they don't necessarily know who it is. The person's doing it behind the screen, so there's no way they can necessarily do something about this person.
>
> (Young man, aged 17)

Various studies have looked at attributes such as risk-taking, rejection of school values, sporting ability and other things that appear to be associated with popularity. Allen and colleagues (2014) followed a group of adolescents through high school, finding that those who engaged in risk-taking at age 13 were more popular at age 15, but that this popularity did not last. This study highlights the shifting nature of peer relationships at this stage. In Foulkes' book *Coming of Age* (2024), many of the interviewees remembered situations at school where there were high status groups such as the "cool kids" and a feeling of envy at wanting to be part of such a group but knowing that one could not aspire to be included.

Turning now to the dynamics of the larger peer group, one of the key themes here has to do with the question of peer influence, or peer pressure. Are all adolescents susceptible to peer pressure – or is this true only of a minority? The answer is closely linked to the issue of social acceptance. Where the need for acceptance is high, peer influence will be more powerful. There are two variables that affect the need for acceptance: one is age and the other has to do with individual differences. As far as age is concerned, studies show that conformity to group norms or influence is at its height in early to middle adolescence – from about the age of 12 to the age of 15. It is at this time that questions of acceptance or rejection loom largest in the minds of young people, and thus they are more susceptible to the pressures that stem from peers (Cotterell, 2007).

> I was in a friendship group a couple of years ago, and it was just so toxic, then it just became, like, we didn't really like each other. So, I'm like, if you're making me angry, then I'll tell you to stop. And if you're asking me to do things that I don't really want to do, then I feel like, no, I'm not doing that. I don't mind confronting people, like, you're doing things I don't like. And I'll be, like, stop, and just cut people out of my life.
>
> (Young woman, aged 17)

As they grow older, adolescents are more able to make up their own minds and to stand up to pressure that might originate from the group. However, it is also the case that individual differences affect susceptibility to peer influence. Some young people will be more autonomous than others, and personality factors play their part in determining acceptance or rejection of peer influence. One further factor that is significant is the degree of support from the family. More will be said about this later, but it is apparent that those who receive low levels of support from parents and other adults are likely to be more open to influence from peers (Steinberg, 2023).

Brown (1999) makes the point that there are different types of peer influence. In his view, direct pressure is relatively rare, but other types of influence include:

- Modelling (where young people seek to emulate the behaviour of others);
- Structuring of opportunities (where peers provide an arena for certain types of behaviour, such as taking drugs at a party);
- Normative regulation (where peers work together to define the norms they are comfortable with, such as working out what is right or wrong in sexual behaviour).

Brown also emphasizes the fact that influence works both ways. As has been noted, relationships are reciprocal, so that adolescents are both recipients and producers of influence. This leads to the important question of whether peer groups are self-selecting. Are those with common interests drawn together, or are peer groups agents of socialization, exerting influence and changing the behaviour of those who wish to belong? Research indicates that both selection and socialization are at work in a variety of different areas (Cotterell, 2007). This process can occur in a range of activities and behaviours, including school engagement, sports and hobbies, antisocial behaviour, the use of substances and so on.

Adolescents who drink or smoke are more likely than others to choose friends who do the same, but similarly spending time with such friends increases the likelihood that the individual will take up these behaviours (Ennett et al., 2006). The question is often asked as to whether the peer group encourages certain behaviours, especially when it comes to anti-social behaviour. Many years ago, I wrote an article entitled "*Who leads who astray*?" (Coleman, 1979). In this, I argued that influence goes both ways. It is true that some peer groups have the power to encourage certain behaviours, especially if individuals are susceptible to such influence. Yet, on the other hand, there are individuals who have the personality or ability to influence the group as a whole, either towards positive or less positive behaviours.

> I think my friends are good at, like, knowing my boundaries. I think they're quite good like that. They wouldn't ask me to do something that I didn't want to do. They're very regarding of all my boundaries.
>
> (Young woman, aged 16)

Parents and peers

Friendships are based on a very different set of structural relationships than those with parents. Friendships are more symmetrical, involve reciprocity and are evolutionary through adolescence. While friendships are important to younger children, there is a change at the beginning of adolescence, with peers assuming greater salience, and taking up more leisure time outside the family. During the adolescent years, obvious alterations take place in relationship patterns and in social contexts. As has already been noted, friends become companions, and providers of advice, support and endorsement. Friends become models of behaviour and sources of comparative information concerning personal qualities and social skills.

Relationships with parents alter also, as we have explored in the previous chapter. There are moves to greater equality and more opportunity for negotiation and discussion. The central question in considering family and peers has to do with whether parents or friends exercise the greater influence during this stage of life. In early writings, this was known as "the parent–peer issue". This is a matter of great significance for parents, and of course for society in general. The idea that parents lose influence over their children, and that young people are in the business of creating a world apart from the family, with different values, is certain to raise anxiety among parents and carers.

Many years ago, James Coleman wrote a book entitled *The Adolescent Society* (1961). In this, he gave prominence to the idea that young people are likely to develop a set of values that are in direct contradiction to the values of adult society. Since that time, this idea has surfaced in many different ways. Indeed, the notion that in some way adolescence is all about overturning the old order and setting up challenges to the established way of doing things is as old as any commentary on adolescence. After all, this suggestion was central to the ideas about youth put forward by Plato and other Greek writers.

> My friends keep me going. So, without them, I don't know where I'd be to be honest. They're not always perfect, and it's not anyway what my parents want to see in a friend, but for me, like, they're amazing.
>
> (Young man, aged 17)

In terms of parenting, this anxiety will be expressed by fears about unsuitable friends and worries about who the young person will be associating with after school. For parents, the notion that their influence will be waning during these years and that they will have less and less influence as time goes on is, not unnaturally, something that is likely to cause much anxiety. However, these ideas are not borne out by the research on adolescent friendships. It is clear, firstly, that the idea of an either-or situation is far too simple. It is not a question of whether parents or peers are more influential, but rather a case of both being influential in different circumstances.

It is also important to note that research evidence indicates that peers fill a vacuum when parents are not engaged or are not involved with their sons and daughters. It is only when parents are not playing a role that friends assume greater significance and may in such situations become more influential. Let me first consider the either-or question. The evidence shows that in general parents and carers remain important in future-orientated domains such as education and career choice, while friends are more influential where social dilemmas, fashion and leisure are concerned (Coleman, 2014; Hendry, 2015).

Some studies have shown that adolescents are more influenced by parents in core values (Steinberg, 2023), while others have argued that in many situations young people will in fact consult both parents and peers before making a decision (Cotterell, 2007). In terms of whether parents or peers are seen as more supportive, the evidence is clear that as young people move through adolescence, friends assume greater and greater significance. However, even though friends become more important, most take the view that, in the great majority of cases, friends never surpass parents (Meeus, 2019: Steinberg, 2023).

It is easy to see how young people would turn to friends for support. Friends are less likely than parents to coerce, criticize or lecture. Friends are more likely to give each other personal validity when it comes to making difficult decisions. Nevertheless, virtually every piece of research that has been carried out underlines the major role that parents and carers play in affecting outcomes for young people. One good example of this can be found in Liza Catan's (2004) report based on 19 different studies which were part of the British Economic and Social Research Council (ESRC) Youth, Citizenship and Social Change programme. As Catan says:

> Studies in the programme moved towards a view of families of origin as the co-ordinating site for many different types of resources central to young people's futures, both economic and material, and social/cultural, as in the studies which highlighted the importance of parental aspirations, parental involvement in children's education, and support for school and college .... For the majority some level of family support lasts throughout their twenties, and provides fundamental personal and material resources, without which the transition to adulthood is highly risky and stressful.
>
> (pp. 24 and 25)

These words have become even more pertinent since this report was written. Chapters included in Hagell's book *Changing Adolescence* (2012) show that over time parents have become even more significant in the provision of support for adolescents and young adults. This trend has received further documentation in the work of Meeus (2019).

Let me turn to the question of whether friends fill a vacuum when parents are not available. The discussion about this notion has been framed in terms of whether support from one relationship can compensate for a lack of support in another relationship. This question can only be understood if a social network approach is taken, as for example in the work of Cotterell (2007). Here a number of studies are documented where low support from parents led to greater involvement with peer-led activities and a higher level of anti-social behaviour. It is also the case that some studies have illustrated the point that even when young people are involved with anti-social friendship groups, having support from parents will cause them to be less susceptible to negative peer group influence (Walker-Barnes and Mason, 2004).

Parents and peers cannot really be looked at in isolation. Each needs to be considered as part of the inter-connected social world of the adolescent. Most of the characteristics that young people bring to their friendships and peer relationships will be learnt in the home. This pattern continues, with parental behaviour and attitudes having an impact on the way young people behave in this sphere. One example that illustrates this is the finding that parenting style affects friendship choice. Those with indifferent parents choose friends who are indifferent to adult values, and those with indulgent parents select friends who fit into the indulgent model (Steinberg, 2023).

It should be noted that young people also influence their parents. Influence goes both ways. Some adolescents will opt for friendship groups that mirror family values, while others will choose friends who annoy or irritate their parents. Some may even select friends who are the exact opposite of what their parents would wish for! As in all situations, parents and young people interact in a reciprocal manner, and this is as true in friendship choice as it is in other domains (Gavazzi, 2011).

Rejection and isolation

In view of the importance of friendship and the peer group, it is well to consider the implications for young people of being solitary, lonely or rejected by the social group which surrounds them. There are a couple of questions to be addressed:

- Does it matter if a young person is without friends?
- Do lonely or rejected individuals share particular personality characteristics?

Loneliness is an emotion which is experienced by everyone at some time. To have experienced loneliness is not to say that the individual is without friends. Everyone spends time alone, and during adolescence there are many positive aspects of solitude. To have private time is important, and opportunities for reflection can allow for growth and well-being. Difficulties arise when solitude is unwanted, and when the individual seeks company but is rebuffed. It is painful to lose friends, or to find that friendship is elusive. In this section, I will focus on situations of unwanted solitude, leading to isolation and rejection.

Looking at the impact of being without friends, there is very little research on this topic. Yet it is one that concerns parents and young people alike, and it deserves greater attention. Research by Ryan (2001) showed that approximately 15% of young adolescents are without friends. It is likely that this is a very mixed group, with many different reasons for being without friends. There are undoubtedly some who go through adolescence as solitary individuals but who cope well with this situation. Among them will be those who get support from other sources, such as a sibling or other family member.

> I'm having a bit of an issue on that at the moment. About friends. Like, I feel I can't talk to them, right? I don't know, maybe I'm masking? They come to me for help, and so I feel I need to help them. But then I feel it's one-sided, because I know they can't help me.
>
> (Young person, aged 16)

A proportion of these individuals will go on to become more socially engaged as they mature. Another group here will be those who are withdrawn, who have a deficit in social skills or experience social anxiety (Hadwin and Magdalena, 2021). Lastly, there will be those who are who are unpopular due to aggressive or inappropriate behaviour (Fairchild, 2021). The impact of being without friends will differ for each of these groups. It is important to emphasize that not all adolescents who lack friends will be damaged or disadvantaged by this situation. Having said this, research findings do, in the main, report negative consequences for those who are rejected by their peers. Steinberg (2023) lists a number of studies showing rejection to be associated with depression, anxiety, low self-esteem and poor academic performance.

Turning now to the characteristics of isolated or rejected adolescents, there are different sub-groups here. These will need to be discussed separately. Before doing so, a general point can be made about age. Age is an important variable here, since loneliness is experienced more often in early adolescence. As young people grow, they develop strategies to cope with loneliness, and report fewer low moods as a result of being on their own. My own work, published in *Relationships in Adolescence* (1974), was one of the first studies to document this. The developing cognitive abilities of the young person may be valuable in helping to manage solitude. It could also be that for the older individual, solitude is useful for self-reflection, emotion regulation and coping.

In considering the characteristics of isolated or rejected individuals, most writers draw a distinction between those who are withdrawn and those who are aggressive. Studies by Crick and colleagues (e.g., Crick and Dodge, 1996) have shown that unpopular aggressive young people are more likely than others to think that other people's behaviour is deliberately aggressive, even when it is not. This attribute has come to be known as *hostile attributional bias*, and it plays a central role in the behaviour of adolescents who are rejected by their peers.

When aggression is mentioned, it is most often boys who are in the frame. However, girls can be just as aggressive, only in a different form. This is often called *social aggression*, involving verbal bullying, trying to cause unhappiness and manipulating social situations to upset or aggravate others. These young people differ from those who are unpopular and withdrawn. The withdrawn group consists of individuals who are likely to be anxious and uncertain of how to behave when they are with others of the same age. Their lack of confidence and low self-esteem makes others feel uncomfortable, and they become easy targets for bullying. They are often especially sensitive to rejection, which in turn makes the situation worse.

Bullying is an important consideration in any outline of rejected or isolated adolescents. This is a topic which has been the subject of considerable research. Foulkes (2024) has a chapter on this topic, and Steinberg (2023) also reviews the literature. He makes the point that bullying varies from country to country and points out that bullying is likely to be higher in countries with greater income inequality. It is also the case that bullying is defined differently in different countries, as is evidenced by Eslea and colleagues (2003).

> School was very annoying, so, I got beaten up multiple times. It wasn't very nice. Sometimes nothing happened, and they did very little towards me, getting beaten up. Sometimes my parents had to go into school, and maybe even call the police, because they would do nothing about it.
>
> (Young man, aged 17)

As far as the characteristics of bullies and victims are concerned, research shows that victims of bullying tend to be depressed and lonely more than others and to have lower self-esteem and more limited social skills than their peers (Hawker and Boulton, 2000). One important study looked at victims of bullying in 48 countries and linked the amount of bullying with suicide attempts (Koyanagi et al., 2019). The evidence here showed a clear link between being bullied and suicidal behaviour. In a group of 12–15-year-olds in a range of countries, it was evident that suicide attempts increased as a function of how frequently the young people were bullied. This is a stark reminder of how damaging bullying can be to the victims.

Bullies on the other hand, while also having social deficits, differ in significant respects. They tend to be more aggressive and to display fewer pro-social behaviours such as cooperation and the ability to share. They are more likely to be at risk for later problem behaviours. Some have argued that in fact bullies do not lack social skills but rather use bullying to obtain social goals that they see as important or useful to them. As Scholte and van Aken (2006) put it: "These bullies may not lack social skills, since they can accurately interpret social cues, but they use socially deviant strategies to obtain their goals" (page 188). It is important to note that there is a small group who are both bullies and victims. It is probable that these young people have more problems than those who are either bullies or victims (Foulkes, 2024).

The virtual world

As I have noted, the involvement of young people in the on-line world is pervasive and is clearly a highly significant feature of life in adolescence. It is also the case that this is a fast-moving picture, so that by the time this is published, new digital platforms and different activities will be available. There has been much discussion of the threats and opportunities offered by the digital world. These have been sufficiently rehearsed elsewhere (see Hayman and Coleman, 2016). It is useful, however, to consider the characteristics of what is known as the "net generation", and I will review the issues raised by having a generation of multi-media producers as well as consumers. Some writers (e.g., Talmud and Mesch, 2020) have talked of the "bedroom culture" and the effects of this on peer relationships.

One argument here concerns what is known as the displacement hypothesis. Does the intensive use of new media lead to time displacement or to activity displacement? In other words, does the involvement in digital activity lead to less social life outside the bedroom, and does it also lead to the possibility that young people have less time for sports or other activities outside the home? Most commentators reject these arguments. It is claimed that the internet facilitates a variety of activities, including many that are peer-oriented, so that such activities reinforce existing relationships. One example of this is that more games are being created that involve relationship building, and most commentators believe that adolescents integrate the tools of the internet into their off-line worlds (Talmud and Mesch, 2020).

Turning now to the idea of time displacement, Talmud and Mesch (2020) put it like this: "Taken together, the most consistent finding was … the absence of any evidence for the time displacement hypothesis. Indeed, internet users formed a group of adolescents more likely to participate in social and extra-curricular activities than non-users" (page 59). Other writers agree with this, although it does depend on how the internet is being used, and whether that activity is linked with activities in the off-line world (Vanucci et al., 2020).

I have discussed the effect of social media on mental health in Chapter 7. As far as peer relationships are concerned, most studies appear to support the idea that the use of social media facilitates friendships and widens the social network. However, this does very much depend on the personal resources that the young person brings to the table. Steinberg put is like this: "... social media sites are a context in which the socially rich get richer and the socially poor get poorer" (2023, page 203). This phrase underlines the point that those who are resilient and have good social skills get a lot out of the extra affordances provided by the internet. On the other hand, those who have low levels of support from their social networks may experience social media as a world that reinforces worries and anxieties (Mikami et al., 2019).

Conclusion

In this chapter, I have outlined in some detail about the social brain, and I have considered the genesis of friendship during this period of life. It is clear that social relationships assume greater importance as young people move through adolescence. In many ways, friends and the peer group offer support, endorsement and recognition. The world of the peer group is also key as a location in which adolescents are able to learn essential social skills. While many believe that the peer group becomes the most important influence during adolescence, we have seen that parents continue to play a vital role in many areas. Key adults can offer support at times of difficulty and remain influential when it comes to education and career. The internet has in some ways enhanced social relationships, allowing for wider and richer experiences. However, there are limits to the positive impact of the internet, and for those with low levels of support elsewhere the virtual world can have serious negative consequences.

Chapter 10

Anti-social behaviour

Introduction

It is a regrettable fact that adolescence is closely associated in the public mind with ideas about anti-social behaviour. It would appear that this has been the case for as long as history has been recorded. We know this from writers in ancient Greece, to the poet John Keats who wrote of adolescents as having *"the character undecided"* and Shakespeare who wrote about youth "*wronging the ancientry*". This is unfortunate, as it has implications for young people, and for their relationships with adults. In general, young people are sensitive to how they are perceived by adults, especially in public spaces, and it is easy to see how the behaviour of a few can have an impact on the majority who are law-abiding. However, there are, of course, young people who do get involved in criminal behaviour, and it is to this topic that I will turn here.

Closely associated with the stereotype of adolescence as creating or causing trouble in one way or another, there is the perception in the public mind that youth crime is on an upward trend. While this was true in the 1980s and 1990s, the situation today is very different. As Steinberg (2023) notes, rates of youth offending in North America are at their lowest level since the 1970s. This change can be seen not just in the USA, but across European countries as reported by Koops and Castro (2006). This may seem contrary to expectations, especially since there has been such a focus on knife crime among young people. This element of criminality remains a small element of the overall picture, although clearly a very worrying one.

Turning now to the age distribution, offending behaviour is not equally distributed among different age groups. This is sometimes known as the age–crime curve and has been remarkably stable over time and is seen in almost all countries (Case, 2025). This curve illustrates the fact that criminal behaviour is seen most commonly among males between the ages of 16 and 20, the peak age being 18. For young women, the peak age is 15. After these

DOI: 10.4324/9781032640433-10

ages, the incidence of offending diminishes as the individual moves into adulthood. The question arises as to why offending is so closely associated with the adolescent stage of life? Why does it decrease markedly as young people reach adulthood?

Theories relating to anti-social behaviour in adolescence

Many theories have been put forward to explain this phenomenon. Emler and Reicher (1995) argued that processes in the peer group played an important part. They put forward the notion of "reputation management", by which they meant the necessity to fit in, or outshine, those who were perceived to be the figures with high status. Others writers (Pitts, 2008; Stoddard et al., 2013) look to the social circumstances, such as poverty and deprivation, as a key explanation for offending. They argue that in these circumstances parents are less able to monitor their adolescents, and that where high levels of deprivation exist, the fabric of neighbourhoods breaks down, leading to the use of drugs and criminal activity among adults.

> So, it's like, if I was in this alleyway, and it was really dark, I've got this lanyard, so if anything was to happen here, say if I said there was someone coming to try and attack me, I would pull this, I would yank this, and it would automatically start flashing. … So, if my friend, was like, trying to rob a shop, and I go: "No, I'm not doing that" And they go: "Yes, let's rob this place, and my friends, they're not good people, and then you have an option, you don't ever come back to this group".
>
> (Young man, aged 15)

Linked to these social circumstances is another important factor seen in recent times, which is the availability of weapons, including guns and knives. As these weapons become more easily accessed by young people, this increases the likelihood that violence will play a part in crime or enable violence to occur more easily. Most writers agree that maturation and age play a central role in the trajectory of youth crime. Writers such as Schaeffer and Uggen (2009) argue that desistance from offending is a function of the processes involved in becoming an adult and assuming adult roles. Having a stable relationship, being in employment and parenthood all contribute to a developmental process operating against involvement in criminal behaviour.

The evidence from longitudinal studies of offending behaviour has given us important insights into the trajectories of this type of behaviour. What is clear is that the earlier offending occurs, the more likely it is that the individual will become a chronic offender and will experience difficulties into adulthood (Case, 2025). One finding that has greatly influenced thinking in this field is that proposed by Moffit (2006). This proposal suggests that there are two groups of young offenders. The two groups are:

- Life-course persistent offenders;
- Adolescence-limited offenders.

On the one hand, there appear a very small number who display serious problem behaviour from an early age – these are the life-course persistent offenders. They account for a majority of the crime committed during the adolescent years. These children, who are predominantly boys, demonstrate aggressive behaviour, are hyperactive and struggle with relationships from an early age. On the other hand, the adolescence-limited group, as the name implies, start their offending behaviour when they reach adolescence and are the ones who are most likely to desist from crime when they reach adulthood.

One excellent example of the research that has underpinned these ideas is that of Stattin and Magnusson (1996). These Swedish researchers showed that males who were designated as life- course persistent represented 14% of the sample who were at some time involved in anti-social behaviour. However, this group accounted for approximately 60% of the crimes committed by the whole cohort, so it is clear that they are the most serious offenders. These findings have implications for interventions, something I will discuss later in the chapter.

Some researchers have suggested that there are other groups of offenders who do not fit into this neat categorization. There may be those who are troublesome in early childhood but do not go on to get involved in anti-social behaviour as adolescents. Alternatively, some young people may start a criminal career as adolescents and then go to be offenders as adults. Another argument is that no one is really a life-course persistent offender, since virtually all adults desist from crime by mid-life. In spite of these arguments, there is no doubt that the basic distinction proposed by Moffit (2006) has remained a central element in our understanding of anti-social behaviour.

As will have been apparent, the longitudinal studies referred to above concentrated on males as the main focus of their attention. Many writers have, however, asked the question as to whether similar trajectories can be identified for females as have been described for males (Fontaine et al., 2009). This question poses significant difficulties, partly because the numbers are so much smaller for females than for males, and partly because early problematic behaviour among girls and young women is not so easily described or classified.

> Like I've got this one friend, she's had mental health problems, and she actually tried to commit suicide one time, and she picked up her knife and she scratched it really hard, and we are trying to calm her down. We'd get the police involved. So, then I made the call, I called the police, and the police went to her house, and then they came to get her in school.
>
> (Young man, aged 14)

In a commentary by Case (2025), he notes that most authors who have discussed the topic of female anti-social behaviour tend to focus on family dysfunction or sexual dysfunction. However, there has also been an interest in the role of the peer group for females, with some arguing that offending among young women is primarily a social phenomenon (Moffitt, 2006). A major advance among criminologists who look at this question from a feminist point of view has been to point to the links between young women's offending and their victimization experiences. Studies of young women in the criminal justice system consistently indicate high rates of exploitation and childhood trauma (Wroe and Pearce, 2022). While the links between these variables are still not well understood, the victimization experiences of young women are clearly a very important area for further research.

Risk factors in anti-social behaviour

The points made above on the victimization of young women takes me on to a review of risk factors in anti-social behaviour. The first topic to be considered here is the role of the family. Every study on this subject has identified the family as being highly significant as a risk factor for anti-social behaviour. Commentators have noted four ways in which the family may be associated with this type of behaviour in young people. The first is neglect. When parents spend too little time with their children, they may fail to provide the boundaries and structure necessary, or they may fail to monitor and supervise in an appropriate manner. Furthermore, if parents are uninvolved or uninterested in the lives of their sons and daughters, this leaves a gap which can be filled by the peer group.

A second possibility is that conflict in the home may lead to children witnessing violence and aggression between parents, or children being the recipient of harsh or erratic punishment. Numerous studies, going right back to those carried out many years ago (e.g., West and Farrington, 1977), have provided supportive evidence for this conclusion.

A third variable to be considered is the behaviour or values of the parents themselves. Thus, for example, Hagell and Newburn's (1996) study of persistent offenders showed that one of the most significant predictors of whether a young person will acquire a criminal record is whether they have a parent who has been convicted. The final variable of the four mentioned here is what has been known as the "disruption paradigm" (Loeber and Stouthamer-Loeber, 1986). By this is meant that neglect, and conflict may arise in the family because of other factors such as bereavement, illness or the absence of one family member. Again, there is a wealth of evidence to support this argument. However, as many writers have pointed out, it is not the event itself which is associated with anti-social behaviour. Rather, it is the consequences that flow from the event, such as parental neglect or domestic violence, which will be significant here (Hill and Maugham, 2001).

> I think a lot of parents, they send us out and go, yeah, go out with your friends. I don't think that is, personally, right. I say because they're 14, they're still teenagers. They can get themselves into trouble, because they can go out end up robbing a place, like doing a shopping centre, and then running off, not coming back. It's trouble man.
>
> (Young man, aged 14)

All analyses of major studies show that it is the first of these – neglect – that has the strongest connection. In addition, there appears to be a cumulative effect, with the greater number of family handicaps, the greater the likelihood of anti-social behaviour being in evidence. Before leaving this topic, it is interesting to note that, just as family factors are significantly associated with the onset of anti-social behaviour, they are also linked with desistance as well. Thus, improved parental relationships can have a critical impact on this type of behaviour. There is some evidence in the literature that marriage or stable partnerships are associated with a reduction in anti-social behaviour. The title of a paper, "*I met this wife of mine and things got on a better track*" (Ronka et al., 2002), is a good illustration of this conclusion.

I have already mentioned the peer group, and I have discussed the role of peers in the previous chapter. For the moment it is important to note that, for many writers, an association between a deviant peer group is a significant risk factor in explaining anti-social behaviour. However, the picture is not entirely clear. It cannot be certain whether young people encourage each other, or whether it is simply the case that much anti-social behaviour tends to occur in groups rather than alone.

> I was friends with kids who weren't the best, right? Like behaviour wise, but I never forced myself to do the stuff they would do. Not only messed around at school, but seriously, like, at McDonalds. They'd be, like, chucking nuggets at each other, climbing on top of roofs and stuff. I wouldn't do that stuff.
>
> (Young man, aged 15)

There may be a third explanation, namely that young people with deviant attitudes tend to cluster together, so that those with similar behaviours and interests are drawn to each other, without anyone exerting an anti-social influence on anyone else (Scholte and van Aken, 2006). That said, there is no doubt that there is a close association between the anti-social activities of a young person and those of their friends. In Osgood et al. (1996), it was shown that having anti-social peers was one of the best predictors of self-reported offending behaviour.

In a similar vein, Moffit (2006) concluded that the association between anti-social behaviour and the peer group was strongest for those who were most attached to peers, and who felt most peer pressure. However, there still remains a question of interpretation. If anti-social behaviour is a group activity, then anti-social adolescents will have anti-social friends. This does not mean that the peer group necessarily leads others to offend. It is safer to conclude that having friends who are engaged in anti-social behaviour is an indicator of such behaviour rather than a cause of it.

Environmental factors in anti-social behaviour

I have already mentioned the roles of poverty and deprivation as contributors to anti-social behaviour. It is clear that the social fabric of the home and the neighbourhood will play a large part in contributing to the likelihood of young people becoming involved in various types of anti-social behaviour. The lack of social capital, poor employment prospects and the impact of limited resources available will all be factors in the life course of any young person. In addition to these central factors, commentators such as Hagell (2007) have pointed to three further environmental factors that may play a part in the development of anti-social behaviour.

The first of these is school effects. There is research evidence to show that schools do make a difference. This may not be a direct effect, but the key is the way schools support the vulnerable and less able adolescents and in the ethos they create. Where schools support a sense of belonging and engagement, they are likely to reduce the chances that young people become involved in activities such as offending and substance misuse. This is sometimes referred to as school connectedness, a variable that has been shown to enhance pro-social behaviour, as well as an interest in learning and educational goals (Frydenberg, 2019, pages 76 ff.)

> So, it was one time when I saw someone with the same bag as me, and I accused them of it, and I don't know, I forgot my bag was in the car, and I started panicking. And I started getting angry, and I started panicking, and then eventually had a real panic attack. And my Head of Year came, and she was trying to restrain me, she was calming me down, and all members of staff they were coming, and they moved everyone away from this corridor.
>
> (Young man, aged 15)

The second factor mentioned by Hagell (2007) is the media. The way in which the media represent young people, and the way in which crime and other anti-social activities are reported, does undoubtedly impact the public perception of adolescence. This is, in turn, influential in affecting attitudes and policies pursued by politicians. In this category also has to be placed the role of the internet. It is clear that messaging on social media sites has the potential to aggravate tensions between groups of young people and to incite conflict and violence due to information (often erroneous) found on such sites.

Finally, there is the increasing availability of guns and other weapons such as knives and other sharp objects. There is no doubt that this trend has an impact on criminal behaviour. If it is known that one group is carrying weapons, this is a clear signal for others to do the same. Thus, the likelihood of conflict which leads to violence is enhanced, as are the chances that those on the periphery get dragged into the criminal justice system.

Adolescent-to-parent abuse

I include this here as it is one aspect of anti-social behaviour that is rarely acknowledged, and about which there is relatively little research or information. One exception to this comes from the work of Holt (2025). She has been persistent in highlighting this as an important element in the spectrum of anti-social behaviour. As she says, this type of abuse upsets the way we normally understand power to operate in abusive relationships, and it involves actors who are not easily categorized as either victims or perpetrators. Abuse in this context can involve verbal attacks and various types of aggression and can include violence towards the parent or to other family members.

This author outlines some of the ways this type of abuse escalates in families. She describes what are called "asking patterns", where the young person requests something which is unreasonable or difficult for the parent to agree to. This then leads to conflict and resentment and continues into aggression or abuse. There is also the opposite of this, where the parent asks something from the young person, only to be met with resistance which leads to anger and abuse.

The pattern of behaviour is usually one that starts with verbal abuse and then leads to more extreme reactions from the young person. This creates intolerable pressure for the parent, and as Holt makes clear, it is extremely difficult for the adult to work out how to respond. It is often the case that, at first, the parent challenges the abuse. However, if that does not work, there then comes a stage of acceptance, or attempts to alter the situation. Holt (2025) discusses abuse in the context of kinship care and in circumstances where the young person is neurodivergent. She also recommends interventions and strategies that parents can adopt to manage these incredibly difficult situations.

Anti-social behaviour in context

The work of Stephen Case (2025) has been significant in emphasizing the importance of context in understanding anti-social behaviour. This author outlines a number of messages which he believes to be essential if there is to be a rounded and helpful approach to this topic. The first of these is the need to challenge the simplistic views of politicians and other commentators. For Case, anti-social behaviour is determined by economic, social and psychological factors, just as I have outlined previously. Next, Case points to the complexity of this behaviour and the need to recognize that no one theory can adequately cover the various forms of anti-social behaviour.

Thirdly, he argues for a child-centred approach. This approach would be one that understands the history of a young offender and takes into account the variables that have led this young person to become involved in such behaviour. Lastly, he points to the need to avoid the stigma that is sometimes attached to offending by adolescents. He stresses the importance of providing interventions that address the circumstances and needs of the young people who become involved in this type of behaviour.

This leads me to the subject of interventions for offending behaviour. Hagell (2007) has provided an excellent summary of the key elements necessary to be effective in reducing or stopping this type of behaviour. The principles that Hagell has drawn from the research literature are as follows:

- Interventions should target specific behaviours where possible, and should include social skills training and problem-solving;
- They should clearly be matched to the particular needs of the young offender;
- They should be well-structured and planned;
- They should be effectively supervised and monitored;
- They should have a clear theoretical model which explains how they are expected to work, and they should remain true to the original model.

These principles are ones that line up closely with an approach that takes into account the needs of the individual and recognizes the importance of professionalism and high standards in the delivery of interventions. Of course, there are many challenges in the provision of interventions that adhere to these standards. However, unless these principles are taken into account, interventions are unlikely to make much impact on offending behaviour.

Conclusion

In this chapter, I have discussed some of the issues relating to the stereotyping of young people, and the assumptions made by the public in general about the likelihood of anti-social behaviour among this age group. However, research data show clearly that rates of offending among the young have fallen significantly over the last few decades. This may be related to the changing nature of crime or with improved safety and security measures now in place for vehicles and other property. I discussed theories of anti-social behaviour and noted that the distinction between life-course persistent and adolescent-limited offending has provided a useful perspective on the origins of this type of behaviour.

I outlined some of major risk factors for anti-social behaviour and noted that there has been increasing concern about the risk factors for young women, which may differ from the risk factors for males in significant ways. I covered some of the key environmental variables that may be linked to anti-social behaviour, such as the role of the school, the influence of the media and the increasing availability of weapons. I concluded the chapter by considering interventions and noted some important principles that need to be in place if interventions are to be effective.

Chapter 11

Risk, resilience and well-being

Introduction

There are many ways to understand adolescence. For some young people it is a stressful time, and yet for others it is a period of growth and opportunity. As I have noted, for many parents it is a stage which raises significant challenges. There are numerous factors that make this a period of pressure and anxiety for both generations. Commentators may point to stress over exams, mental health difficulties, the climate emergency, problems relating to social media and many other possible obstacles to healthy maturation. Yet communities and neighbourhoods are full of adolescents getting on with their lives, coping with problems that adults might find daunting, enjoying their leisure, preparing for and taking exams and doing their utmost to become independent.

The movement known as "positive youth development" (Benson et al., 2004) has sought to emphasize a strengths-based model of adolescence rather than one which highlights the problems and difficulties of this stage. Another term that is used in this context is an asset framework (Flanagan, 2004; Salusky et al., 2014), again underlining the positive contributions that young people can make to families, schools and society generally. Approaches such as these are interested in the building blocks that underlie healthy development. They are linked to concepts such as agency, competence and connectedness, ideas to which I will return later in the chapter.

> Like, death, that is a huge stress of mine. And, like, as a kid it really kept me up at night. I'd be so worried about it, like, you'd just be sitting there in bed, and think about it, and I'd, like, really get into it. And I think you just have to, like, step away from it, and take a deep breath, and focus on something else. Because, like, I have realized you can't control that. Like, it's not in our hands. So, you just have to forget about it, well, you can't really forget about it, but you just have to back up from it, as you can't change the outcome.
>
> (Young woman, aged 17)

DOI: 10.4324/9781032640433-11

Risk and protective factors

While it is extremely important to highlight the adaptive capabilities of young people, it would be wrong to underestimate the impact of stress and disadvantage and to minimize the challenges and obstacles faced by some young people during this stage of their lives. I want to conclude this book with a focus on the strengths and resources of young people. However, studies of resilience make the point that this concept cannot be fully understood without an examination of risk factors as well. Risk and protective factors have to be studied together (Stevenson, 2022). As is clear from the work of Sir Michael Rutter and his colleagues, the two are bound up together, with resilience and coping impacted directly by the degree of risk experienced by the individual.

Based on the work of Rutter and others in this field (e.g., Luthar, 2003), any understanding of resilience and coping needs to include an awareness of both risk and protective factors. In view of this, I will first address risk factors and the part they play in determining how young people respond to stress and disadvantage. Following this, I will turn to the role of protective factors. Readers will be aware that I discussed the question of risk in Chapter 2, when I explored the role of brain development in facilitating, or reducing, the possibility of risk-taking behaviour in adolescence. In this chapter, I will consider risk in a wider context as it pertains to resilience and coping.

Risk is a complex term, especially as it applies to young people. Coleman and Hagell (2007) identified a variety of different uses of the term *risk*, among which the following three are of the greatest importance:

- *Risk* factors: As noted in the previous chapter on anti-social behaviour, these are factors that contribute to poor outcomes for young people. Some examples might include poverty, deprivation, ill health and dysfunctional family relationships.
- *Risk* behaviour: This applies to potentially harmful behaviour such as having unsafe sex, abusing substances or engaging in actions that harm others.
- Young people at *risk*: This term is used to refer to those who are potentially vulnerable, such as those who are subject to abuse or neglect or those in custody or in care.

These three terms all refer to somewhat different meanings of the word *risk*. It is important to keep this in mind as I explore the first of these terms, that of risk factors. Landmark studies of risk and resilience have considered the impact of poverty, war, natural disasters, health problems, physical and emotional abuse and so on. These factors represent some but not all of the established risk factors that are known to be associated with negative outcomes for children and young people. Early studies of risk tended to focus on one factor, such as poverty. Later studies have recognized that these factors tend to cluster or co-occur, and research has moved to include more than one factor.

> I'd say the time I probably struggled most mentally was with a physical injury. Because it meant I couldn't play football, or see my friends. So, it wasn't the physical side so much. It hurt, but that happens. It was more the missing out on different things. It's stopped you from going out, and seeing your friends, going to the gym, which makes you feel better physically, right?
>
> (Young man, aged 17)

An example of such a situation might include the fact that parents living in poverty may have higher rates of depression or other mental health difficulties. This might in turn lead to less effective parenting, so that adult depression, financial hardship and parenting behaviour all impact on the young people in such a family. In this way, the impact of risk can multiply, and later studies have looked at what is known as cumulative risk, where risk indicators have been aggregated (Masten and Powell, 2003). All writers in this field agree that, in general, the more risks the individual is exposed to, or the greater the risk gradient, the greater the likelihood of a poor outcome (Stevenson, 2022).

Another approach to the understanding of risk factors is to consider them in terms of whether they are within the individual, the family or the community. Of course, not all factors can be classified in this way, and many of these will interact with each other, but some of the following examples are useful:

- *Individual factors:* anxious temperament, low intelligence, poor health, limited attention span and low levels of tolerance of frustration;
- *Family factors*: parental ill-health, parental conflict, parental involvement in crime, harsh or erratic discipline and loss of a parent due to death or divorce;
- *Community factors*: economic disadvantage, poor housing, quality of schooling and other services, availability of drugs and levels of crime.

Another approach here is to consider this in the context of stress, rather than in terms of risk. A good example of this may be found in the work of Compas (2004). He notes that stress will vary depending on whether it is normative or atypical, large or small, chronic or acute. Experiences such as a change of school or daily hassles with adults are sometimes known as normative stress. Acute stress would refer to such things as being in a car accident or the death of someone close.

Two key factors that have been noted in the literature are the timing of events and the number of stressful events experienced by the young person. Readers will recognize these ideas from the discussion of turning points and developmental contextualism in Chapter 1. Here I pointed out that the greater number of stressful events, the more resources will be needed to deal with these. This is particularly true in adolescence, when there may be both normative and non-normative events to manage.

> Like, obviously, social media isn't all that good in a lot of ways. As well as, like, older generations, like, pooping on our parade and stuff, like a lot of them, so we're lazy, and we don't do this, and we don't do that. But I feel we're more hard working than they are. And also, for us to be hard working, because we've got, like, our phones that distract us so easily. So, it's hard to get out of that world, and actually pay attention to reality.
>
> (Young woman, aged 16)

For a young person who has to move to a new school, deal with puberty, make new friends, as well as having an acute problem to manage at home (illness of a parent for example), this is going to be very different from someone who only has one stressful event to which to respond. This notion is similar to that of a risk gradient, mentioned previously, where the example given was of poverty interacting with parental depression and the responses of parents to adolescent behaviour.

The number of events is linked to the question of timing. The way normative and non-normative events cluster together is a major factor in determining the individual's ability to cope. If difficulties impinge on the individual all at the same time, this will obviously make it that much more problematic than if stressful events occur one at a time.

It is time now to turn to the role of protective factors. While it may be the case from what I have said that those exposed to more risk or stressful events will have poorer outcomes, studies of resilience indicate that this is not true of all. The major studies of risk and resilience (e.g., Fergusson and Horwood, 2003; Werner and Smith, 1992) point out that there are some who, despite being exposed to major adversity and many stressful experiences, appear to cope well and to show remarkable resilience in the face of huge odds.

The key here lies in the role of protective factors. What are these protective factors? Many writers believe it is helpful to draw a distinction as has already been done with risk factors, between those which are individual attributes, those which originate from within the family and those that depend on resources in the neighbourhood or community. This distinction is one that was first described by authors I have already mentioned, including Rutter and his colleagues (e.g., Garmezy and Rutter, 1983). These factors are as follows:

- *Individual attributes*: good intellectual skills, positive temperament, positive self-image;
- *Family attributes*: high warmth, cohesion, high expectations, parental involvement;
- *Community attributes*: good schools, resources such as sports facilities, low levels of crime, adequate housing.

Readers will be aware that this classification is remarkably similar to the one proposed for risk factors. The relation between risk and protective factors is one that inspires continuing debate. Further consideration will be given to this question in due course, but for the moment it is time to turn to the major studies of risk and resilience, so that a picture can be gained of the findings from these ground-breaking investigations. One of the most interesting challenges for social scientists working in this field has been to try and understand how it is that, even in situations where there is a high level of adversity, some children and young people appear to cope well and to overcome the extreme risks to which they are exposed.

Two landmark studies are often quoted when considering this question. The first is one that was carried out in Hawaii during the 1980s by Werner and colleagues (Werner and Smith, 1992). In this research, the investigators managed to track down over 500 individuals who had been studied as part of a large cohort when they were children. They found that out of the group who had experienced major risk factors (chronic poverty, parents lacking education, troubled family environments), two-thirds had developed serious problems by the age of 18. However, approximately one-third appeared to have survived well and to be functioning effectively as adults.

This group was distinguished by high levels of achievement orientation, as well as having alternative care-givers during middle childhood. Other factors that were prominent included sociability, good communication skills, a supportive neighbourhood, and good peer relationships. Of considerable importance also was the presence or absence of additional stresses experienced later on, especially during adolescence. Those who were exposed to a high number of risk factors in childhood, and who also experienced further adversity as adolescents, did worst of all. As was noted earlier, when the risk gradient becomes steeper, the individual is at greater disadvantage.

The second study is known as the Christchurch Health and Development study, carried out in New Zealand. The lead researcher on this study was David Fergusson, although many others have worked with him and contributed to the scientific excellence of the investigation. In essence, this is a longitudinal study of an unselected sample of 1,200 children born in 1977. The cohort was studied at a number of points between birth and 21 years of age. A particular focus of the research was to identify those children exposed to major risk factors. The study shows that, as with the Hawaii investigation, some who experience high-risk environments do survive and overcome adversity.

Fergusson and others (Fergusson and Horwood, 2003) report that, with increasing exposure to childhood adversities, there were marked increases in mental health problems in adolescence. Yet not all individuals developed such disorders. Some showed a capacity to overcome the risk environment, and most of the protective factors already mentioned were present in those young people who could be described as resilient.

> Like a lot of the time my bad days don't have a reason. I'm like, I just feel lost today. I don't know why. And my Mum's like, it's ok. Do you want to talk it through or whatever? And often we'll just sit and watch TV or something. So, it's a bit less. I think it's having company makes me feel a bit better. But then sometimes it's nice to have no company as well, to shut myself in my room and lock myself away.
>
> (Young woman, aged 17)

One particular protective factor highlighted time and time again by the researchers was the presence of one key adult during childhood and adolescence. This adult did not need to be a parent. It could be another relative or even someone outside the family. However, the role played by one adult who cared about the child or young person, and who was available at significant turning points, appears to be absolutely central to the development of resilience in the face of adversity.

In discussions of the interplay between risk and protective factors (e.g., Olsson et al., 2003; Rutter, 2003), there is a strong emphasis on the importance of considering dynamic processes rather than looking simply at a catalogue of static variables. Rutter has been keen to emphasize the role of gene–environment interactions, as well as the importance of biological factors such as brain structures and the neuro-endocrine system. He argues that psychological variables, such as personal agency, coping mechanisms and so on interact with the genetic and physiological characteristics of an individual, and that all these variables contribute to a dynamic process of adaptation to adverse environmental conditions.

One last point on questions of risk is that to with the pre-eminence of early childhood experiences in determining outcomes for vulnerable young people. Are risk factors in childhood more powerful than those that occur at later ages? Is it the case, as Bynner (2001) has put it: "The earlier the disadvantage occurred, and the longer it has persisted, the lower the likelihood that these factors (the protective factors) would counter it?" This is an assumption that is generally accepted by social scientists and policy makers. Many of the results of the longitudinal studies on resilience do appear to support this conclusion.

In spite of this, the evidence is not entirely clear. It may be that there are exceptions to the rule that the earlier the exposure to risk factors, the more difficult it is to alter the course of development. It is the case that, even for those who have suffered high levels of adversity at an early age, there are some protective factors that operate in adolescence and in early adulthood. Studies of young offenders, as well as those brought up in the care system, have shown that changes in relationships in adulthood, especially marriage to a stable partner, can act as a powerful protective factor. There is also evidence that, during adolescence, involvement with positive peer groups, as well as the impact of a caring and supportive adult, can act to counter early exposure to risk factors (Luthar, 2003). One academic paper, which I have already mentioned in the previous chapter, captures this point neatly. Ronka et al. (2002) gave their article the title: *"I met this wife of mine, and things got on a better track".*

Up to this point the nature of risk has been considered, as well as the role played by protective factors in modifying experiences of adversity. Various questions regarding risk and adversity have been explored, and the results of major studies in this field have been summarized. The question has been considered as to whether protective factors can be effective in adolescence and early adulthood despite early adversity. I will now take a closer look at coping, resilience and well-being.

Coping

Those who write about stress in adolescence are also interested in coping (Frydenberg, 2019). There have been a wide range of theoretical approaches to coping, stretching back to the nineteenth century. Most commentators focus on how individuals deal with their environments and what resources they bring to the interaction. In theory, there is no such thing as good or bad coping. It will depend on the judgement of the individual and the context of the circumstances. However, it is clear from research that there are some coping strategies that are mostly helpful and some that are, in the majority of cases, unhelpful.

There have been many attempts to classify coping strategies. One such attempt was first proposed by Lazarus (1966), and has been widely used by later researchers. This distinguishes between emotion-focussed and problem-focussed coping. The function of both types of coping is to modify the relation between the stressor and the individual. In problem-focussed coping, however, the individual attempts to alter, reduce or get rid of the stress. In emotion-focussed coping, there is an attempt to change the emotional state, such as anxiety, which is created by the stressor.

> Taking time alone really works for me. I like to sit on my own and not have to talk to people for, like, say 15 minutes or so, or even an hour or so. Just sitting there and not having everybody talking to me, or just even being around me, just sitting on my own slice, that's pretty much what I think is best.
>
> (Young woman, aged 17)

Others writers, such as Hampel and Peterman (2005), in their studies of German adolescents, use the distinction between emotion-focussed and problem-focussed coping, but they introduced a third category – that of maladaptive coping. In their view, this includes such things are rumination, aggression and denial. Frydenberg (2019) has outlined a similar approach, as she draws a distinction between productive and non-productive coping.

She also adds a further dimension, which she calls reference to others. Thus, productive coping would include looking for the positives in a situation, seeking relaxing diversions and so on. Non-productive coping includes worry, self-blame and ignoring the problem. Lastly, reference to others covers such things as seeking social support, asking help from key adults and looking to community resources such as the church.

There are a range of variables that will have an impact on the coping strategies selected by individual adolescents. In terms of age, Frydenberg (2019) reports that older young people are more likely to blame themselves and to use tension-reduction strategies. These strategies can be adaptive, such as listening to music or taking exercise, or they can be maladaptive, such as using alcohol or drugs. In terms of gender, most of the studies into this aspect of coping are rather dated, and it is questionable as to how relevant these findings are today.

> I feel that boys are less supported, I think, because people think that they should just be, like, "get along with life and stuff". I think they have less support. Speaking to my brother he has had less support at home because my parents didn't know how to help him, and they just expected him to know what's going on. Boys are scared to ask for help, because it's stigmatized, so they find it harder to actually ask for help.
>
> (Young woman, aged 19)

One example is the work of Seiffge-Krenke (1995), who reported that boys are more likely to use active coping, while girls are more likely to use emotion-focussed coping strategies. In this study, it was also noted that girls were more likely to seek help and to use social support in the face of stressful experiences. Interestingly, boys are more at risk since they are less likely to seek support, yet on the contrary girls may be more at risk as they depend on the advice and support of others, whether this is helpful or not. These distinctions are supported by later reviews, such as that of Frydenberg (2019).

As far as culture and ethnicity is concerned, studies on coping here are few and far between. Alsaker and Flammer (1999) looked at coping among young people in 12 European countries and concluded that one of the key variables was the context in which young people were growing up. Thus, time spent in school, leisure activities and the role of the family all varied across countries. These in turn influenced the style of coping displayed by adolescents in the various countries. Another example (D'Anastasi and Frydenberg, 2005) investigated coping in Anglo-Australian and minority group Australian young people. One of their findings was that becoming involved in social action and seeking spiritual support were two coping strategies used more often by minority-group Australians than by Anglo-Australians. This finding illustrates the importance of context, so that background experiences as well as the sources of support available determine the styles of coping adopted by different groups.

The work of Frydenberg (2019) is especially important here, as she and her colleagues are responsible for the only validated measure of coping in adolescence. This is known as the Adolescent Coping Scale (ACS), which has been widely used in research, especially in Australia, where it was created. The ACS has been further developed into the ACS2, and there is also a short form with only 20 items rather than the original 60 items. The scale also has an addition which allows the researcher to explore both the frequency of the use of a strategy but also its effectiveness. This development has enabled the study of coping to progress significantly.

Resilience

I now want to turn to an outline of the concept of resilience. As will be apparent from all that has been said so far, resilience is clearly linked to notions of risk and adversity, as well as to our understanding of coping and the management of stressful or traumatic experiences. There is much debate about the nature of resilience, and questions arise continually as to how to understand this concept (Higgen et al., 2022; Luthar, 2003). Is resilience a personality trait, or is it a process of adjustment? Does it continue over the lifespan, or is it a response to particular circumstances? Is resilience always a positive thing, or can it have negative connotations?

Some commentators argue that resilience can apply both to processes and to outcomes. It is therefore essential to keep these two things distinct. Thus, the concept can be used to consider the types of behaviour and the psychosocial outcomes seen in young people exposed to adversity. Here one might be looking at educational performance, avoidance of criminal behaviour or other measures of "good" functioning. The problem with this is that there are many different possible outcomes and therefore numerous possible criteria for resilience.

On the other hand, studies that look at processes are more likely to be interested in the way that risk and protective factors interact. Here there is less of a concern with outcome measures and more of an interest in how the spectrum of risk and protective factors work together to produce an adaptation in particular circumstances. Recent discussions of resilience are focussing on this as a process, having psychosocial, environmental and biological elements in it (Ungar, 2021).

> I think it is very stressful, like, with all the things happening at school, course work, exams and stuff, in your life. I kind of, like, isolate myself out to my room, and I'll be there, sit for a bit, maybe have a little cry. But I feel like, that is a good thing. I don't know if it is necessarily healthy, to be by yourself while doing it, but it is definitely a good outlook for me.
>
> (Young woman, aged 16)

An example here would be resilience in young people growing up in very disadvantaged communities (Macdonald, 2007). In such circumstances, a commonly used measure of resilience might be avoidance of substance misuse or good school performance. However, in a situation where there is little motivation to achieve at school, or where substance misuse is common amongst young people, a better measure of resilience might be something like optimism or caring behaviour.

This point is made by Higgen et al. (2022) when discussing resilience in the Global South. These authors suggest that resilience is often conceived as influenced by Western cultures. However, processes that could prove beneficial for young people in Western cultures may be neutral or even negative for young people in other cultures. These authors note a range of resources that may enhance or enable resilience in a variety of cultures. These include such things as adherence to cultural traditions and access to material resources. In these circumstances, resilience could be understood as the ability to navigate towards such resources, and the capacity of the individual to negotiate for them in the context of exposure to adversity (Ungar, 2021).

A further issue mentioned already is the question of whether resilience has any negative consequences. This query is raised in a paper by Ehrlich et al. (2023) and discussed in Luthar (2006). Here the subject of the investigation was resilience in Black and Latino young people growing up in the USA in disadvantaged communities. Luthar (2006) makes the point that what he calls "high-effort coping" was associated with greater risk for various health conditions in such populations. Thus, navigating disadvantage and adversity in these environments has consequences, and developing resilience to stressful events and experiences may well lead to further disadvantages in later life.

In summary, it can be stated that resilience is not a stable personality characteristic but a process depending on many variables. Resilience arises as an interaction between risk and protective factors. It is often seen as an outcome, but this is misleading. Good school performance or avoidance of crime is an outcome. Resilience is not something that people have or do not have, but rather it is a response to difficult or adverse circumstances. There are many different types of resilience, depending on the particular individual. Some types of resilience may be considered "more healthy" than others, but it will depend on the situation of the individual. Resilience is not static, but it can change over the lifespan. It may not be apparent at one stage, but may develop at another stage because of the availability of protective factors.

One of the key questions has to do with the interaction between risk and resilience. This is not a simple relation, but some conclusions can be drawn from the research evidence and summaries by noted authors, such as Luthar (2003), Masten (2014) and Ungar (2021). These conclusions are:

- There is strong evidence from longitudinal studies that, where protective factors are present, most children and young people do recover from short-term adversity. In this sense, it can be said that the majority have the capacity for resilience so long as the risk factors are limited and protective factors are in place.

- Where risk factors are continuous and severe, only a minority manage to cope. The more serious the adversity, the stronger the protective factors need to be. Thus, under conditions of major risk, resilience is only apparent among a minority who can draw on the strengths gained from the protective factors.
- The major risk factors for young people tend to lie within chronic and transitional events rather than in the acute risks. Thus, adolescents show greater resilience when faced with acute adversities such as bereavement or short-term illness and less resilience when exposed to chronic risks such as continuing family conflict, long-term poverty and multiple changes of home or school.
- Resilience can only develop in circumstances where there is risk or stress. Resilience is most likely to develop through gradual exposure to difficulties at a manageable level of intensity, and at points in the life cycle where protective factors can operate. Rutter (2003) called these "steeling experiences".

One of the powerful attractions of the emphasis on resilience is that it reflects a positive approach, encouraging adults to keep the strengths and assets of the young person in mind at all times. All of the authors mentioned above (Luthar, Masten and Ungar) make the point that in all models of change it is essential to include predictors of positive outcomes. In any assessment of a young person, it should be mandatory to identify the capabilities and resources of the individual alongside the risks. A useful outline of a "strengths-based approach" can be found in Hutchinson (2013), in which she places the capabilities of the individual young person at the centre of all social work interventions.

A number of writers have considered the question of how to promote resilience in circumstances where the adolescent is likely to be faced with adversity (e.g., Frydenberg, 2019). The first strategy is to reduce the young person's exposure to risk. This may seem obvious, but it is often hard to achieve. An example here might be the role of the school in combating high levels of poverty or low levels of parental care. Thus, by providing breakfast clubs, the school can offer support to those who have poor nutrition at the start of the day. After-school clubs offer a quiet space to do homework or an alternative for those who might be unsupervised and out in the community after school.

A second strategy is to find ways of interrupting the chain reaction of negative events. As has been noted, the presence of one risk factor increases the likelihood that others will be present. As a result, if the impact of one risk factor can be diminished or reduced, it may follow that other positive consequences flow from this. The provision of safe places for young people to meet with the non-custodial parent following a divorce is a good example. Many such parents find it hard to keep up regular contact with their sons or daughters if they live at a distance, or if there is nowhere for them to meet on neutral ground. Yet regular contact with the non-custodial parent following family breakdown is, in most cases, a protective factor. Innovative schemes which provide contact centres make it possible for relationships to be maintained in spite of experiences of disruption and loss.

The third strategy is to offer the young person positive experiences in order to enhance the impact of potential protective factors. Finding ways for young people to discover their talents and strengths leads to enhanced self-esteem. This process can also make possible positive relationships with key adults. Results from the Christchurch study (Fergusson and Horwood, 2003) underline the role played by one key adult in combating serious adversity, and a further example of this strategy may be taken from the literature on divorce.

Where parental separation may initially appear to be a risk factor for a young person, new opportunities for growth can occur in such situations. The adolescent may have the opportunity to take on new roles, or to assume new responsibilities that would normally fall to adults in the family. Research indicates that such experiences, as long as they are not onerous, can give young people confidence and assist them to develop new skills, thus bolstering protective factors for their development.

The question of how to build resilience in young people is one that exercises all who have anything to do with this age group. It is a challenge for schools to provide a curriculum that addresses this problem. It is of obvious concern to parents and care-givers, and it is something that preoccupies government officials. Yet there is no easy answer. Resilience is a complex phenomenon, and one that is often misunderstood. As we have noted, it is not a characteristic, nor is it an outcome. Rather, it is best seen as an adaptation to challenging circumstances or as the capacity to bounce back from adversity. Whether someone can be said to be resilient will depend on the level of risk and the type of protective factors that are present. I will now turn to the topic of well-being, one closely related to both coping and resilience.

Well-being

Well-being in young people is a subject that is attracting greater interest today than has been the case in the past. The concept has grown out of the positive psychology movement, and a good place to start is the work of Martin Seligman. His book *Flourish* (2011) and his writings on this topic have generated a considerable amount of discussion. According to Seligman, there are five elements that go to make up well-being. These are:

- Positive emotion;
- Engagement;
- Meaning;
- Positive relationships; and
- Accomplishment.

Of course, these five elements can be interpreted in many different ways, and in respect of young people, would no doubt have to be rephrased if they were to make sense in the context of adolescence. It is also important to note that well-being has not been subjected to rigorous measurement or to scientific research in the normal sense of that term. This is in contrast to the concepts of coping and resilience. At the beginning of discussions about well-being, the focus tended to be on the absence of distress and negative experiences. More recently, concepts such as positive affect and mental and physical good health have come to the fore in debate over well-being (Frydenberg, 2019).

> I've always thought that everything that you experience just, like, becomes part of you. I always love the idea that "Oh! I'm everything I've always loved". Like, I feel that anyone you meet, like, they become part of you, and I love that idea. You'll always be finding new parts of yourself, like, when you experience something, or you go to new places, it all becomes part of you. I feel you are discovering new things about yourself, and that's really nice.
>
> (Young woman, aged 17)

In much of the literature on well-being, there is a clear overlap with concepts such as emotional resilience and emotional literacy. Thus, Ogden and Hagen (2019) talk about coping strategies and emotion regulation, while Hoyos (2021) writes about emotional literacy in the context of education. These authors all cover the same ground. This is well described by Bailey and Tsoflias (2025) when they outline emotional well-being as having the ability to:

- Understand, regulate and express emotions;
- Control and understand impulses to act unhelpfully;
- Have empathy and compassion for others; and
- Take action to recover and replenish energy.

As readers will appreciate, well-being can be described as a "catch-all" concept. It has grown to be popular, but it has strayed somewhat from its roots in positive psychology, where it has had strong links with notions of happiness. It is valuable in the context of education, if in its use it helps to focus the ethos of schools on the management of emotions and on the importance of having a positive approach to life.

> I don't worry too much about things. I more care about, like, getting my dreams and stuff, and making them happen. So, other things, they don't really bother me. I've got my friends. I've been friends with them since I was little. I'm quite a laid-back person, so nothing really bothers me.
>
> (Young woman, aged 18)

In my own work I have concentrated on well-being in the school setting (Coleman, 2009). In this I explored various ways in which well-being has been introduced into the classroom. I have been concerned that, with the focus on the well-being of students, there has been too little attention paid to the well-being of the teaching staff. In this context, the work of Webb et al. (2009) was refreshing, as they were able to show that, in the school setting, the well-being of students is closely linked to that of the staff.

There is one further point to be made concerning well-being in the classroom, and that concerns the curriculum that is used to bolster or enhance well-being in students. I discussed this in Chapter 7, when I mentioned mental health literacy, and the evaluation of different curricula. The organization Bounce Forward (www.bounceforward.com) has been involved in the development of a curriculum entitled "Healthy Minds". This has been subject to well-designed trials in England, and the results are encouraging. It is to be hoped that more work will be carried out on this topic.

Conclusion

The topics I have covered in this chapter are appropriate as a way of ending the book. It is important for me to bring this book to a conclusion by emphasizing the positive and adaptive capacities of young people. For too long, adolescence has been seen as a "problem" stage, and there has been a continuing focus on troubled and troubling behaviour. In this final chapter, I have covered a range of topics, including risk, resilience, coping and well-being. It will be apparent that these topics relate to each other and may well have similar underlying conceptual foundations. Coping and resilience are central to the ability to function well during the adolescent stage of development.

There has been far too little recognition of the ability of young people to demonstrate coping skills and to show their determination to contribute in a positive fashion to their own development and to the communities around them. However we want to define the concept of well-being, it is right that, as a society, we wish our adolescents to experience well-being as they move through this stage of their lives. In this way, they will become happier and more fulfilled as adults.

In Chapter 1, I outlined the concept of agency in relation to the developing young person. I wanted to emphasize the fact that adolescents are able to make decisions about their path through this stage of life. This seems important for all who are involved with this age group. They are no longer children, and if adults are able to recognize this, and to engage with the needs of young people as they mature, they will traverse this stage more easily.

I also believe that our knowledge of the brain in adolescence can make a significant difference to the outcomes for young people. I have noted that the more key adults show understanding of the impact of the changes in the brain, the easier it will be for adolescents to adapt to these changes. In Chapter 2, I included a blog about why secondary school pupils should be taught about brain development. I believe this should be a priority. Young people tell me that this knowledge makes a great difference to them. It makes it easier to cope with the emotional ups and downs that are an inevitable part of this stage. As for older students, they tell me they wish they had had this information when they were younger.

I will end this book with three messages to readers. The first has to do with the role of adults. All the research points to the importance of parents and carers in the lives of young people. Where parents and carers are engaged and supportive, young people are most likely to thrive. Adults matter. Indeed, many adults around the adolescent can make a difference, but parents and carers have a hugely significant role to play.

The second message has to do with knowledge of the brain. Understanding what happens in the adolescent brain can change relationships and can alter the outcomes for young people. It is my hope that this knowledge will gradually be more and more widely disseminated, both to adults and to young people. Lastly, I will emphasize once again that this is a stage. This means that things will not remain the same. The young person is going through a process, a transition from childhood to maturity. It is a process that takes time and may have some bumpy periods. I hope that the information contained in this book will assist all who live and work with adolescents to understand them better.

A word about the interviews

In order to ensure that the voices of young people are included, a number of interviews have been carried out with a wide variety of individuals from different backgrounds aged between 14 and 18. Their voices are included in all chapters and undoubtedly add a vivid perspective on what it is like to be an adolescent in 2025. As I have said, I am hugely grateful to Fiona Factor. She carried out 26 interviews with young people between the ages of 14 and 18. She included those from a secondary school, those from a youth club and those from an education authority's alternative provision for those who, for whatever reason, were finding ordinary secondary school difficult to manage.

In the text, I have provided the age and gender of the individual. Where the young person identified as non-binary or trans, I have described them as 'young person' rather than 'young man' or 'young woman'. In some cases, where it is relevant to the quote, I have provided further information on identity or sexual orientation.

Appendix

Interview schedule 2025

- To get us started, can you tell us about something that you really enjoy? Something really enjoyable about your life at the moment.
- We want to know what it is like being a teenager. So how would you describe the life of a teenager? What is it like being a teenager?
- Do you think it is harder for a boy or girl growing up today?

Self-identity

1. We often talk of the teenage years as a time when you think about your identity – like who you are, or what sort of a person you are. Has this happened to you?
2. What kind of issues about your identity have you considered? Gender identity? Sexual orientation?
3. Was this a difficult time – sometimes referred to as an identity crisis?
4. Thinking now about puberty – do you remember what happened when your body started changing, or how it happened for you? Was it a good or bad experience?

Challenges

- The teenager years are often described as a time of "storm and stress". Does that make sense to you?

- What do you think is most stressful about this time of life?
    a. For example, do you worry about things that happen in the world or you see on the news?
    b. Your future – career, income, family etc.?
- Lots of young people have had difficulties with their mental health, e.g. greater anxiety, panic attacks etc.
    a. Have you or any of your friends experienced this? What kind of support has been helpful?
    b. Why do you think there has been an increase in mental health difficulties for young people?

Peer relationships

1. Turning to friends – in what ways are friends important?
2. Do friends ever ask or expect you to do things you don't want to do? If so, how do you deal with that?
3. Social media is so important now – how does it affect your life? Do you think it is good or bad?
4. Are you in a relationship? Are there any particular challenges or difficulties in maintaining a relationship in today's world?

Parents/carers

1. Now that you are a teenager do you think it is easier or harder to talk to your parents?
2. In what way are parents important for young people like you?
3. What or who helps you to deal with problems and challenges in your life?

Lastly, how would you describe the life of a teenager today? – The best and the worst?

Further reading

Chapter 1

Foulkes, L (2024) *Coming of age: how adolescence shapes us*. The Bodley Head. London.
Haidt, J (2024) *The anxious generation*. Allen Lane. London.
Meeus, W (2019) *Adolescent development: longitudinal research into the self and personal relationships*. Routledge. Abingdon.
Steinberg, L (2015) *Age of opportunity: lessons from the new science of adolescence*. Houghton Mifflin Harcourt. New York.
Steinberg, L (2023) *Adolescence*. 13th Edition. McGraw Hill. New York.

Chapter 2

Blakemore, S-J (2019) *Inventing ourselves: the secret life of the teenage brain*. Penguin Random House. London.
Jensen, F E (2015) *The teenage brain: a neuroscientist's survival guide to raising adolescents and young adults*. Harper. New York.
Galvan, A (2017) *The neuroscience of adolescence*. Cambridge University Press. Cambridge.
Morgan, N (2013) *Blame my brain: the amazing teenage brain revealed*. Walker Books. London.

Chapter 3

Foster, R (2022) *Life time: the new science of the body clock and how it can revolutionize your sleep and health*. Penguin Life. London.
Goodyear, V and Armour, K (Eds.) (2019) *Young people, social media and health*. Routledge. Abingdon.
Hadley, A (2025) *Teenage pregnancy and young parenthood*. 2nd Edition. Routledge. Abingdon.

Kang, M, Coyne, I and Gray, N (2025) *Adolescent health and well-being: meeting challenges old and new*. Routledge. Abingdon.

Riccardelli, L and Yager, Z (2016) *Adolescence and body image*. Routledge. Abingdon.

Chapter 4

Coleman, J (2021) *The teacher and the teenage brain*. Routledge. Abingdon.

Dehaene, S (2020) *How we learn: the new science of education and the brain*. Penguin Books. London.

Devine, R and Lecce, S (2021) *Theory of mind in middle childhood and adolescence*. Routledge. Abingdon.

Howard-Jones, P (2018) *The evolution of the learning brain*. Routledge. Abingdon.

Thomas, M, Mareschal, D and Dumontheil, I (Eds.) (2020) *Educational neuroscience: development across the lifespan*. Routledge. Abingdon.

Chapter 5

Brady, M (2016) *The body in adolescence: psychic isolation and physical symptoms*. Routledge. Abingdon.

Erikson, E (1968) *Identity, youth and crisis*. Faber. London.

Ferrer-Wreder, L and Kroger, J (2020) *Identity in adolescence: the balance between self and other*. 4th Edition. Routledge. Abingdon.

Foulkes, L (2025) *Coming of age: how adolescence shapes us*. The Bodley Head. London.

Steinberg, L (2023) *Adolescence*. 13th Edition. McGraw Hill. New York.

Chapter 6

Behun, R and Owens, E (2020) *Youth and internet pornography: the impact and influence on adolescent development*. Routledge. Abingdon.

Hadley, A (2025) *Teenage pregnancy and young parenthood*. 2nd Edition. Routledge. Abingdon.

Kang, M, Coyne, I and Gray, N (2025) *Adolescent health and well-being: meeting challenges old and new*. Routledge. Abingdon.

Temple-Smith, M, Moore, S and Rosenthal, D (2016) *Sexuality in adolescence: the digital generation*. Routledge. Abingdon.

Chapter 7

Campbell, S, Morley, D and Catchpole, R (2016) *Critical issues in child and adolescent mental health*. Palgrave Macmillan. London.

Laver-Bradbury, C, Thompson, M, Gale, C and Hooper, C (Eds.) (2021) *Child and adolescent mental health: theory and practice*. Routledge. Abingdon.

Ogden, T and Hagen, K (Eds.) (2019) *Adolescent mental health: prevention and intervention.* Routledge. Abingdon.

Chapter 8

Abela A and Walker, J (Eds.) (2014) *Contemporary issues in family studies.* Wiley Blackwell. Chichester, Sussex.
Coleman, J (2019) *Why won't my teenager talk to me?* 2nd Edition. Routledge. Abingdon.
Hill, R (2025) *Raising confident teenagers.* Karnac Books. Bicester, Oxon.
Holt, A (2025) *Adolescent to parent abuse.* 2nd Edition. Policy Press. Bristol.
Livingstone, S and Blum-Ross, A (2020) *Parenting for a digital future.* Oxford University Press. Oxford.
Sisler, A and Ittel, A (2015) *Siblings in adolescence: emerging individuals, lasting bonds.* Psychology Press. Hove, Sussex.

Chapter 9

Cotterell, J (2007) *Social networks in youth and adolescence.* 2nd Edition. Routledge. Abingdon.
Foulkes, L (2024) *Coming of age: how adolescence shapes us.* The Bodley Head. London.
Hagell, A (Ed.) (2012) *Changing adolescence: social trends and mental health.* Policy Press. Bristol.
Steinberg, L (2023) *Adolescence.* 13th Edition. McGraw Hill. New York.
Talmud, I and Mesch, G (2020) *Wired youth: the online social world of adolescence.* Routledge. Abingdon.

Chapter 10

Case, S (2025) *Youth offending in context: challenges and solutions.* Routledge. Abingdon.
Hagell, A (Ed.) (2012) *Changing adolescence: social trends and mental health.* Policy Press. Bristol.
Le Blanc, M (2021) *The development of anti-social behaviour and crime.* Springer Publishing. New York.

Chapter 11

Bailey, L and Tsoflias, V (2026) *Raise resilience: teach your teenager well.* Routledge. Abingdon.
Frydenberg, E (2019) *Adolescent coping.* 3rd Edition. Routledge. Abingdon.
Luthar, S (Ed.) (2003) *Resilience and vulnerability.* Cambridge University Press. Cambridge.
Masten, A (2014) *Ordinary magic: resilience in development.* The Guilford Press. London.
Steinberg, L (2015) *Age of opportunity: lessons from the new science of adolescence.* Houghton Mifflin Harcourt. New York.

References

Abela, A and Walker, J (Eds.) (2014) *Contemporary Issues in family studies.* Wiley Blackwell. Chichester, Sussex.

Adelson, J (1971) The political imagination of the young adolescent. *Daedalus.* Fall. 1013–1050.

Adelson, J (1972) The political imagination of the young adolescent. In Kagan, J and Coles, R (Eds.) *Twelve to sixteen: early adolescence.* Norton. New York.

Adelson, J, Green, B and O'Neill, R (1969) Growth of the idea of law in adolescence. *Developmental Psychology.* 1. 327–332. https://psycnet.apa.org/doi/10.1037/h0027705

Adelson, J and O'Neill, R (1966) The development of political thought in adolescence. *Journal of Personality and Social Psychology.* 4. 259–308.

Allen, J, Schad, M, Ouderkerk, B and Chango, J (2014) Whatever happened to the 'cool' kids? *Child Development.* 85. 1866–1880. https://doi.org/10.1111/cdev.12250

Alsaker, F and Flammer, A (1999) Time use by adolescents in an international perspective. In Alsaker, F and Flammer, A (Eds.) *The adolescent experience: European and American adolescents in the 1990s.* Lawrence Erlbaum. Hillsdale, New Jersey.

Anthony, R, Young, H, Hewitt, G … Cook, S (2023) Young people's online communication and its association with mental well-being. *Child and Adolescent Mental Health.* 28(1). 4–11. https://doi.org/10.1111/camh.12610

Armitage, J, Newlove-Delgado, T, Ford, T and Collishaw, S (2025) Characteristics of children with a psychiatric disorder in 1999, 2004, and 2017: An analysis of the national child mental health surveys of England. *Journal of Child Psychiatry and Psychology.* 66(2). 167–177. https://doi.org/10.1111/jcpp.14040

Auger, N, Steiger, H, Ayoub, A and Israel, M (2023) Shifting age of child eating disorder hospitalizations during the Covid-19 pandemic. *Journal of Child Psychology and Psychiatry.* 64(8). 176–184. https://doi.org/10.1111/jcpp.13800

Azzopardi, P, Stephen, J, Hearps, K … Patton, G (2019) Progress in adolescent health and well-being: Tracking twelve headline indicators for 195 countries and territories: 1990 to 2016. *The Lancet.* 393(10176). 1101–1118. https://doi.org/10.1016/S0140-6736(18)32427-9

References

Bailey, L and Tsoflias, V (forthcoming) *Raise resilience: Teach your teenager well.* Routledge. Abingdon.

Bancroft, J and Reinisch, J (1990) *Adolescence and puberty.* Oxford University Press. Oxford.

Bao, Z, Zhang, W, Lai, X and Wang, Y (2015) Parental attachment and Chinese adolescents' delinquency: The mediating role of moral disengagement. *Journal of Adolescence.* 44. 37–47. https://doi.org/10.1016/j.adolescence.2015.06.002

Baron-Cohen, S (2017) Neurodiversity: A revolutionary concept for autism and psychiatry. *Journal of Child Psychology and Psychiatry.* 58(6). 744–747. https://doi.org/10.1111/jcpp.12703

Barter, C, McCarry, M, Berridge, D and Kerry, K (2009) *Partner exploitation and violence in teenage intimate relationships.* NSPCC. London. www.nspcc.org.uk

Baumrind, D (1971) Current patterns of parental authority. *Developmental Psychology Monographs.* 4. 1–102.

Becht, A, Spitzer, J, Grapsas, S ... Thomaes, S (2024) Feeling anxious and being engaged in a warming world: climate anxiety and adolescents' pro-environmental behaviour. *Journal of Child Psychology and Psychiatry.* 65(10). 1270–1282. https://doi.org/10.1111/jcpp.14035

Behun, R and Owens, E (2020) *Youth and internet pornography.* Routledge. Abingdon.

Beltz, A, Corley, R, Wadsworth, S and Berenbaum, S (2019) Does puberty affect the development of behaviour problems as a mediator, moderator or unique predictor? *Development and Psychopathology.* 32(4):1473–1485. https://doi.org/10.1017/S095457941900141X

Benson, P, Mannes, M, Pitman, K and Ferber, K (2004) Youth development, developmental assets, and public policy. In Lerner, R and Steinberg, L (Eds.) *Handbook of adolescent development* (2nd Edition). Wiley. New York.

Berk, M (2022) Suicide prevention in youth. *Child and Adolescent Mental Health.* 27(4). 325–327. https://doi.org/10.1111/camh.12604

Berrington, A, Diamond, I, Ingham, R and Stevenson, J (2005) *Consequences of teenage parenthood: pathways that minimize the long-term negative impacts of teenage childbearing.* Final report submitted to the Department of Health in London. University of Southampton.

Blakemore, S-J (2019) *Inventing ourselves: the secret life of the teenage brain.* Penguin Random House. London.

Bleidorn, W (2015) What accounts for personality maturation in early adulthood? *Current Directions in Psychological Science.* 24. 245–252. https://doi.org/10.1177/0963721414568662

Brady, M (2016) *The body in adolescence.* Routledge. Abingdon.

Brauner, E, Busch, A, Lind, C, Hickey, M and Juul, A (2020) Trends in the incidence of precocious puberty and normal variant puberty among children in Denmark 1998–2010. *JAMA Network Open.* 3(10). e2015665. https://doi.org/10.1001/jamanetworkopen.2020.15665

Bronfenbrenner, U (1979) *The ecology of human development.* Harvard University Press. Cambridge, MA.

Brooks-Gunn, J and Warren, M (1985) The effects of delayed menarche in different contexts: dance and non-dance students. *Journal of Youth and Adolescence.* 14. 285–300. https://doi.org/10.1007/BF02089235

Brown, B (1999) 'You're going out with who?' Peer group influences on adolescent romantic relationships. In Furman, W, Brown, B and Feiring, S (Eds.) *Contemporary perspectives on adolescent romantic relationships*. Cambridge University Press. Cambridge.

Brown, B and Larson, J (2009) Peer relationships in adolescence. In Lerner, R and Steinberg, L (Eds.) *Handbook of Adolescent Psychology* (3rd Edition). Wiley. New York, NY.

Buchanan, C, Maccoby, E and Dornbusch, S (1996) *Adolescents after divorce*. Harvard University Press. Cambridge, MA.

Bussey, K (2011) Gender identity development. In Schwartz, S, Luyckx, K and Vignoles, V (Eds.) *Handbook of identity theory and research* (pp. 603–628). Springer Science. New York, NY.

Bynner, J (2001) Childhood risks and protective factors in social exclusion. *Children and Society*. 15. 285–301.

Byrnes, J (2003) Cognitive development during adolescence. In Adams, G and Berzonsky, M (Eds.) *Blackwell handbook of adolescence*. Blackwell Publishing. Oxford.

Call, C and Mortimer, J (2001) *Arenas of comfort in adolescence; a study in adjustment in context*. Lawrence Erlbaum. Mahwah, New Jersey.

Calzo, J, Sonneville, K, Haines, J, Blood, E and Austin, B (2012) The development of associations among body mass index, body dissatisfaction, and weight and shape concern among adolescent boys and girls. *Journal of Adolescent Health*. 51(5). 517–523. https://doi.org/10.1016/j.jadohealth.2012.02.021

Carlson, E, Sroufe, L and Byron, E (2004) The construction of experience: A longitudinal study of representation and behaviour. *Child Development*. 75. 66–83. https://doi.org/10.1111/j.1467-8624.2004.00654.x

Case, S (2025) *Youth offending in context*. Routledge. Abingdon.

Catan, L (2004) *Becoming adult: changing youth transitions in the 21st century: final report*. Economic and Social Research Council. London.

Chao, R (2001) Extending research on the consequences of parenting style for Chinese Americans and European Americans. *Child Development*. 72. 1832–1843.

Ching, B, Downs, J, Zhang, S … Simonoff, E (2025) The impact of the Covid-19 pandemic on the mental health of children and young people with pre-existing mental health conditions. *Journal of Child Psychology and Psychiatry*. 66(8). 1274–1298. https://doi.org/10.1111/jcpp.14117

Christie, A (2021) Post-traumatic stress disorder (PTSD). In Laver-Bradbury, C, Thompson, M and Hooper, C (Eds.) *Child and Adolescent Mental Health*. Routledge. Abingdon.

Chua, T and Chang, L (2016) Follow me and like my beautiful selfies: Singapore teenage girls' engagement in self-presentation. *Computers in Human Behaviour*. 55. 190–197. https://doi.org/10.1016f/j.chb.2015.09.011

Coleman, J (1974) *Relationships in adolescence*. Routledge and Kegan Paul. London.

Coleman, J (1978) Current contradictions in adolescent theory. *Journal of Youth and Adolescence*. 7. 1–11.

Coleman, J (1979) Who leads who astray? Causes of anti-social behaviour in adolescence. *Journal of Adolescence*. 2. 179–185.

Coleman, J (2001) *Sex and your teenager*. Wiley. Chichester, Sussex.
Coleman, J (2009) Well-being in schools: empirical measure or politician's dream? *Oxford Review of Education*. 35. 281–292. https://doi.org/10.1080/03054980902934548
Coleman, J (2011) *The nature of adolescence* (4th Edition). Routledge. Abingdon.
Coleman, J (2014) Parenting teenagers. In Abela, A and Walker, J (Eds.) *Contemporary issues in family studies*. Wiley Blackwell. Chichester, Sussex.
Coleman, J (2019) *Why won't my teenager talk to me?* (2nd Edition). Routledge. Abingdon.
Coleman, J (2021) *The teacher and the teenage brain*. Routledge. Abingdon.
Coleman, J (2024) *The psychology of the teenage brain*. Routledge. Abingdon.
Coleman, J and Brooks, F (2009) *Key data on adolescence: 2009*. Association for Young People's Health. London.
Coleman, J and Hagell, A (Eds.) (2007) *Adolescence, risk and resilience: against the odds*. Wiley. Chichester, Sussex.
Coleman, JS (1961) *The adolescent society*. The Free Press. New York, NY.
Coleman, L and Coleman, J (2002) The measurement of puberty: a review. *Journal of Adolescence*. 25. 535–550. https://doi.org/10.1006/jado.2002.0494
Coles, B (1996) *Youth and social policy*. UCL Press. London.
Compas, B (2004) Processes of risk and resilience during adolescence. In Lerner, R and Steinberg, L (Eds.) *Handbook of adolescent psychology* (2nd Edition). Wiley. New York, NY.
Cotterell, J (2007) *Social networks in youth and adolescence*. Routledge. Abingdon.
Crenshaw, K (1991) Mapping the margins: intersectionality, identity politics, and violence against women of colour. *Stanford Law Review*. 43. 1241–1299.
Crick, N and Dodge, K (1996) Social information processing mechanisms in reactive and proactive aggression. *Child Development*. 67. 993–1002. https://doi.org/10.1111/j.1467-8624.1996.tb01778.x
Crocetti, E (2017) Identity formation in adolescence: the dynamic of forming and consolidating identity commitments. *Child Development Perspectives*. 11. 145–150. https://doi.org/10.1111/cdep.12226
Crone, E (2017) *The adolescent brain*. Psychology Press/Routledge. Abingdon, Oxon.
D'Anastasi, T and Frydenberg, E (2005) Ethnicity and coping: what young people do and what young people should learn. *Australian Journal of Guidance and Coping*. 15. 43–59.
Daddis, C and Randolph, C (2010) Dating and disclosure: adolescent management of information regarding romantic involvement. *Journal of Adolescence*. 33. 309–320. https://doi.org/10.1016/j.adolescence.2009.05.002
Daha, M (2011) Contextual factors contributing to ethnic identity development of second-generation Iranian-American adolescents. *Journal of Adolescent Research*. 26. 543–569. https://doi.org/10.1177/0743558411402335
Davies, C and Eynon, R (2013) *Teenagers and technology*. Routledge. Abingdon.
Deater-Deckard, K, Godwin, J, Lansford, JE … Al Hassan, S (2018) Within and between-person and group variance in behaviour and beliefs in cross-cultural data. *Journal of Adolescence*. 62. 207–217. https://doi.org/10.1016/j.adolescence.2017.06.002
Dehaene, S (2020) *How we learn*. Penguin Allen Lane Science Education. London.

Demetriou, A, Christou, C, Spanoudis, G and Platsidou, M (2002) The development of mental processing, efficiency, working memory and thinking. *Monographs of the Society for Research in Child Development*. 67. 1–53.

Devine, R and Lecce, S (Eds.) (2021) *Theory of mind in middle childhood and adolescence*. Routledge. Abingdon.

Diamond, L (2005) A new view of lesbian sub-types: stable versus fluid identity trajectories over an 8-year period. *Psychology of Women Quarterly*. 29. 119–128. https://doi.org/10.1111/j.1471-6402.2005.00174.x

Diamond, L (2008) Female bisexuality from adolescence to adulthood. Results from a 10-year longitudinal study. *Developmental Psychology*. 44. 5–14.

Diamond, L and Butterworth, M (2008) Questioning gender and sexual identity: dynamic links over time. *Sex Roles: A Journal of Research*. 59. 365–376. https://doi.org/10.1007/s11199-008-9425-3

Dillon, F, Worthington, R and Moradi, B (2011) Sexual identity as a universal process. In Schwartz, S, Lucyckx, K and Vignoles, V (Eds.) *Handbook of identity theory and research* (pp. 649–670). Springer Science. New York, NY.

Dimitrova, R, Ferrer-Wreder, L and Trost, K (2015) Intergenerational transmission of ethnic identity and life satisfaction of Roma minority adolescents and their parents. *Journal of Adolescence*. 45. 296–306. https://doi.org/10.1016/j.adolescence.2015.10.014

Dotterer, A and Day, E (2019) Parental knowledge discrepancies: examining the roles of warmth and self-disclosure. *Journal of Youth and Adolescence*. 48. 459–468. https://doi.org/10.1007/s10964-018-0926-2

Douglass, S and Umana-Taylor, A (2015) A brief form of the ethnic identity scale: development and empirical validation. *Identity: An International Journal of Theory and Research*. 15. 48–65. https://doi.org/10.1080/15283488.2014.989442

Douvan, E and Adelson, J (1966) *The adolescent experience*. John Wiley. New York, NY.

Dunphy, D (1972) Peer group socialization. In Hunt, F (Ed.) *Socialization in Australia*. Angus and Robertson. Sydney.

Eccles, J and Roeser, R (2003) Schools as developmental contexts. In Adams, G and Berzonsky, M (Eds.) *Blackwell handbook of adolescence*. Blackwell Publishing. Oxford.

Edwards, H, Wright, S, Sargeant, C and Wood-Downie, H (2024) A systematic review and meta-analysis of sex differences in narrow constructs of restricted and repetitive behaviours. *Journal of Child Psychology and Psychiatry*. 65(1). 4–17. https://doi.org/10.1111/jcpp.13855

Ehrlich, K, Lyle, S, Corallo, K … Brody, G (2023) Socio-economic disadvantage and high-effort coping in childhood: evidence of skin-deep resilience. *Journal of Child Psychology and Psychiatry*. 64. 5. https://doi.org/10.1111/jcpp.13840

Eisenberg, N and Morris, A (2004) Moral cognitions and prosocial responding in adolescence. In Lerner, R and Steinberg, L (Eds.) *Handbook of adolescent psychology* (2nd Edition). Wiley. New York.

Elder, G (1998) The life course as developmental theory. *Child Development*. 69. 1–12. https://doi.org/10.1111/j.1467-8624.1998.tb06128.x

Elkind, D (1966) Conceptual orientation shifts in children and adolescents. *Child Development.* 37. 493–498. https://doi.org/10.2307/1126673

Elkind, D (1967) Egocentrism in adolescence. *Child Development.* 1025–1034. https://doi.org/10.2307/1127100

Emler, N and Reicher, S (1995) *Adolescence and delinquency.* Blackwell. Oxford.

Ennett, S, Bauman, K, Hussong, K and Du Rant, R (2006) The peer context of adolescent substance misuse: findings from social network analysis. *Journal of Research on Adolescence.* 16. 159–186.

Erikson, E (1968) *Identity, youth and crisis.* Norton. New York.

Eslea, M, Menesini, E, Morita, Y … Smith, P (2003) Friendship and loneliness among bullies and victims: data from seven countries. *Aggressive Behaviour.* 30. 71–83. https://doi.org/10.1002/ab.20006

Eveleth, P and Tanner, J (1977) *Worldwide variation in human growth.* Cambridge University Press. Cambridge, UK.

Fairchild, G (2021) Juvenile disruptive behaviour disorders: Chapter 41. In Laver-Bradbury, C, Thompson, M, Gale, C and Hooper, C (Eds.) *Child and adolescent mental health: theory and practice.* Routledge. Abingdon.

Fergusson, D and Horwood, L (2003) Resilient children in adversity: results of a 21-year study. In Luthar, S (Ed.) *Resilience and vulnerability.* Cambridge University Press. Cambridge.

Ferrer-Wreder, L and Kroger, J (2020) *Identity in adolescence: the balance between self and other* (4th Edition). Routledge. Abingdon.

Flanagan, C (2004) Volunteerism, leadership, political socialization and civic engagement. In Lerner, R and Steinberg, L (Eds.) *Handbook of adolescent psychology* (2nd Edition). Wiley. New York.

Fleary, S, Joseph, P and Pappagianopoulos, J (2018) Adolescent health literacy and health behaviours: a systematic review. *Journal of Adolescence.* 62. 116–127. https://doi.org/10.1016/j.adolescence.2017.11.010

Fonagy, P, Target, M, Cottrell, D, Phillips, J and Kurtz, Z (2015) *What works for whom? A critical review of treatments for children and adolescents.* The Guilford Press. London.

Fontaine, N, Carbonneau, R, Vitaro, F and Tremblay, R (2009) Research review: a critical review of studies on the developmental trajectories of anti-social behaviour in females. *Journal of Child Psychology and Psychiatry.* 50. 363–385. https://doi.org/10.1111/j.1469-7610.2008.01949.x

Forster, V (2021) Developmental trauma. In Laver-Bradbury, C, and Hooper, C (Eds.) *Child and adolescent mental health.* Routledge. Abingdon.

Foster, R (2022) *Life time: the new science of the body clock.* Penguin Life. London.

Foulkes, L (2022) Not such a class act. *New Scientist.* 25. 24–25.

Foulkes, L (2024) Chapter 6 "Sex education". In *Coming of age: how adolescence shapes us.* Bodley Head. London.

Frank, A (1993) *The diary of a young girl.* Bantam. New York.

Franke, B, Fombonne, E and Ronald, A (2021) The new genetics of autism. *Journal of Child Psychology and Psychiatry.* 62(11). 1271–1273. https://doi.org/10.1111/jcpp.13527

Frankel, R (1998) *The adolescent psyche.* Routledge. London.

Freud, A (1937) *The ego and the mechanisms of defence.* Hogarth Press. London.

Frydenberg, E (2019) *Adolescent coping* (3rd Edition). Routledge. Abingdon.

Gale, C (2021) Attachment theory. In Laver-Bradbury, C, Thompson, M, Gale, C and Hooper, C (Eds.) *Child and adolescent mental health: theory and practice.* Routledge. Abingdon.

Galvan, A (2017) *The neuroscience of adolescence.* Cambridge University Press. Cambridge, UK.

Gardner, F, Collishaw, S, Maugham, B ... Hagell, A (2012) Trends in parenting. In Hagell, A (Ed.) *Changing adolescence: social trends and mental health.* Policy Press. Bristol.

Garmezy, N and Rutter, M (Eds.) (1983) *Stress, coping and development in children.* McGraw Hill. New York, NY.

Gavazzi, S (2011) *Families with adolescents.* Springer. New York, NY.

Ghirardi, L, Kuja-Halkola, R, Butwicka, A ... Taylor, M (2021) Familial and genetic associations between autism spectrum disorder and other neurodevelopmental and psychiatric disorders. *Journal of Child Psychology and Psychiatry.* 62(11). 1274–1284. https://doi.org/10.1111/jcpp.13508

Gilligan, C, Lyons, N and Hammer, T (1990) *Making connections: the relational worlds of adolescent girls at Emma Willard School.* Harvard University Press. Cambridge, MA.

Golm, D and Kreppner, J (2021) The effect of child maltreatment on brain development. In Laver-Bradbury, C, Thompson, M and Hooper, C (Eds.) *Child and adolescent mental health.* Routledge. Abingdon.

Goodfellow, C, Macintyre, A and Sosu, E (2023) Associations between mental health literacy and adolescent help-seeking intentions. *Child and Adolescent Mental Health.* 28(3). 285–392.

Goodyear, V and Armour, K (2019) *Young people, social media and health.* Routledge. Abingdon.

Goossens, L (2006) The many faces of autonomy. In *Handbook of adolescent development.* Psychology Press. Hove, Sussex.

Graber, J and Brooks-Gunn, J (1996) Transitions and turning points: navigating the passage from childhood to adolescence. *Developmental Psychology.* 32. 768–776. https://doi.org/10.1016/j.adolescence.2005.08.003

Gray, N, Desmond, A, Beadle, S and Bundle, D (2022) Breaking down silos between health and education to improve adolescent well-being. *British Medical Journal.* 379. 1472–1486.

Greenspan, L and Deardorff, J (2014) *The new puberty.* Rodale. New York.

Grolnick, W, Beiswenger, K and Price, C (2008) Stepping up without over-stepping: disentangling parenting dimensions and their implications for adolescent development. In Kerr, M, Stattin, H and Engels, R (Eds.) *What can parents do?* Wiley. Chichester, Sussex.

Grotevant, H and Cooper, C (1986) Individuation in family relationships: a perspective on individual differences. *Human Development.* 29. 82–100.

Gummerson, M, Keller, M and Mata, J (2008) To give or not to give: children and adolescents' sharing and moral negotiations in economic decision situations. *Child Development.* 79. 562–576. https://doi.org/10.1111/j.1467-8624.2008.01143.x

References

Guzman-Holst, C, Davis, R, Andrews, J and Foulkes, L (2025) Scoping review; potential harm from school-based group mental health interventions. *Child and Adolescent Mental Health.* 30(3). 208–222. https://osf.io/preprints/psyarxiv/we6bz

Hadley, A (2025) *Teenage pregnancy and young parenthood: effective policy and practice.* Routledge. Abingdon.

Hadwin, J and Magdalena, R (2021) Fear and anxiety: Chapter 45. In Laver-Bradbury, C, Thompson, M, Gale, C and Hooper, C (Eds.) *Child and adolescent mental health: Theory and practice.* Routledge. Abingdon.

Hagell, A (2007) Anti-social behaviour. In Coleman, J and Hagell, A (Eds.) *Adolescence, risk and resilience.* Wiley. Chichester, Sussex.

Hagell, A (Ed.) (2012) *Changing adolescence: social trends and mental health.* Policy Press. Bristol.

Hagell, A and Newburn, T (1996) Family and social contexts of adolescent re-offenders. *Journal of Adolescence.* 19. 5–18.

Hagell, A and Shah, R (2019) *Key data on young people: 2019.* Association for Young People's Health. London.

Haidt, J (2024) *The anxious generation.* Allen Lane. London.

Hall, GS (1904) *Adolescence: its relation to physiology, anthropology, sociology, sex, crime, religion and education.* Appleton. New York.

Hammack, P (2006) Identity, conflict and coexistence: life stories of Israeli and Palestinian adolescents. *Journal of Adolescent Research.* 21. 323–269. https://doi.org/10.1177/0743558406289745

Hammack, P (2014) Theoretical foundations of identity. In McClean, K and Syed, M (Eds.) *Oxford handbook of identity development* (pp. 1–37). Oxford University Press. New York. NY.

Hampel, P and Peterman, F (2005) Age and gender effects on coping in children and adolescents. *Journal of Youth and Adolescence.* 34. 73–83.

Hari, J (2022) *Stolen focus.* Bloomsbury. London.

Harter, S (1990) Self and identity development. In Feldman, S and Elliot, G (Eds.) *At the threshold: the developing adolescent.* Harvard University Press. Cambridge, MA.

Hawker, D and Boulton, M (2000) Twenty years research on peer victimization and psychosocial maladjustment. *Journal of Child Psychology and Psychiatry.* 41. 441–455. https://doi.org/10.1111/1469-7610.00629

Hawkes, D (2010) Just what difference does teenage motherhood make? Evidence from the Millenium Cohort Study. In Duncan, S and Alexander, C (Eds.) *Teenage parenthood: what's the problem?* Tufnell Press. London.

Hayman, S and Coleman, J (2016) *Parents and digital technology.* Routledge. Abingdon.

Hendry, L (2015) *Developmental transitions across the life span.* Psychology Press. Hove, Sussex.

Herman-Giddens, M, Steffes, J, Harris, D, Hussey, M and Reiter, E (2012) Secondary sexual characteristics in boys. *Paediatrics.* https://doi.org/10.1542/peds.2011-3291

Higgen, S, Mueller, J and Mosko, M (2022) Universal health interventions for young students in adverse environments: a systematic review of evaluated interventions. *Child and Adolescent Mental Health.* 3. 281–293. https://doi.org/10.1111/camh.12493

Hill, J and Maugham, B (Eds.) (2001) *Conduct disorders in childhood and adolescence.* Cambridge University Press. Cambridge.

Hill, R (2025) *Raising confident teenagers.* Karnac Publishing. Bicester, Oxon.

Hinshaw, S (2018) Attention-deficit hyperactivity disorder: controversy, developmental mechanisms, and multiple levels of analysis. *Annual Review of Clinical Psychology.* 14. 291–316. https://doi.org/10.1146/annurev-clinpsy-050817-084917

Hinshaw, S, Nguyen, P, O'Grady, M and Rosenthal, E (2022) Attention-deficit/hyperactivity disorder in girls and women: underrepresentation and key directions. *Journal of Child Psychology and Psychiatry.* 63(4). 484–496. https://doi.org/10.1111/jcpp.13480

Hinshaw, S and Scheffler, R (2014) *The ADHD explosion: myths, medication, money, and today's push for performance.* Oxford University Press. New York, NY.

Hirsch, B and DuBois, D (1991) Self-esteem in early adolescence: the identification and prediction of contrasting longitudinal trajectories. *Journal of Youth and Adolescence.* 20. 53–72. https://doi.org/10.1007/BF01537351

Holmes, D (Ed.) (2022) *Safeguarding young people: risks, rights and resilience.* Jessica Kingsley. London.

Holt, A (2025) *Adolescent to parent abuse* (2nd Edition). Policy Press. Bristol.

Hoyos, C (2021) Early access: emotional literacy and first aid in schools. In Laver-Bradbury, C, Thompson, M, Gale, C and Hooper, C (Eds.) *Child and adolescent mental health.* Routledge. Abingdon.

Hulbert, S, Eida, T, Ferris, E and Kendall, S (2023) HBSC Study for England. National Report. Findings from 2001 to 2022. University of Kent.

Hutchinson, A (2013) Strengths-based/resilience theory. In Davies, M (Ed.) *The Blackwell companion to social work* (4th Edition). Wiley-Blackwell. Chichester, Sussex.

Inhelder, B and Piaget, J (1958) *The growth of logical thinking.* Routledge and Kegan Paul. London.

Jansen, L and Leitjen, P (2025) Each unhappy family is unhappy in its own way: a call for clearer conceptualization of adverse family factors in biosocial research on child and adolescent mental health problems. *Journal of Child Psychology and Psychiatry.* 66(6). 771–774. https://doi.org/10.1111/jcpp.14174

Jenkins, J, Simpson, A, Dunn and O'Connor, T (2005) Mutual influence of marital conflict and children's behaviour problems. *Child Development.* 76. 24–39. https://doi.org/10.1111/j.1467-8624.2005.00827.x

Jones, G (1995) *Leaving home.* Open University Press. Milton Keynes.

Kail, R and Ferrer, E (2007) Processing speed in childhood and adolescence. *Child Development.* 78. 1760–1770. https://doi.org/10.1111/j.1467-8624.2007.01088.x

Kang, M, Coyne, I and Gray, N (2026) *Adolescent health and well-being.* Routledge. Abingdon.

Kaplan, A and Garner, J (2017) A complex dynamic systems perspective on identity and its development. *Developmental Psychology.* 53. 2036–2051.

Kauhannen, W, and Yunus, W (2023) A systematic review of the mental health changes in children and young people before and during the Covid 19 pandemic. *European Child and Adolescent Psychiatry.* 32. 995–1013. https://doi.org/10.1007/s00787-022-02060-0

References

Keating, D (2011) Cognitive development. In Brown, B and Prinstein, M (Eds.) *Encyclopedia of adolescence* (Volume 1, pp. 106–114). Academic Press. New York.

Keijsers, L and Laird, R (2010) Introduction to special issue: careful conversations: adolescents managing their parents' access to information. *Journal of Adolescence*. 33. 255–260. https://doi.org/10.1016/j.adolescence.2009.10.009

Kelleher, E (2025) Annual research review: psychosis in children and adolescents: key updates. *Journal of Child Psychology and Psychiatry*. 66(4). 460–476. https://doi.org/10.1111/jcpp.14088

Kerr, M and Stattin, H (2000) What parents know, how they know it, and several forms of adolescent adjustment. *Developmental Psychology*. 36. 366–380.

Kerr, M, Stattin, H and Engels, R (Eds.) (2008) *What can parents do? New insights into the role of parents in adolescent problem behaviour*. Wiley. Chichester, Sussex.

Keyes, K and Platt, J (2024) Sex, gender and internalizing conditions among adolescents in the 21st century: trends, causes and consequences. *Journal of Child Psychology and Psychiatry*. 65(4). 384–407. https://doi.org/10.1111/jcpp.13864

Kim, Y and Stattin, H (2019) Parent-youth discussions about politics from age 13 to 28. *Journal of Applied Developmental Psychology*. 62. 249–259. https://doi.org/10.1016/j.appdev.2019.04.001

Kloep, M (1999) Love is all you need. Focusing on adolescents' life concerns from an ecological perspective. *Journal of Adolescence*. 22. 49–62. https://doi.org/10.1016/j.adolescence.2009.10.009

Kohlberg, L (Ed.) (1981) *The philosophy of moral development* (Volume 1). Harper and Row. San Francisco, CA.

Kohlberg, L (Ed.) (1984) *The philosophy of moral development* (Volume 2). Harper and Row. San Francisco, CA.

Kohlberg, L and Gilligan, C (1971) Twelve to sixteen: early adolescence. *Daedalus*. 100(4). 1068–1072.

Kolto, A, Young, H, Burke, L … Gabhainn, S (2018) Love and dating patterns for same- and both-gender attracted adolescents across Europe. *Journal of Research on Adolescence*. 28. 772–778. https://doi.org/10.1111/jora.12394

Koops, W and Castro, B 2006) Development of aggression and its linkages with violence and delinquency. In Jackson, S and Goossens, L (Eds.) *Handbook of adolescent development*. Psychology Press. Hove, Sussex.

Koyanagi, A, Oh, H, Carvalho, A … DeVylder, J (2019) Bullying victimization and suicide attempt among adolescents aged 12–15 years from 48 countries. *Journal of the American Academy of Child and Adolescent Psychiatry*. 58. 907–918. https://doi.org/10.1016/j.jaac.2018.10.018

Kuhn, D (2009) Adolescent thinking. In Lerner, R and Steinberg, L (Eds.) *Handbook of adolescent psychology* (3rd Edition, Volume 1), pp.152–186. Wiley. New York, NY.

Lansen, L and Leitjen, P (2025) Each unhappy family is unhappy in its own way: a call for clearer conceptualization of adverse family factors in biosocial research on child and adolescent mental health problems. *Journal of Child Psychology and Psychiatry*. 66(6). 771–774. https://doi.org/10.1111/jcpp.14174

Laver-Bradbury, C (2021) Parenting programmes. In Laver-Bradbury, C, Thompson, M, Gale, C and Hooper, C (Eds.) *Child and adolescent mental health: theory and practice: Chapter 70.* Routledge. Abingdon.

Laver-Bradbury, C, Thompson, M, Gale, C and Hooper, C (2021) *Child and adolescent mental health: theory and practice.* Routledge. Abingdon.

Lazarus, R (1966) *Psychological stress and the coping process.* McGraw-Hill. New York, NY.

Li, G and Davis, J (2020) Sexual experimentation in heterosexual, bisexual, lesbian/gay and questioning adolescents aged 11 to 15. *Journal of Research on Adolescence.* 30. 423–439. https://doi.org/10.1111/jora.12535

Lila, M, van Aken, M, Musito, G and Buelga, S (2006) Families and adolescents. In Jackson, S and Goossens, L (Eds.) *Handbook of adolescent development.* Psychology Press. Hove, Sussex.

Livingstone, S, Orben, A and Odgers, C (2023) Should academics collaborate with digital companies to improve young people's mental health? *Child and Adolescent Mental Health.* 28(1). 150–152. https://doi.org/10.1111/camh.12630

Loeber, R and Stouthammer-Loeber, M (1986) Family factors as correlates and predictors of juvenile conduct problems and delinquency. In Morris, M and Tonry, M. (Eds.) *Crime and justice: Volume 7.* University of Chicago Press. Chicago.

Luthar, S (Ed.) (2003) *Resilience and vulnerability.* Cambridge University Press. Cambridge.

Luther, S (2006) Resilience in development: a synthesis of research across five decades. In Cicchetti, D and Cohen, D (Eds.) *Developmental psychopathology: risk, disorder and adaptation.* Wiley. New York, NY.

Maccoby, E and Martin, J (1983) Socialization in the context of the family: parent–child interaction. In Hetherington, E (Ed.) *Handbook of child psychology.* Wiley. New York, NY.

Macdonald, R (2007) Social exclusion, risk and young adulthood. In Coleman, J and Hagell, A (Eds.) *Adolescence, risk and resilience: against the odds.* Wiley. Chichester, Sussex.

Maheux, A, Burnell, K, Maza, M and Prinstein, M (2025) Annual research review: adolescent social media is not a monolith. *Journal of Child Psychology and Psychiatry.* 66(4). 440–459. https://doi.org/10.1111/jcpp.14085

Marcia, J (1966) Development and validation of ego-identity status. *Journal of Personality and Social Psychology.* 3. 551–558. https://psycnet.apa.org/doi/10.1037/h0023281

Marcia, J (1993) The relational roots of identity. In Kroger, J (Ed.) *Discussions on ego-identity.* Lawrence Erlbaum. Hillsdale, NJ.

Marshall, S, Tilton-Weaver, L and Bosdet, L (2005) Information management: considering adolescents' regulation of parental knowledge. *Journal of Adolescence.* 28. 633–648. https://doi.org/10.1016/j.adolescence.2005.08.008

Marston, C and Lewis, R (2014) Anal heterosex among young people and the implications for health promotion: a qualitative study in the UK. *BMJ Open.* 4(8). https://doi.org/10.1136/bmjopen-2014-004996

Mason, G, Auerbach, R and Stewart, J (2025) Predicting the trajectory of non-suicidal self-injury among adolescents. *Journal of Child Psychology and Psychiatry.* 66(2). 189–201. https://doi.org/10.1111/jcpp.14046

References

Masten, A (2014) *Ordinary magic: resilience in development.* The Guilford Press. London.

Masten, A and Powell, J (2003) A resilience framework for research, policy and practice. In Luthar, S (Ed.) *Resilience and vulnerability.* Cambridge University Press. Cambridge.

McCrory, E, Gerin, E and Viding, E (2017) Child maltreatment, latent vulnerability, and the shift to preventative psychiatry: the contribution of functional brain imaging. *Journal of Child Psychology and Psychiatry.* 58. 338–357. https://doi.org/10.1111/jcpp.12713

Meeus, W (2019) *Adolescent development.* Routledge. Abingdon.

Mendelson, M and Aboud, F (1999) Measuring friendship quality in late adolescents and young adults. *Canadian Journal of Behavioural Science.* 31. 130–132.

Mendle, J (2014) Beyond pubertal timing: new directions for studying individual differences in development. *Current Directions in Psychological Science.* 23. 215–219. https://doi.org/10.1177/0963721414530144

Mendle, J and Ferrero, J (2012) Detrimental psychological outcomes associated with pubertal timing in adolescent boys. *Developmental Review.* 32. 49–66. https://doi.org/10.1016/j.dr.2011.11.001

Meng, X, Li, S, Duan, W, Sun, Y and Jia, C (2017) Secular trend of age of menarche in Chinese adolescents born from 1973–2004. *Paediatrics.* 140. https://doi.org/10.1542/peds.2017-0085

Mikami, AY, Szwedo, DE, Khalis, A, Jia, M and Na, JJ. (2019) Online social interactions predict academic and emotional adjustment in the transition to university. *Journal of Research on Adolescence.* 29. 210–224. https://doi.org/10.1111/jora.12377

Miller, G (1956) The magical number seven, plus or minus two: some limits to our capacity to process information. *Psychological Review.* 63(2). 81–89.

Mills, M (2014) Globalization and family life. Chapter 17. In Abela, A and Walker, J (Eds.) *Contemporary issues in family studies.* Routledge. Abingdon.

Mitchell, A, Patrick, K, Heywood, W … Pitts, M (2014) *Fifth National Survey of Australian Secondary School Students and Sexual Health, 2013.* ARCSHS Monograph Series No. 97. La Trobe University. Melbourne.

Moffit, T (2006) Life-course persistent versus adolescent-limited anti-social behaviour. In Cicchetti, D and Cohen, D (Eds.) *Developmental psychopathology* (Volume 2). Wiley. New York, NY.

Montagna, W and Sadler, W (Eds.) (1974) *Reproductive Behaviour.* Plenum. New York.

Moore, S and Rosenthal, D (2006) *Sexuality in adolescence: current trends.* Routledge. Abingdon.

Morgan, N (2013) *Blame my brain: the amazing teenage brain revealed.* Walker Books. London.

Mounts, N (2002) Parental management of adolescent peer relationships in context. *Journal of Family Psychology.* 16. 58–69. 446–467. https://doi.org/10.1177/0743558403258854

Mounts, N (2004) Adolescents' perceptions of parental management of peer relationships in an ethnically diverse sample. *Journal of Adolescent Research.* 19. 446–467.

Murray, F (1990) The conversion of truth into necessity. In Overton, W (Ed.) *Reasoning, necessity and logic: developmental perspectives.* Lawrence Erlbaum. Hillsdale, NJ.

Murray, M, Obeid, N, Gunnell, K … Goldfield, G (2023) Appearance satisfaction mediates the relationship between recreational screen time and depressive symptoms in adolescents. *Child and Adolescent Mental Health.* 28(1). 12–21. https://doi.org/10.1111/camh.12576

Muuss, R (1996) *Theories of adolescence* (6th Edition). McGraw-Hill. New York.

Neves S (2025) Exploring the landscape of sexuality. *The Psychologist*. 50–51.

Nicholls, D (2023) A perfect storm: how and why eating disorders in young people have thrived in lockdown, and what is happening to address it? *Journal of Child Psychology and Psychiatry*. 64(2). 335–338. https://doi.org/10.1111/jcpp.13676

Nicholson, J, D'Esposito, F, Lucas, N and Westrupp, M (2014) Raising children in single-parent families. In Abela, A and Walker, J (Eds.) *Contemporary issues in family studies*. Wiley Blackwell. Chichester, Sussex.

Nutbeam, D (2000) Health literacy as a public health goal. *Health Promotion International*. 15(3). 259–267.

Offer, D (1969) *The psychological world of the teenager*. Basic Books. New York.

Offer, D, Ostrov, D, Howard, K and Dolin, S (1992) *The offer self-image questionnaire for adolescents – revised*. Western Psychological Services. Los Angeles, CA.

Ogden, T and Hagen, K (2019) *Adolescent health: prevention and intervention*. Routledge. Abingdon.

Olsson, C, Bond, L, Burns, J and Sawyer, S (2003) Adolescent resilience: a concept analysis. *Journal of Adolescence*. 26. 1–11. https://doi.org/10.1016/S0140-1971(02)00118-5

Oosterhoff, B, Wray-Lake, L, Palmer, C and Kaplow, J (2019) Historical trends in concerns about social issues across four decades among U.S. adolescents. *Journal of Research on Adolescence*. 30(S2). 485–498. https://doi.org/10.1111/jora.12493

Orth, U and Robins, R (2014) The development of self-esteem. *Current Directions in Psychological Science*. 23. 381–387. https://doi.org/10.1177/0963721414547414

Osgood, D, Wilson, J and Johnson, L (1996) Routine activities and individual deviant behaviour. *American Sociological Review*. 61. 635–655.

Over, H, Bunce, C and Zendle, D (2025) What do we need to know about the manosphere and young people's mental health. *Child and Adolescent Mental Health*. 30(3). 272–275. https://doi.org/10.1111/camh.12747

Parent, A-S, Teilman, G, Juul, A and Toppari, N (2003) The timing of normal puberty and the age limits of sexual precocity: variations around the world. *Endocrine Review*. 24. 668–693. https://doi.org/10.1210/er.2002-0019

Pathmendra, P, Raggatt, M, Lim, M and Skinner, R (2023) Exposure to pornography and adolescent sexual behaviour. *Journal of Medicine and Internet Research*. 25. https://doi.org/10.2196/43116

Patton, G, Sawyer, S and Santelli, J (2016) Our future: a Lancet commission on adolescent health and well-being. *The Lancet*. 387(10036). 2423–2478.

Pearce, J (2017) Preventing child sexual exploitation: would an international age of consent to sexual activity help secure the welfare of children? In Dolan, P and Frost, N (Eds.) *The Routledge handbook of global child welfare*. Routledge. Abingdon.

Pearce, J (2019) *Child sexual exploitation: why theory matters*. Policy Press. Bristol.

Peters, S (2021) The development of executive functions in childhood and adolescence: their relation to school performance. In Thomas, MSC, Mareschal, D and Dumontheil, I (Eds.) *Educational neuroscience: development across the lifespan*. Routledge. Abingdon.

Phinney, J (1993) A three-stage model of ethnic identity development. In Bernal, M and Knight, G (Eds.) *Ethnic identity: formation and transmission among Hispanics and other minorities.* State University of New York Press. Albany, NY.

Phinney, J and Devich-Navarro, M (1997) Variations in bi-cultural identification among African-American and Mexican-American adolescents. *Journal of Research on Adolescence.* 7. 3–32. https://doi.org/10.1207/s15327795jra0701_2

Piaget, J (1932) *The moral judgement of the child.* Routledge and Kegan Paul. London.

Pickett, K and Wilkinson, R (2024) Socio-economic inequality and child and adolescent mental health. *Child and Adolescent Mental Health.* 29(3). 308–310. https://doi.org/10.1111/camh.12699

Pirrone, L (2022) Pornography use profiles and emergence of sexual behaviour in adolescence. *Archives of Sexual Behaviour.* 51. 1141–1156. https://doi.org/10.1007/s10508-021-02140-3

Pitts, J (2008) *Reluctant gangsters: the changing face of youth crime.* Willan Publishing. Cullompton, Devon.

Pryor, J (2014) Mariage and divorce in the Western world. In Abela, A and Walker, J (Eds.) *Contemporary issues in family studies.* Chapter 4. Routledge. Abingdon.

Putwain, D (2025) *Understanding and helping to overcome exam anxiety.* Routledge. Abingdon.

Rask, C, Duholm, C, Poulsen, C and Wright, K (2024) Health anxiety in children and adolescents – developmental aspects and cross-generational influences. *Journal of Child Psychology and Psychiatry.* 65(4). 413–430. https://doi.org/10.1111/jcpp.13912

Reitz, E, Dekovic, M and Meijer, A (2006) Relations between parenting and externalizing and internalizing problem behaviour. *Journal of Adolescence.* 29. 419–436. https://doi.org/10.1016/j.adolescence.2005.08.003

Ricciardelli, L and Yager, Z (2016) *Adolescence and body image.* Routledge. Abingdon.

Rieger, S, Gollnar, R and Roberts, B (2016) Low self-esteem prospectively predicts depression. *Journal of Personality and Social Psychology.* 110. e16–e22. https://psycnet.apa.org/doi/10.1037/pspp0000037

Rivas-Drake, D and Umana-Taylor, A (2019) *Below the surface: talking with teens about race, ethnicity and identity.* Princeton University Press. Princeton, NJ.

Rivas-Drake, D, Umana-Taylor, A, Schaeffer, D and Medina, M (2017) Ethnic-racial identity and friendships in early adolescence. *Child Development.* 88. 710–724. https://doi.org/10.1111/cdev.12790

Robertson, C, Kennedy, G, McIntosh, L and McKechnie, A (2025) Home Fae home: a case study in co-designing trauma-informed safe spaces with young people in Dundee. *Child and Adolescent Mental Health.* 30(2). 131–139. https://doi.org/10.1111/camh.12765

Roker, D and Coleman, J (Eds.) (2007) *Working with parents of young people.* Jessica Kingsley. London.

Roker, D and Coleman, J (Eds.) (2007) *Working with parents of young people: research, policy and practice.* Jessica Kingsley. London.

Ronka, A, Oravala, S and Pulkinnen, L (2002) 'I met this wife of mine and things got on a better track': turning points in risk development. *Journal of Adolescence.* 25. 47–64. https://doi.org/10.1006/jado.2001.0448

Rosenberg, M (1965) *Society and the adolescent self-image.* Princeton University Press. Princeton, NJ.

Rosenberg, M (1979) *Concerning the self.* Basic Books. New York.

Ruiz S, Roosa, M and Gonzalez, M (2002) Predictors of self-esteem for Mexican-American and European American youths. *Journal of Family Psychology.* 16. 70–80.

Rusk, S, DiBari, J, Mason, D … Wang, X (2024) The impact of Covid-19 on psychiatric clinical encounters among low-income racially diverse children. *Journal of Child Psychology and Psychiatry.* 65(5). 631–643. https://doi.org/10.1111/jcpp.13809

Rutter, M (2003) Genetic influences in risk and protection: implications for understanding resilience. In Luthar, S (Ed.) *Resilience and vulnerability.* Cambridge University Press. Cambridge.

Ryan, R (2001) The peer group as a context for the development of young motivation and achievement. *Child Development.* 72. 1135–1150. https://doi.org/10.1111/1467-8624.00338

Salusky, L, Larson, R, Griffiths, A … Guzman, M (2014) How adolescents develop responsibility: what can be learned from youth programs. *Journal of Research on Adolescence.* 24. 417–430. https://doi.org/10.1111/jora.12118

Sanson, A and Dubicka, B (2022) The climate and ecological mental health emergency: evidence and action. *Child and Adolescent Mental Health.* 27(1). 1–4. https://doi.org/10.1111/camh.12540

Sanson, A, Van Hoorn, J and Burke, S (2019) Responding to the impacts of the climate crisis on children and youth. *Child Development Perspectives.* 13. 201–207. https://doi.org/10.1111/cdep.12342

Savage, J (2007) *Teenage: the creation of youth 1875–1945.* Chatto and Windus. London.

Schaeffer, S and Uggen, C 2009) Juvenile delinquency and desistance. In Furlong, A (Ed.) *Handbook of youth and young adulthood.* Routledge. London.

Schaffer, R (2006) *Key concepts in developmental psychology.* Sage. London.

Schmidt, J and Padilla, B (2003) Self-esteem and family challenge: an investigation of their effects on achievement. *Journal of Youth and Adolescence.* 32. 37–46. https://doi.org/10.1023/A:1021080323230

Scholte, R and van Aken, M (2006) Peer relations in adolescence. In Jackson, S and Goossens, L (Eds.) *Handbook of adolescent development.* Psychology Press. Hove, Sussex.

Schwartz, SJ, Unger, JB, Meca, A … Pattarroyo, M (2017) Personal identity development in Hispanic immigrant adolescents. *Journal of Youth and Adolescence.* 46. 898–913. https://doi.org/10.1007/s10964-016-0615-y

Scott, J (2007) The role of the family. In Coleman, J and Hagell, A (Eds.) *Adolescence, risk and resilience.* John Wiley. Chichester, Sussex.

Seiffge-Krenke, I (1995) *Stress, coping and relationships in adolescence.* Lawrence Erlbaum. Mahwah, New Jersey.

Seligman, M (2011) *Flourish: a new understanding of happiness and well-being.* Nicholas Brealey. London.

Sherman, R, Illingworth, G and Harvey, C (2020) The neuroscience of sleep. In Thomas, M, Mareschal, D and Dumontheil, I (Eds.) *Educational neuroscience.* Routledge. Abingdon.

Shaw, J and Frost, N (2013) *Young people and the care experience.* Routledge. London.

Shmuel, S and Seiffge-Krenke, I (1997) *Fathers and adolescents.* Routledge. Abingdon.

Sibley, M, Flores, S, Murphy, M ... van Dreel, S (2025) Pharmacological and non-pharmacological treatments for adolescents with attention deficit/hyperactivity disorder. *Journal of Child Psychology and Psychiatry.* 66(1). 132–149. https://doi.org/10.1111/jcpp.14056

Silberman, S (2015) *Neurotribes: the legacy of autism.* Allen and Unwin. London.

Simmons, R and Blyth, D (1987) *Moving into adolescence: the impact of pubertal change and school context.* Aldine de Gruyter. New York.

Sisler, A and Ittel, A (2015) *Siblings in adolescence.* Psychology Press. London.

Smetana, J (2002) Culture, autonomy and personal jurisdiction in parent-adolescent relationships. *Advances in Child Development and Behaviour.* 29. 51–87. https://doi.org/10.1016/S0065-2407(02)80051-9

Smetana, J and Chuang, S (2001) Middle class African-American parents' conceptions of parenting in the transition to adolescence. *Journal of Research on Adolescence.* 11. 177–198. https://doi.org/10.1111/1532-7795.00009

Smetana, J and Villalobos, M (2009) Social cognitive development in adolescence. In Lerner, R and Steinberg, L (Eds.) *Handbook of adolescent psychology* (3rd Edition). Wiley. New York, NY.

Soller, B (2014) Caught in a bad romance: adolescent romantic relationships and mental health. *Journal of Health and Social Behaviour.* 55(1). 56–72. https://doi.org/10.1177/0022146513520432

Sonuga-Barke, E and Fearon, P (2021) Do lockdowns scar? Three putative mechanisms through which Covid-19 mitigation policies could cause long-term harm to young people's mental health. *Journal of Child Psychology and Psychiatry.* 62(12). 1375–1378. https://doi.org/10.1111/jcpp.13537

Stattin, H and Kerr, M (2000) Parental monitoring: a reinterpretation. *Child Development.* 71. 1070–1083. https://doi.org/10.1111/1467-8624.00210

Stattin, H and Magnusson, D (1996) Anti-social development: a holistic approach. *Development and Psychopathology.* 8(4):617–645. https://doi.org/10.1017/S0954579400007331

Steinberg, L (2016) *Age of opportunity: lessons from the new science of adolescence.* Mariner Books. Boston, MA.

Steinberg, L (2023) *Adolescence* (13th Edition). McGraw-Hill. New York.

Steinberg, L and Silverberg, S (Eds.) (1986) The vicissitudes of autonomy in early adolescence. *Child Development.* 57. 841–851. https://doi.org/10.2307/1130361

Stevenson, J (2022) Editorial perspective: how Sir Michael Rutter revolutionized our understanding of human development: an introduction to a systematic digest of his work. *Journal of Child Psychology and Psychiatry.* 63(1). 4–7. https://doi.org/10.1111/jcpp.13559

Stoddard, S, Whiteside, L, Zimmerman, M ... Walton, M (2013) The relation between cumulative risk promotive factors, and adolescent violent behaviour among urban adolescents. *American Journal of Community Psychology.* 51. 57–65. https://doi.org/0.1007/s10464-012-9541-7

Stumper, A, Olino, T, Abramson, L and Alloy, L (2019) Pubertal timing and substance abuse in adolescence. *Journal of Abnormal Child Psychology*. 47. 1509–1520. https://doi.org/10.1007/s10802-019-00524-7

Sunshine, A and McClennan, J (2023) Psychosis in children and adolescents. *The Journal of Child Psychology and Psychiatry*. 64(7). 980–988. https://doi.org/10.1111/jcpp.13777

Talmud, I and Mesch, G (2020) *Wired youth: the online social world of adolescence*. Routledge. Abingdon.

Tanner, J (1962) *Growth at adolescence*. Blackwell Scientific Publications. Oxford.

Tanner, J (1978) *Foetus into man*. Open Books. London.

Tanton, C, Jones, K, Macdowall, W and Mercer, C (2015) Patterns and trends in sources of information about sex among young people in Britain: evidence from three national surveys. *BMJ Open*. 5. e007834. https://doi.org/10.1136/bmjopen-2015-007834

Temple-Smith, M, Moore, S and Rosenthal, D (2016) *Sexuality in adolescence: the digital generation*. Routledge. Abingdon.

Temple-Smith, MM and Rosenthal, D (2016) *Sexuality in adolescence: the digital generation*. Routledge. Abingdon.

Thomas, M, Mareschal, D and Dumontheil, I (Eds.) (2020) *Educational neuroscience: development across the lifespan*. Routledge. Abingdon.

Tilton-Weaver, L, Kerr, M and Stattin, H (2010) Open up or close down: how do parental reactions affect youth information management? *Journal of Adolescence*. 33. 333–346.

Timimi, S (2025) *Searching for normal: a new approach to understanding mental health, distress and neurodiversity*. Penguin. London.

Townsend, E, Ness, J, Waters, K … Hawton, K (2022) Life problems in children and adolescents who self-harm: findings from the multi-centre study of self-harm in England. *Child and Adolescent Mental Health*. 27(4). 352–360. https://doi.org/10.1111/camh.12544

Troiden, R (1989) The formation of homosexual identities. In Herdt, G (Ed.) *Gay and lesbian youth*. Haworth Press. New York, NY.

Umana-Taylor, A, Quintana, S, Lee, R, Cross, W and Seaton, E (2014) Ethnic and racial identity during adolescence and into young adulthood. *Child Development*. 85. 21–39. https://doi.org/10.1111/cdev.12196

Ungar, M (Ed.) (2021) *Multi-systemic resilience: adaptation and transformation in contexts of change*. Oxford University Press. Oxford.

Upchurch, D, Lillard, L and Li, N (2002) Inconsistencies in reporting the occurrence and timing of first intercourse among adolescents. *Journal of Sex Research*. 39. 197–206. https://doi.org/10.1080/00224490209552142

Van Lawick, J (2014) Couple and family dynamics and escalation in violence. In Abela, A and Walker, J (Eds.) *Contemporary issues in family studies*. Wiley Blackwell. Chichester, Sussex.

Vannucci, A, Simpson, E, Gagnon, S and Ohanessian, C (2020) Social media use and risky behaviours in adolescence: a meta-analysis. *Journal of Adolescence*. 79. 258–274. https://doi.org/10.1016/j.adolescence.2020.01.014

Walker, L, Gusfafson, P and Hennig, K (2001) The consolidation/transition model in moral reasoning development. *Developmental Psychology*. 37. 187–197. https://psycnet.apa.org/doi/10.1037/0012-1649.37.2.187

Walker, M (2018) *Why we sleep*. Penguin. London.

Walker-Barnes, C and Mason, C (2004) Delinquency and substance misuse among gang-involved youth: the moderating role of parenting practices. *American Journal of Community Psychology*. 34. 235–250.

Ward, S and Overton, W (1990) Semantic familiarity, relevance and the development of deductive reasoning. *Developmental Psychology*. 26. 488–493.

Watson, K, Coiro, M, Ciriegio, A, Dakkak, A, Jones, M and Compas, B (2023) Covid-19 stressors and symptoms of anxiety and depression in a community sample of children and adolescents. *Child and Adolescent Mental Health*. 28(1). 172–179. https://doi.org/10.1111/camh.12598

Webb, R, Vulliamy, G, Sarja, A and Poikonen, P (2009) Professional learning communities and teacher well-being. *Oxford Review of Education*. 35. 405–422. https://doi.org/10.1080/03054980902935008

Webster, C (2009) Young people, race and ethnicity. In Furlong, A (Ed.) *Handbook of youth and young adulthood*. Routledge. London.

Wellings, K, Mercer, C, Tanton, S … Johnson, A (2013) The prevalence of unplanned pregnancy and associated factors in Britain: findings from the third national survey of sexual attitudes and lifestyle. *Lancet*. 382(9907). 1807–1816.

Werner, E and Smith, R (1992) *Overcoming the odds: high risk children from birth to adulthood*. Cornell University Press. New York, NY.

West, D and Farrington, D (1977) *The delinquent way of life*. Heinemann. London.

White, A, Moeller, J and Brackett, M (2018) Gender identity and sexual labels used by US high school students: a co-occurrence network analysis. *Psychology of Sexual Orientation and Gender Diversity*. 5. 243–252. https://psycnet.apa.org/doi/10.1037/sgd0000266

Wilson, P (2016) What evidence works for whom? In Campbell, S, Morley, D and Catchpole, R (Eds.) *Critical issues in child and adolescent mental health*. Palgrave. London.

Witt, K, Stewart, A and Hawton, K (2025) Treatments for young people who self-harm: challenges and recommendations. *Journal of Child Psychology and Psychiatry*. 66(1). 122–131. https://doi.org/10.1111/jcpp.14052

World Health Organization (2021) Making every school a health-promoting school. Global standards and indicators.

Wroe, L and Pearce, J (2022) Young people negotiating intra- and extra-familial harm and safety: social and holistic approaches. In Holmes, D (Ed.) *Safeguarding young people: risks, rights and resilience*. Jessica Kingsley. London.

Wu, L, Mendola, P and Buck, G (2002) Ethnic differences in the presence of secondary sexual characteristics and menarche among US girls. *Paediatrics*. 110. 47–63. https://doi.org/10.1542/peds.110.4.752

Yan Ma, K, Burn, A-M and Anderson, J (2023) School-based mental health literacy interventions to promote help-seeking. *Child and Adolescent Mental Health*. 28(3). 408–424. https://doi.org/10.1111/camh.12609

Yau, J and Smetana, J (2003) Adolescent–parent conflict in Hong Kong and Shenzhen. *International Journal of Behavioural Development*. 27. 201–211. https://doi.org/10.1080/01650250244000209

Yeager, D (2017) Dealing with social difficulty during adolescence. *Child Development Perspectives*. 11. 196–201. https://doi.org/10.1111/cdep.12234

Yonker, L, Zan, S and Kinane, T (2015) Friending' teens: a systematic of social media in adolescent and young adult health care. *Journal of Medical Internet Research*. 17(1). https://doi.org/10.2196/jmir.3692

Youniss, J and Smollar, J (1985) *Adolescent relations with mothers, fathers and friends*. University of Chicago Press. Chicago.

Zhang, C, Zaleski, G, Kailley, J ... Robillard, J (2024) Social media content mediation may do more harm than good more harm than good. *Child and Adolescent Mental Health*. 29(1). 104–106. https://doi.org/10.1111/camh.12689

Zhang, X, Wei, X, Ji, L, Chen, L and Deater-Deckard, K (2017) Reconsidering parenting in Chinese culture. *Journal of Youth and Adolescence*. 46. 1117–1136. https://doi.org/10.1007/s10964-017-0664-x

Zhong, Y, Patel, N, Ferris, M and Rak, E (2019) Health literacy, nutrition knowledge, and health care readiness in youth with chronic kidney disease. *Journal of Child Health Care*. https://doi.org/10.1177/1367493519831493

Zimmerman, M, Copeland, L, Shope, J and Dielman, T (1997) A longitudinal study of self-esteem: implications for adolescent development. *Journal of Youth and Adolescence*. 26. 117–142. https://link.springer.com/article/10.1023/A:1024596313925#citeas

Index

Note: Page references in *italics* denote figures.

For Product Safety Concerns and Information please contact our
EU representative GPSR@taylorandfrancis.com Taylor & Francis
Verlag GmbH, Kaufingerstraße 24, 80331 München, Germany